QUOTATIONS
FROM
A LIFE OF READING

Compiled by *Raphael* Ryan

You know when you are reading a book and you come across an idea that is very well expressed, or a phrase that aptly portrays what the writer wanted to convey? It stops you in your tracks, and you mull it over in your mind, you think about it and allow it to delight your imagination.

Throughout many years of reading, I got into the habit of jotting down quotations that struck me as either being very well expressed or capturing a particular viewpoint.

I collected these erudite sayings under theme, in alphabetical order, and by dipping in and out of them have found them very useful when called upon to give a talk or to inspire a piece of fiction I would be writing. Quotations like those gathered here often provided a thoughtful starting point. They can also serves as a thoughtful take on life, an idea to be contemplated or a viewpoint worthy of consideration.

Where possible the page number I use is from the edition I was reading. Very early quotations in my quest might not have that accuracy.

As Alexander Pope once observed, *what oft was thought, but ne'er so well express'd* in his "Essay on Criticism, I hope you, too, will find these quotations a journey to somewhere, or at least a diversion along this path of life.

Raphael Ryan

CATEGORIES:

ACTORS & ACTING
ADVENTURE
AGITATION
ALLEGORY
AMBITION
AMERICAN
ANIMALS
ARGUMENT
ART
ATMOSPHERE
AWARENESS
BEAUTY
BEHAVIOUR
BELIEF
BIBLE
BIOGRAPHY
BLAME
BLINDNESS
BOOKS
CERTAINTY
CHANCE
CHARACTER
CHARITY
CHILDREN & CHILDHOOD
CHILDREN
CHOICE
CHRISTMAS & NEW YEAR
CITIES
CIVILIZATION
CLASS
CLOTHES
CONFLICT
CONSCIENCE
COURAGE
CREATIVITY
CRIME
CRITICS & CRITICISM
CURIOSITY
DANGER
DAWN
DEATH
DEFEAT
DEFINITIONS
DREAMS
DRUGS

EDUCATIONEQUALITY
EXCUSE
FAME
FAMILY
FANATICS
FATE & DESTINY
FEAR
FEELINGS
FOLLY
FOOD & DRINK
FORGIVENESS
FREEDOM
FRIENDSHIP
FUTURE
GENERATION
GOD & PROVIDENCE
GOOD
GOSSIP
GRANDPARENTS
HANDICAPPED
HAPPENINGS
HAPPINESS & ENJOYMENT
HATE
HOME
HOPE
HUMAN OBSERVATIONS
HUMOUR
IDENTITY
IGNORANCE
ILLUSIONS
IMAGES
IMAGINATION
INFORMATION
INNOCENCE
IRELAND
ISOLATION
JEALOUSY
JEWS
JOURNEYS
KNOWLEDGE
LANGUAGE
LAWS
LIFE
LITERATURE
LONELINESS
LOVE
LOYALTY
LUCK

MACHINES
MANNERS
MARRIAGE
MATHEMATICS
MEDICINE
MEMORY
MEN &WOMEN
MEN
MONEY
MORALITY
MOTHERS
MUSIC
NATURE, HUMAN
NATURE
NEWS & REPORTING
NOSTALGIA & SADNESS
NOVELS & NOVELISTS
OLD AGE
OPPORTUNITY
OPTIMISM
ORDER & CHAOS
OSTENTATION
OWNERSHIP
PARENTS
PAST & HISTORY
PATRIOTISM
PEOPLE
PHILOSOPHERS & THEOLOGIANS
PHOTOGRAPHY
PLACES
POETRY
POLITICS
POVERTY
POWER
PREJUDICE
PROVERBS & SAYINGS
QUARRELS
RACISM & BLACKS
READING
REALITY
REASON
RELATIONSHIPS
RELIGION
RESPONSIBILITY
ROUTINE
RUMOUR

SADNESS
SAFETY
SARCASM
SCIENCE
SECRETS
SELF ANALYSIS
SEXUALITY
SHAKESPEARE
SHAME
SICKNESS
SILENCE
SOCIETY
SPEECH
STORY-TELLING
SUCCESS & FAILURE
SUFFERING
SUICIDE & DESPAIR
SUNSET
SURVIVAL
TALENT
TASTE
TERRORISM
THEATRE & PLAYS
THOUGHT
TIME
TOLERATION
TRAVEL & TOURISM
TRUTH
UNDERSTANDING
UNIVERSE
UTOPIA
VENGEANCE
VIOLENCE
VIRTUE
WEAPONS
WORDS & PHRASES
WORK
WORLD
WRITING
WRONG
YOUTH

ACTORS & ACTING

Often it's the material that will define an actor, but you didn't do that. You defined yourself with what you chose to do.
Paul Haggis to Charlize Theron. Subday Independent, 6/7/2008.

"You know, for a certain sort of actor it's an advantage to have a rather indefinite sense of self. It makes it much easier to get into various parts."
Alison Lurie. FOREIGN AFFAIRS, p144.

(Hollywood film stars) analphabetic humanoids......irreverently gilded with adventitious photogeneity.
Anthony Burgess. HOMAGE TO QWERT YUIOP.

The true purpose of masks, as any actor will tell you, is not concealment, but transformation. A culture of masks is one that understands a good deal about the process of metamorphosis.
Salman Rushdie. THE JAGUAR SMILE, p26.

James Bond movies - 'technological entertainment.'
Anthony Burgess. I.I. 4/7/87.

The important thing in drama is to have a metaphor which means that people who aren't part of the particular reality portrayed on the stage can identify with it.
Colin Teevan, Gallowglass Theatre Company. Irish Times, 31/7/90.

ADVENTURE

Ever since Joyce we have been aware of the fact that the greatest adventure in our lives is the absence of adventure. Odysseus fought at Troy, made his way home on a ship he himself piloted, had a mistress on every island - no, such is not the life we live. Homer's 'Odyssey' now takes place within man. The islands, the sea, the sirens seducing us, the Ithaca calling us home - they have all been reduced to voices within us.
Milan Kundera. THE BOOK OF LAUGHTER & FORGETTING, p90.

No act is so private it does not seek applause.
John Updike. COUPLES, p132.

Probably no job is done well unless done instinctively.
Anthony Powell.

AGITATION

Agitation in one corner is often mirrored by a similar hubbub in another. There is no rhyme or reason to this. Correlation is not cause. It is just 'the music of chance' as one prominent American novelist has phrased it.
Siri Hustvedt. THE SUMMER WITHOUT MEN, p166.

ALLEGORY

Sometimes the fluffy bunny of incredulity zooms round the bend so rapidly that the greyhound of language is left agog, in the starting cage.
David Mitchell. CLOUD ATLAS, p170.

All games have morals; and the game of Snakes and Ladders captures, as no other activity can hope to do, the eternal truth that for every ladder you climb, a snake is waiting around the corner; and for every snake, a ladder will compensate. But it's more than that; no mere carrot-and-stick affair; because implicit in the game is the unchanging twoness of things, the duality of up against down, good against evil; the solid rationality of ladders balances the occult sinuosities of the serpent; in the opposition of staircase and cobra we can see, metaphorically, all conceivable oppositions, Alpha against Omega.......
Salman Rushdie. MIDNIGHT'S CHILDREN, p141.

AMBITION

If you always do what you always did, you'll always get what you always got!
David Corkery/Hugh O'Donovan, Irish Independent 14/2/2014.

We live on the flat, on the level, and yet – and so – we aspire. Groundlings, we can sometimes reach as far as the gods. Some soar with art, others with religion; most with love. But when we soar, we can also crash. There are few soft landings. We may find ourselves bouncing across the ground with leg-fracturing force, dragged towards some foreign railway line. Every love story is a potential grief story. If not at first, then later. If not for one, then for the other. Sometimes, for both.
Julian Barnes. LEVELS OF LIFE, p36.

We are what we pretend to be, so we must be careful about what we pretend to be.
Kurt Vonnegut, MOTHER NIGHT.

He said any ambition to put things right was subject to the doom of unintended consequences.
Tessa Hadley. THE LONDON TRAIN, p253.

To be a poet and not know the trade,
To be a lover and repel all women,
Twin ironies by which great saints are made,
The agonising pincer-jaws of heaven.
Patrick Kavanagh.

One of the most important things I had learnt at Auschwitz was that one must always avoid being a nobody. All roads are closed to a person who appears useless, all are open to a person who has a function, even the most fatuous.
Primo Levi. THE TRUCE, p235.

The goals we pursue are always veiled. A girl who longs for marriage longs for something she knows nothing about. The boy who hankers after fame has no idea what fame is. The thing that gives our every move its meaning is always totally unknown to us.
Milan Kundera. THE UNBEARABLE LIGHTNESS OF BEING, p122.

There's no stopping a man in the pursuit of his own ambition, particularly if he's read God's mind and found that they think alike.
J Rizkalla. THE JERICHO GARDEN, cf S.T. 10/4/88.

We live such a short time in the world, it seems a pity not to do the jobs we're suited for.
Anthony Powell. THE SOLDIER'S ART, p49.

No doubt our accepting what we are must always inhibit our being what we ought to be.
John Fowles. THE MAGUS, p164.

"Pity we didn't get here first," he said.
"We the Russians?"
"Not only Russians," he shook his head. "Slavs, Hungarians, Germans even. Any people who could cope with wide horizons. Too much of this country (Australia) went to islanders. They never understood it. They're afraid of space."
Bruce Chatwin. THE SONGLINES, p128.

(an aim that miscarried due to the dampness, which - punishment of the camel that stubbornly insists on passing through the eye of the needle - ravaged the throats and bronchia of the Peruvian aristocracy)
Mario Vargas Llosa. AUNT JULIA AND THE SCRIPTWRITER, p279.

The goal set by Dr. Townsend still motivates the linguists to continue the patient labour they have undertaken. I have always been both moved and frightened by the strong, unshakable faith that leads men to dedicate their lives to that faith and accept any sacrifice in its name; for heroism and fanaticism, selfless acts and crimes alike can spring from this attitude.
Mario Vargas Llosa. THE STORYTELLER, p87.

These days you can be what you like: the trick is to have enough identities to meet each occasion.
Brian Thompson. CLEVER GIRL: a sentimental education.

Ambition – an overture to disappointment!
Sandi Toksvig, 24/1/2010.

AMERICAN

Billy has noticed that audiences don't seem to mind anyway. All the fakeness just rolls right off them, maybe because the nonstop sales job of American life has instilled in them exceptionally high thresholds of sham, puff, spin, bullshit and outright lies, in other words for advertising in all its forms. Billy himself never noticed how fake it all is until he'd done time in a combat zone.
Ben Fountain, BILLY LYNN'S LONG HALFTIME WALK, p131.

'America runs on extremes. The latest craze and a tank of gas will get you about anywhere. Today the Kremlin is a messianic movement and you're better dead than Red. Tomorrow they'll decide the real mischief is cigarettes and sugar in your coffee. The culture is built on hyperbole.
Barbara Kingsolver. THE LACUNA, p425.

Maybe this was what it meant to be American. Everything and everyone struck him as young – the movie, badly acted, poorly written, was a puerile and impossible fantasy; these buildings, all hurriedly constructed, were like the makeshift toys of a precocious child. Nobody intended things to still be relevant years from now. For better or worse, these people did what they wanted and it made them happy.
J Robert Lennon. THE LIGHT OF FALLING STARS, p217.

That was the stark thing you discovered about America – it was civilized round the edges, but fifty miles inland from any major city… you really did go into another world.
Keith Richards. LIFE, p155.

ANIMALS

(on possible sighting of a panther in a snowy landscape on Ridgeway Path, Wilts) I wish we had pulled over and gone back with torches to examine the ground, searching for pug marks in the snow and mud. And then I thought that perhaps it was better – after crossing that other worldly landscape on that ancient path – to have not proof or disproof, but instead a certain image of uncertain origin: the fierce light of those two eyes scorching out of the darkness.
Robert Macfarlane, THE OLD WAYS, p304.

I always adored horses, noblest of creatures, such wounded sensitivity in their wise eyes, such rational restraint of energy at their high-strung hindquarters.
Angela Carter. "The Tiger's Bride" in THE BLOODY CHAMBER, p62.

...he told them of horses killed under him and he said that the souls of horses mirror the souls of men more closely than men suppose and that horses also love war. Men say they only learn this but he said that no creature can learn that which his heart has no shape to hold.
Cormac McCarthy. ALL THE PRETTY HORSES, p111.

ARGUMENT

She could see this was going the way of all their arguments, poised to step from the ground of true complaints into the quicksand of trivial nonsense.
Barbara Kingsolver, FLIGHT BEHAVIOUR, p46.

ART

'Bad artists copy, good artists steal.'
Picasso

The power of art was to express the *cultures of emotions* and help the 'individual understand his fellow human beings'.
Illia Ehrenberg quoted in Orlando Figgis, THE WHISPERERS, p590.

Art is imagination. Imagination changes, fuses. Without imagination you have stupid details on one side and empty dreams on the other.
Iris Murdoch. THE BLACK PRINCE, p50.

There are only three questions asked in art: who am I? And who are you? And what the fuck's going on?
John Lanchester.   THE DEBT TO PLEASURE, p159.

Modernism is about finding out how much you could get away with leaving out. Post-modernism is about how much you can get away with putting in.
John Lanchester.   THE DEBT TO PLEASURE, p159.

Hamlet is words, and so is Hamlet. He is as witty as Jesus Christ, but whereas Christ speaks Hamlet is speech. He is the tormented empty sinful consciousness of man seared by the bright light of art, God's flayed victim dancing the dance of creation.
Iris Murdoch.   THE BLACK PRINCE, p199.

Art is a vain and hollow show, a toy of gross illusion, unless it points beyond itself and moves ever whither it points.
Iris Murdoch. THE BLACK PRINCE, p392.

Defeated by holiness, the medieval illuminators stood their saints in a world of gold, then later, as perhaps - vision - became more selective, set a saintly head against an aureole. Beauty too, I think; which is what the old men saw as they sat on the wall, their voices thin and dry as the stridulation of crickets.
William Golding. THE PAPER MEN, p62.

Hitler and Behan were both unfulfilled house painters.
John Ryan. REMEMBERING HOW WE STOOD.

One should never have oneself portrayed except in youth.
John Ryan. REMEMBERING HOW WE STOOD, p47.

It is not the function of art to solve problems but to present them clearly.
Chekhov.

Painting......involves one in a more laboured relationship with a subject - or at least in a more conscious and immersed relationship with a medium - than drawing does. Drawing is closer to the pure moment of perception.
Seamus Heaney. GOVERNMENT OF THE TONGUE, p13.

(re the architecture of a Southern town) It is optimistic architecture. It expects the future to make as much sense as the past.
Don De Lillo. LIBRA, p23.

The Union building....had been designed in an appropriately depressing blind-cubist-with-a-hangover style.
Iain Banks. ESPEDAIR STREET, p17.

When you look at a painting it's something that's over, isn't it? it's a record of what's really passed through the painter's mind, both the event of seeing and the concept that arises from it the imagining are fixed in paint. So a picture is always abstract, to me the style of painting hasn't much to do with it.....
Nadine Gordimer. BURGER'S DAUGHTER, p286.

We have art so that we shall not die of reality.
Nietzsche.

This portrait is my most-loved, but not for beauty: Miss Hannah Heddin (now lately deceased) was sixty years of age when this portrait was taken: her mouth shows a severity - she was never known to smile; but her eyes - see how their hooded lids conceal beneath them a natural gaiety, that is not quite quenched! See how the hands, resting upon the hem of her simple (and threadbare) shawl, for all their chapped sturdiness, and arthritic curves, speak of younger days still - in that brass ring about which the skin has folded up, as a field folds about a boulder. Only the Gainsboroughs amongst the painters can hope to emulate this poignant entrapment of the years - in which the face itself is, as it were, its own artist; and the photographer the humble recorder with his trends of glass and light.
Adam Thorpe. ULVERTON, p179.

'An object in a museum case', he wrote, 'must suffer the de-natural existence of an animal in the zoo. In any museum the object dies - of suffocation and the public gaze - whereas private ownership confers on the owner the right and the need to touch. As a young child will reach out to handle the thing it names, so the passionate collector, his eye in harmony with his hand, restores to the object the life-giving touch of its maker.'
Bruce Chatwin. UTZ, p20.

Art is an attempt to give man a consciousness of his own hidden greatness.
Malraux.

ATMOSPHERE

Grey desks and fluorescent lighting: 1950s functionalism.
J M Coetzee. DUSKLANDS, p7.

A dull pulse lit the oily timbers. The flames wavered in the vivid light, uncertain how to find their way back to the sun.
J G Ballard. THE DAY OF CREATION, p20.

(At a children's football match).....to the sound of first names and obscenities shouted in urgent falsetto, high balls were fought for in the air.
Ian McEwan. THE CHILD IN TIME, p140.

The street lamps were white and stretched away like a necklace of light.
Carlo Gebler. WORK AND PLAY, p69.

Their voices are a faint, background murmur, like the twittering of mice behind a wainscot.
John Banville. MEFISTO, p12.

wet, institutional asphalt.
Graham Swift. WATERLAND, p284.

Rainbow veil of petroleum tremble on puddles of water.
Primo Levi. IF THIS IS A MAN.

The bush resounded with splendid avian music; a noisy tropical hosanna was floating upward.
Ryszard Kapuscinski. ANOTHER DAY OF LIFE, p80.

It was as fine a day as the region could contrive at the time of year - a sky as blue as a baby's eyeball; pale, reticent sunshine that offered the bitter-sweet, Slavonic pleasure of evanescence, for it would be gone so very soon; and, today, the snow did not look a killing blanket but like a tender coverlet designed to keep the cold away from germinating seeds.
Angela Carter. NIGHTS AT THE CIRCUS, p267.

In the neuter austerity of that terrain all phenomena were bequeathed a strange equality and no one thing nor spider nor stone nor blade of grass could put forth claim to precedence.
Cormac McCarthy. BLOOD MERIDIAN, p247.

From a high curve in the road, Yonathan caught sight of the peaks of the mountains of Edom shrouded in a veil of blue haze. A band of titans from some distant star who had lost their way and sunk down at last in this place, flashing blindingly from the sun-drunk surface of the Dead Sea.
Amos Oz. A PERFECT PEACE, p264.

And as we drove towards the widening dawn, that now streaked half the sky with a wintry bouquet of pink roses, orange tiger-lilies, as if my husband had ordered me a sky from a florist. The day broke around me like a cool dream.
Angela Carter. THE BLOODY CHAMBER, p13.

The floor was carpeted. The colour of things, chosen to fit an insipid, undemanding cycle of tastes, had faded and blended in the grime of post-war London.
Bruce Arnold. A SINGER AT THE WEDDING, p79.

In the quietness of the room, disturbed only by the faint hiss of a damp log which had recently been added to the fire, the words had about them the sombre ring of eternity knocking at the doors of all our lives.
Bruce Arnold. A SINGER AT THE WEDDING, p177.

Their marriage-house was a statement of intent. It was a big and, when they moved into it, empty of almost everything except possibility. At night Ellen dreamt of silk threads spinning out from it into the darkness, and other threads, from other, imaginable sources, spinning in towards it until their beginnings and their endings had woven the entire blank space of the house into a block of dazzling colour.
Glenn Patterson. FAT LAD, p268.

AWARENESS

She was Christmas-morning-when-you're-eight kind of aware.
Denis Lehane. MYSTIC RIVER, p61.

BEAUTY

And I think of what Hobie said: beauty alters the grain of reality. And I keep thinking too of the more conventional wisdom: namely, that the pursuit of pure beauty is a trap, a fast track to bitterness and sorrow, that beauty has to be wedded to something more meaningful.
Donna Tartt, THE GOLDFINCH, p760.

The boy was beautiful as his mother. In words, beauty can only be suggested by its immediate signal. Theirs was of clarity. Their identical round brows were clear horizons, their nostrils and ear lobes appeared translucent, their skin, lips and eyes had the colouring of portraits in stained glass.
Nadine Gordimer. A JOURNEY.

A single line of poetry or a single paragraph of prose was sufficient to make him happy, not only because they were beautiful but because they were magic doors opening into the realm of the elect, those whose souls are sensitive to things hidden from others.
Milan Kundera. LIFE IS ELSEWHERE, p48.

To live in Havana was to live in a factory that turned out human beauty on a conveyor-belt.
Graham Greene. OUR MAN IN HAVANA, p108.

She was as far from ugliness as she was from beauty.
John McGahern. AMONGST WOMEN, p102.

As soon as Mario laid eyes on Fulvia he thought she was the most beautiful woman he had ever seen, though he realised, in forming this opinion, that her charm was strictly personal, for there was nothing particularly striking about her, just a soft harmony of sweet, warm colours - a blend of caramel, honey and ripe peach. She was not very tall, but her firm, slender body seemed to be that of a woman who carried her own suitcases and was capable of fixing a short circuit. Her placid smile was neither coy nor frivolous; she emanated peace, strength and health.
Francesca Duranti. THE HOUSE ON MOON LAKE, p30.

A beautiful Simone Weil said, seeing herself in the mirror, knows 'This is I'. An ugly woman knows, with equal certainty, 'This is not I'.
A.S. Byatt. POSSESSION, p57.

Because the daughter of his brother Roberto was as perfect a specimen of young womanhood as Richard was of young manhood: one of those beauties who do honor to the species and who make figures of speech comparing teeth to pearls, eyes to stars, hair to flax, and complexions to peaches and cream sound far too pedestrian.
Mario Vargas Llosa. AUNT JULIA AND THE SCRIPTWRITER, p22.

She was young, with the svelte physique of a banty rooster, a complexion tanned by exposure to the elements, hair cut in bangs like a *jeune premier* ballet dancer.
Mario Vargas Llosa. AUNT JULIA AND THE SCRIPTWRITER, p286.

She looked like a fashion model, and Keith generally preferred the other kind, the glamour kind. The demeanour of the model proclaimed that you do what you liked with her. The demeanour of the fashion model proclaimed that she could do what she liked with you.
Martin Amis. LONDON FIELDS, p45.

Beauty is in the eye of the beholder. Which is fun for the beholder; but what about the owner, the tenant? Nicola wondered whether she'd ever had a minute's pleasure from it. Even at sixteen, when you're excitedly realizing what you've got (and imagining it will last forever), you're still noticing what you haven't got, and will never get. Beauty's hand is ever at its lips, bidding adieu. Yes, but bidding adieu 'in the mirror'.
Martin Amis. LONDON FIELDS, p127.

It's very hot still and she wears just a sleeveless T-shirt on the way to the flic. The clear lineaments of her embarrassing perfection spread agony on the street.
Martin Amis. LONDON FIELDS, p135.

"There exists a certain external shapeliness in a woman, which small-town taste mistakenly considers beauty. And then there exists the genuinely erotic beauty of a woman. Of course, it is no small matter to recognise this at a mere glance. It is an art."
Milan Kundera. LAUGHABLE LOVES, p187.

Eugenie, tall and strongly made, possessed nothing of that prettiness with which the generality of mankind is pleased, but she was beautiful in that style of beauty which is so easily misunderstood, and with which artists alone are captivated.
Honore de Balzac. EUGENIE GRANDET, p81.

...The best models are those with the emptiest faces, for the simple reason that a vacant space becomes the site of the onlookers' desires.
Declan Kiberd. Irish Times, 28/12/91.

Beauty, the last triumph possible for man who can no longer hope.
Milan Kundera. THE ART OF THE NOVEL, p122.

At some point in life the world's beauty becomes enough. You don't need to photograph, paint or even remember it. It is enough. No record of it needs to be kept and you don't need someone to share it with or tell it to. When that happens - that letting go - you let go because you can. The world will always be there - while you sleep it will be there - when you wake it will be there as well. So you can sleep and there is reason to wake. A dead hydrangea is as intricate and lovely as one in bloom. Bleak sky is as seductive as sunshine, miniature orange trees without blossoms or fruit are not defective: they are that.
Toni Morrison. TAR BABY, p244.

Her real beauty was in her eyes. Although brown, they seemed black because of the lashes and her look came at you frankly, with a candid boldness.
Gustave Flaubert.   MADAME BOVARY, p25.

BEHAVIOUR

....pacing the deck, with the same intense bigotry of purpose in his aspect.
Herman Melville. MOBY DICK, p147 (Kindle)

How can I not know today your face tomorrow, the face that is there already or is being forged beneath the face you show me or beneath the mask you are wearing, and which you will only show me when I am least expecting it?
Javier Marias. YOUR FACE TOMORROW 1, p155.

We search for patterns (in people's behavior), only to find where the patterns break. And its there, in that fissure, that we pitch our tents and wait.
Nicole Krauss. GREAT HOUSE, p89.

I was relieved to find myself growing bored and impatient with my situation. Boredom is a sentiment not available to the Hottentot: it is a sign of higher humanity.
J M Coetzee. DUSKLANDS, p85.

The lovely thing about humanity is that at times one may be unaware of doing right, but one is always aware of doing wrong.
Vladimir Nabokov. THE ASSISTANT PRODUCER.

The fascination of royalty lies in the teasing suggestion of the internality of those whose lives are presented as, by definition, pure externality, so that even the internal is, by mere fact of its presentation, instantly externalised. Paradoxically, the most 'natural' footage was some old newsreel which congratulated itself on having caught the King and Queen in a relaxed moment feeding ducks; but what came across as natural, at this remove, was their 'effort' to behave naturally, which contrasted with the effortless unnaturalness of their normal self-projection: a gap opened only accidentally, by the warping and drying of representational conventions..
Dai Vaughan. COTTEGE RUBBINGS.

The "wanna-be-in-my-gang" syndrome is the Eighties phenomenon of "multiple conformity.
Desmond Morris.

A human being hardly ever thinks about other people. He contemplates phantasms which resemble them and which he has decked out for his own purpose.
Iris Murdoch. BRUNO'S DREAM, p222.

Discipline was the molecular pattern that attracted them back to their particular association.
Nadine Gordimer. SOMETHING OUT THERE, p178.

The barometer of his emotional nature was set for a spell of riot.
James Joyce. "Counterparts" in DUBLINERS.

It's part of commonplace strategy of adultery to appear in company where both wife and mistress are present. It's accepted as merely a way of hiding, by displaying there's nothing to hide.
Nadine Gordimer. MY SON'S STORY, p92.

We traffic in mockery.
W.B. YEATS.

That which you have done - whether it be only once in your life, in a moment of stupidity or in an outburst of anger - that which you were capable of doing - even if you have forgotten, or have chosen to forget how and why you did it - that which you have done and regretted bitterly, you may never do again. But you are capable of doing it. You may do it. It is curled up inside you.
Amos Oz. THE SLOPES OF LEBANON, p23.

We all make fictions. None of us is what we seem. We arrange our memories to suit our present understanding of ourselves, and not to account accurately for the past. When we meet other people we try to project an image of ourselves that will please or influence them in some way. When we fall in love we blind ourselves to what we do not wish to see.
Christopher Priest. THE GLAMOUR, p212.

(In Auschwitz) There they go, to their day's work, with their heads bent back. I was puzzled at first but now I know why they are doing it, why they stretch their throats like that. They are looking for the souls of their mothers and their fathers, their women and their children, gathering in the heavens - awaiting human form, and union....The sky above the Vistula is full of stars. I can see them now. They no longer hurt my eyes.
Martin Amis. TIME'S ARROW, p131.

Should we expect everything from the power of reason, and nothing from the easy ways of habit?
Montesquieu. PERSIAN LETTERS, p128.

(Two learned men) The first one's conversation, correctly described, could be reduced to this: 'What I have said is true, because I said it.' The second's conversation was about something else: 'What I did not say is not true, because I didn't say it.'
I rather liked the first one, for if a man is opinionated it doesn't matter at all to me; but if he is arrogant it matters a great deal. The first is defending his own ideas: they belong to him; the second is attacking other men's ideas, and they belong to everybody.
Montesquieu. PERSIAN LETTERS No 144.

Somewhat as prisoners beguile their days by training a spider, the reformed drunkard makes an interest out of abstaining from intoxicating drinks, and may live for that negation. There is something, at least, not to be done each day; and a cold triumph awaits his every morning.
R L Stevenson. THE AMATEUR EMIGRANT, p36.

The body is a house of many windows: there we all sit, showing ourselves and crying on the passersby to come and love us. But this fellow has filled his windows with opaque glass, elegantly coloured. His house may be admired for its design, the crowd may pause before the stained windows, but meanwhile the poor proprietor must lie languishing within uncomforted, unchangeably alone.
R L. Stevenson. VIRGINIBUS PUERISQUE, p81.

Its facile to blame the Supreme Court for the pornographic bookstores and the live sex shows. They usually exist because somebody on the zoning board is getting greased. Kids don't do dope because their parents and teachers are permissive. They do it because adults sell it to them. No psychological complexities, no sociological mysteries.
James Lee Burke. THE NEON RAIN, p168.

They carry the arrogance of their master but not the substance of it.
Brian Keenan. TURLOUGH.

BELIEF

The pilot at the end of the runway believes in flight. It's not just a question of knowledge, of understanding aerodynamics; it's also a question of belief.
Julian Barnes. STARING AT THE SUN, p108.

In a secular age, an authentic miracle must purport to be a hoax, in order to gain credit in the world.
Angela Carter. NIGHTS AT THE CIRCUS, p17.

The longer you do a thing, the less certain you are how you do it. One moment it seems impossible; the next you can see that with a bit of luck you might manage it.
Nina Bawden. CIRCLES OF DECEIT, p70.

Yes, suddenly I saw it clearly: most people deceive themselves with a pair of faiths: they believe in *eternal memory* (of people, things, deeds, nations) and in *redressibility* (of deeds, mistakes, sins, wrongs). Both are false faiths. In reality the opposite is true: everything will be forgotten and nothing will be redressed. The task of obtaining redress (by vengeance or by forgiveness) will be taken over by forgetting. No one will redress the wrongs that have been done, but all wrongs will be forgotten.
Milan Kundera. THE JOKE, p294.

What is faith?
Faith was a longing that pretended to be a conviction.
Ivan Klíma. WAITING FOR THE DARK, WAITING FOR THE LIGHT, p152.

The difference between a theory and a belief rested not on proof but on the possibility of disproof. No matter how many observations appeared to corroborate the theory of relativity, for example, it could never conclusively be proved to be true. Its scientific respectability rested on the fact that it could instantly be proven false should contradictory evidence come to light.
Michael Dibdin. MEDUSA, p74.

BIBLE

The Bible has nothing to do with God. The Bible is an account of our waking up, an atavistically dreamed recovery of how we first learned shame in the garden and first considered ourselves different from animals, and Cain was the first to discover that part of us will never wake up. Part of us will act according to instinct, and that will never change. And one of our first instincts is to kill. The Ten Commandments is a list of our instincts that will never leave us.
David Vann. GOAT MOUNTAIN, p140.

To me the Bible is perhaps the greatest book ever written. Not as a step-by-step guide to life or as a travel brochure of the afterlife. In that respect, it is positively dangerous. But as a tightly written work of fiction, it is magnificent.
Shehan Karumatilaka. CHINAMAN, p38.

BIOGRAPHY

I do find biography a very strange activity - the notion that there could be a single truth about a life. By extension, because history is about people, I am fascinated by the way in which there is no absolute interpretation of the past.
Penelope Lively. Good Book Guide 10/88.

It is common knowledge that nobody is born with a decalogue already formed, but that everyone builds his own either during his life or at the end, on the basis of his own experiences, or on those of others which can be assimilated to his own; so that everyone's moral universe, suitably interpreted, comes to be identified with the sum of his former experiences, and so represents an abridged form of his biography.
Primo Levi. THE TRUCE, p224.

Whoever undertakes to write a biography binds himself to lying, to concealment, to flummery.....
Truth is not accessible.
Sigmund Freud. (quoted in Tim O'Brien, IN THE LAKE OF THE WOODS, p291)

BLAME

It is one of the most detestable habits of a Lilliputian mind to credit other people with its own malignant pettiness.
Honore de Balzac. OLD GORIOT, p17.

BLINDNESS

And then it occurred to her how strange it was to be looking at someone who could not return that look: the horror of blindness lay less in being unable to see than in not knowing when you were being watched.
Peter Ackroyd. CHATTERTON, p30.

My methods are new and are causing surprise.
To make the blind see I throw dust in their eyes.
James Joyce. Ulysses, p522.

BOOKS

Books are like love letters. They seem right at the time, but you'd really rather they were destroyed - or you'd had the sense to keep them to yourself in the first place.
Len Deighton. Mail on Sunday, 15/3/87.

What is packaged and pushed and promoted for multi-national fast-sales is the sort of books which Sean O Faolain once described as "utterly without merit except as gob-stoppers for the perpetual adolescent."
Michael Finlan, Irish Times, 24/2/89.

(re. books and reading) the air of duty is less healthy to breathe than the air of innocent enjoyment. The qualities that make a book easily discussable - worse still, easily 'teachable' - are not always, or often, the same as those that make it just a good book.
John Wain. S.T. 11/9/88.

Every book is an image of solitude. It is a tangible object that one can pick up, put down, open, and close, and its words represent many months, if not many years, of one man's solitude, so that with each word one reads in a book one might say to himself that he is confronting a particle of that solitude. A man sits alone in a room and writes. Whether the book speaks of loneliness or companionship, it is necessarily a product of solitude.
Paul Auster. THE INVENTION OF SOLITUDE, p136.

(thrillers and romances) These books open a little square window on the world and set puppets parading outside for you to observe. They bear little resemblance to human beings, to anyone you have ever met or are likely to meet. These characters exist for purposes of plot, and the books they appear in do not threaten the reader in any way; they do not suggest that he or she should reflect, let alone change. But then, of course, being so safe, they defeat themselves, they can never enlighten. And because they don't enlighten, they are unimportant.
Fay Weldon. LETTERS TO ALICE, p12.

People read them (my books) and I don't have any idea who they are. Without even knowing it, I enter the lives of strangers, and for as long as they have my book in their hands, my words are the only reality that exists for them.
Paul Auster. LEVIATHAN, p4.

CERTAINTY

Lodis snorts; too easy. At least ten times a day he has to prove that certitude is the hallmark of the true moron.
Ben Fountain, BILLY LYNN'S LONG HALFTIME WALK, p13.

Why do we care about Lee Harvey Oswald, or Little Big Horn? Because of all that cannot be known. And what if we did know? What if it were proved – absolutely and purely - ... that Oswald acted alone?... Nothing more would beckon, nothing would tantalize. The thing about Custer is this: no survivors. Hence, the eternal doubt, which both frustrates and fascinates. It's a standoff. The human desire for certainty collides with our love of enigma. And so I lose sleep over mute facts and frayed ends and missing witnesses.... So I toss and turn... Would it help to announce the problem early on? To plead for understanding? To argue that solutions only demean the grandeur of human ignorance? To point out that absolute knowledge is absolute closure? To issue a reminder that death itself dissolves into uncertainty, and that out of such uncertainty arise great temples and tales of salvation?
Tim O'Brien. IN THE LAKE OF THE WOODS, p266.

CHANCE

It may be that events constantly take us by surprise, or perhaps traces of what is to become of us are present in our past, and we only need to look behind us to see what we have become, and there is really no need for amazement.
Abdulrasak Gurnah. THE LAST GIFT, p216.

"Why nor," Vinnie echoed, marveling at the long fuse of chance that had blasted this unhappy jobless ex-delinquent from rural Oklahoma into the seat next to hers at Covent Garden.
Alison Lurie. FOREIGN AFFAIRS, p157.

"You should stick to tellin' tomorrow's temperature from today's tap water."
Philip Davison. TWIST AND SHOUT. p21.

Occupying an area rich in double-think, Brian de Palma is simply the innocent beneficiary of a cultural joke.
Martin Amis. THE MORONIC INFERNO, p88.

Most of what matters in our lives takes place in our absence.
Salman Rushdie. MIDNIGHT'S CHILDREN.

Fate holds terrible forfeits for those who gamble on certainties.
Winston Churchill.

It was Paul who said: one lives forward; understanding goes backwards......Whatever happens at any given moment may have been lying dormant in the blood for years.
Andre Brink. THE WALL OF THE PLAGUE., p12.

The crises of our lives do not come, I think, accurately dated; they crop up unexpected and out of turn, and somehow or other arrange themselves according to a calendar we cannot control.
Elizabeth Bishop. quoted Independent Review. 20/5/90.

It was unlikely - I won't say impossible because the archaeology of the mind is mysterious; who can be certain what lurks in that dark, buried city?
Nina Bawden. CIRCLES OF DECEIT. p71.

In all the great events and occurrences of our life, the mind becomes strangely impressed by the localities in which we may happen to be at the precise moment when the pleasures or miseries in question overwhelm us with their weight.
Honore de Balzac. EUGENIE GRANDET, p107

Our lives carry us along in ways we cannot control, and almost nothing stays with us. It dies when we do, and death is something that happens to us every day.
Paul Auster. THE NEW YORK TRILOGY, p199.

In the end, each life is no more than the sum of contingent facts, a chronicle of chance intersections, of random events that divulge nothing but their own lack of purpose.
Paul Auster. THE NEW YORK TRILOGY, p216.

Bobby was waiting for us at lunch the following day. Or, rather, he managed to turn up next to us in line again. He had a particular talent for investing his actions with the quality of randomness - his life, viewed from a distance, would have appeared to be little more than a series of coincidences.
Michael Cunningham. A HOME AT THE END OF THE WORLD, p42.

A river flows by the power of its current, not the confinement of its banks.
Brian Keenan. TURLOUGH, p103.

CHARACTER

Brooke is a very good fellow, but pulpy; he will run into any mould, but he wont keep shape.
George Eliot. MIDDLEMARCH, p43.

Whenever she complained of being so small, Cub told her she was a sports car: no junk in the trunk, but all you need for speed.
Barbara Kingsolver, FLIGHT BEHAVIOUR, p50.

(Mr Gray) He had about him permanently an air of troubled inadequacy, seeming incompetent to deal with the practicalities of everyday life.
John Banville. ANCIENT LIGHT, p103.

Don't be feeling sorry for him. He could steal the stink off shit and not get the smell on his hands.
James Lee Burke. THE GLASS RAINBOW, p3.

Incidentally, it's funny how often the miseries of this world are caused by short people – they are so much more quick-tempered and difficult to get on with than tall ones.
Erich Maria Remarque. ALL QUIET ON THE WESTERN FRONT, p11.

Re the cranky waitress in Bangor, Maine:
She could make eternity and infinity melt and run out through your fingers.
John Steinbeck. TRAVELS WITH CHARLEY, p41.

A nutcracker face – chin and nose trying to come together over a sunken mouth.
Conrad. YOUTH.

Edwin gives his *sole veronique* a concupiscent glance, then delicately attacks it.
Alison Lurie. FOREIGN AFFAIRS, p55.

When the heart speaks, the mind finds it indecent to object.
Milan Kundera. THE UNBEARABLE LIGHTNESS OF BEING. p250.

He is used to patients waiting in queues to see him, but he is not used to waiting in queues himself. A queue, to him, means a man being denied the right to be where he wants to be at a time of his own choosing, which is at the front, now.
Blake Morrison. AND WHEN DID YOU LAST SEE YOUR FATHER? p9.

All that mattered to him was the saying, not what was said: words were the empty rituals with which he held the world at bay.
John Banville. DOCTOR COPERNICUS, p188.

Isn't it funny that for everybody there seems to be just one age at which they are really themselves?
Elizabeth Bowen. THE HOTEL.

What good to us are political doctrines which claim to make man flourish, if we do not know what type of man they will engender?
Antoine de Saint-Exupery. TERRES DES HOMMES.

'You always assumed Stanley knew something you didn't know.'
Warren Beatty on Stanley Kubrick, meeting him on or off the set.

Actions are important only to the degree we invest them with importance.
Gore Vidal. WILLIWAW, p9.

If, however, you can truly see, you will comprehend that that which is your opposite is in possession of something which you lack, which may in fact be your complement.
Timothy O Grady. MOTHERLAND, p77.

"....I read somewhere in Dostoyevsky that if a man wants to stay really honest, he'd better die before he turns forty. From forty they're all scoundrels. On the other hand, they say that Dostoyevsky was a scoundrel himself, a drunken swine and a petty egotist."
Amos Oz. A PERFECT PEACE, p51.

The only evidence of femininity to which Mrs Naa's grooming could respond (as owners of the same make of vehicle, one humble, one a luxury model, passing on a highway silently acknowledge one another with a flick of the headlights) was the Indian dingly-dangley's the girl wore in her ears, answering the big fake pearls sitting on Mrs Naa's plump lobes.
Nadine Gordimer. SOMETHING OUT THERE, p133.

She never stood still for a moment, as with elbow grease, she rubbed out the emptiness of her days.
Moy McCrory. THE O'TWOMEY SISTERS AND THE DAY OF RECKONING.

There is authority in what he says: he bathes daily in a running tap of words inspired by fear and greed, in secret reports of unwary talk, in denunciations inspired by hatred, words spoken after torture.
Brian Moore. THE COLOUR OF BLOOD, p33.

Character is fate. You build your character and you can control your fate.
Jodi Foster. S.T. 12/5/91.

He had that incongruity of common and elegant in which the habitually vulgar think they see the revelation of an eccentric existence, of the perturbations of sentiment, the tyrannies of art, and always a certain contempt for social conventions, that seduces or exasperates them.
Gustave Flaubert. MADAME BOVARY, p156.

Hauser wore a white coat and trousers but with no shirt or vest under the coat. Beneath the antiseptic smells of his chemicals and preserving spirits it was just possible to distinguish the thin vinegar reek of his body odour, a noisome seam in the olefactory strata.
William Boyd. BRAZZAVILLE BEACH, 35.

Adults were boring, with their rationality, their deference, their refusal to punish you as severely as you knew you ought to be punished. Adults were useful because they were boring; they were raw material; they were predictable in their responses. They may be wet and kindly, or sour and vicious; but they were always predictable. They made you believe in advance in the integrity of character.
Julian Barnes. METROLAND, p66.

If Herod's troops were on a house-to-house search for ambiguity they would not sojourn long at La Maison de Val. She is the type of being for whom the phrase "Would you like to come in for coffee?" is gnomic to the point of incomprehensibility, and who would find the apothegm 'Is that a pine-cone in your pocket?' worthy of the Tantric masters.
Julian Barnes. TALKING IT OVER, p188.

In the way that you never see a movie star straining on the lavatory, there were certain human functions which seemed to pass Donovan by, at least in my observation. He defied, as far as I was able to tell, the forces of gravity that anchor the rest of us down to earth, the downward tug of the kids, the dishes, the emotions. Donovan was up there in the atmosphere, in that azure above the weather zone, occasionally touching down to resolve the frictions of nations. It seemed almost unnatural, unwholesome even, for a man like that, or astral sailor, to be earthbound by something as prosaic as a father.
Joesph O'Neill. THIS IS THE LIFE, p60.

The Squire, when intoxicated, glares across the dining-table as if intent on finding in one's waistcoat the horizon that might settle him, and his voice has no need of a speaking-trumpet were it to be issuing instructions on a battlefield. He has eyes like a cotter's windows under thatch - suspicious, yet promising warmth that on further exploration - turns to a chill - and grows damper by the hour, until it altogether hisses into a kind of well, dark and dismal. Yet on the morrow he will be in a crumpled cheerfulness, and all bustle - if the weather allows it.
Adam Thorpe. ULVERTON, p151/2.

The Squire was sporting a white bl;azer and trousers, with a gold watch hanging lustrously from his white waistcoat.... Nothing about the Squire betokened a military demeanour: his shape was that of a William pear, his pence-nez sported a red silk ribbon, his hair was mounted above his head in two polished waves either side of a deep trough, each wave ending in a small curl over the forehead.... there was a general air of dissipation about him, most especially in the creamy pallor of his face, which blurred the edge of neatness and admonished his attempts at moral heartiness. His vigorous fury spluttered with an element of indignation, lacking the cool deadliness of the true autocrat.
Adam Thorpe. ULVERTON, p226.

(assassination of Kirov).... Stalin's friend and ally, Stalin's comrade. For Stalin to have ordered Kirov's death was not just 'out of character', but beyond our understanding of what character might comprise. Which was precisely the point. We have moved into an era when 'character' is a misleading concept. Character has been replaced by ego, and the exercise of authority as a reflection of character has been replaced by the psychopathic retention of power by all possible means and in mockery of all implausibilities. Stalin had Kirov killed: welcome to the modern world.
Julian Barnes. THE PORCUPINE, p106.

Beside the thick-necked bulk of Urville of Urville... sat neither of his two daughters, Diana and Helen - those long-legged visions of money-creamed, honey-skinned globe-trotting loveliness - but instead his niece, the stunning, the fabulous, the golden-haired, vellus-faced, diamond-eyed Verity, upwardly nubile scionette of the house of Urville, the jewel beside the jowls; the girl who, for me, had put the lectual into intellectual, the phany into epiphany, and the ibid in libidinous.
Iain Banks. THE CROW ROAD, p14.

Diddy Shovel's skin was like asphalt, fissured and cracked, thickened by a lifetime of weather, the scurf of age. Stubble worked through the craquelured surface. His eyelids collapsed in protective folds at the outer corners. Bristles eyebrows; enlarged pores gave the nose a sandy appearance.
E Annie Proulx. THE SHIPPING NEWS, p79.

He's as smooth as a fresh-laid turd and gives off the same smell.
Ian Rankin, THE FALLS, p186.

CHARITY

"..you're very kind."
"What else can we be?" The words burst from him. "What sort of people would we be if we weren't kind?" Then he got back in the bus, started the engine and drove off.
James Robertson. THE PROFESSOR OF TRUTH, p35.

Charity.... is the opium of the privileged.... While we do our good works let us not forget that the real solution lies in a world in which charity will have become unnecessary.
Chinua Achebe. ANTHILLS OF THE SAVANNAH, p155.

We should beware of the grand gestures which it costs us nothing to make.
A J Cronin. DEAD AS DOORNAILS, p104.

CHILDREN & CHILDHOOD

He read the alphabet book, that staple of childhood learning, the first philosophy we are exposed to – the simplicity of language, the articulation of a letter that sounds exactly how it looks.
Tea Obreht. THE TIGER'S WIFE, p103.

Do you approach your daughter and tell her that no man has the right to track his feet through a father's memories of his daughter's young life?
James Lee Burke. THE GLASS RAINBOW, p49.

…The passion for destruction is part of how a child discovers the world.
Paulo Coelho. ELEVEN MINUTES, p132.

Children aren't colouring books. You don't get to fill them in with your favorite colors.
Kallid Hosseini. THE KITE RUNER, p19.

For the reality of things, children - be thankful - only visit us for a brief while.
Graham Swift. WATERLAND, p28.

Bertolucci on Sergio Leone: He was completely like a child who has access to the Olympus of his imagination.

We could never have loved the earth so well if we had no childhood in it -..... what novelty is worth that sweet monotony where everything is known, and loved because it is known.
George Eliot. THE MILL ON THE FLOSS, p44.

The child's laughter is pure until he first laughs at a clown.
Angela Carter. NIGHTS AT THE CIRCUS, p119.

You see, when you're a child, you tend to live blindly. It's only afterwards, once you have your own children, that you look back on yourself through them. And for the first time you begin to understand what happened to you, and why it happened.
Andre Brink. A DRY WHITE SEASON, p29.

"You must remember: there was a time when we were inseparable."
"Children always live in a paradise."
Andre Brink. LOOKING ON DARKNESS, p348.

It is the subversive that appeals to children, and it is the subversive that becomes classic children's fiction.
Alison Lurie.

Children learn from modeling themselves on others, mimicking at first the forms of maturity they see in their parents and then coming to perform them cognitively as their capacities grow; why should they not be learning something about themselves, by mimicking the responsibilities recognised precociously by certain other children - their siblings.
Nadine Gordimer. MY SON'S STORY, p26.

How will we teach the children when all the animals are gone? Because animals are what they want to talk about first. Yes, and buses and food and Mama and Dada. But animals are what they break their silence for.
Martin Amis. LONDON FIELDS, p97.

Children love to touch their toys because their toys are the only things they can touch; the only things they can touch freely. Man-made objects, blunted, detoxified, with pleasure possible and pain counterindicated. Or that was the idea.
Martin Amis. LONDON FIELDS, p219.

As a child one wonders about others, not about oneself, since the reality and importance of others is greater. The problem is how to understand them, and how to relate to them. Perhaps, even, how to like them.
Bruce Arnold. A SINGER AT THE WEDDING, p163.

Trouble with mothers is that they fall for everyone - all their children that is, even the ones they haven't got. Yet. It's always yet when they get to that stage.
Evelyn Conlon. "As good a reason as any" from MY HEAD IS OPENING, p32.

We embrace to be embraced. We embrace our children to be folded in the arms of the future, to pass ourselves beyond death, to be transported.....We bear children in order to be mothered by them.
J. M. Coetzee. AGE OF IRON, p5.

It is the roaming gangs of fear, the sullen-mouthed boys, rapacious as sharks, on whom the first shade of the prison house is already feigning to close. Children scorning childhood, the time of wonder, the growing time of the soul. Their souls, their organs of wonder, stunted, petrified.
J.M. Coetzee. AGE OF IRON, p6.

I look back now and understand that the prime function of a mother is to protect and shelter the unformed malleable character of her child. A mother's constant unquestioning love gives the child a bland but fertile mulch of normality and ordinariness in which to grow and flourish.
William Boyd. THE NEW CONFESSIONS, p20.

I have often thought what a melancholy world this would be without children, and what an inhuman world without the aged.
S.T. Coleridge. Lectures 1811-12. No. VII.

Nothing is more useful than to adopt the status of a child: A child can do whatever it likes, for it is innocent and inexperienced: it need not observe the rules of social behaviour for it has not yet entered a world ruled by form; it may show its feelings, whether they are appropriate or not.
Milan Kundera. IMMORTALITY, p66.

Children are living messages we send into the future, a future we will not see. We understand enough about them now to have a fairly good idea of what they need. In effect we are building the house of tomorrow day by day, not out of bricks or steel, but out of the stuff of children's bodies, hearts and minds.
Melvin Konner. CHILDHOOD. NY Times Book Review. 9/2/92.

Mr Tench's father had been a dentist too - his first memory was finding a discarded cast in a wastepaper basket - the rough toothless gaping mouth of clay, like something dug up in Dorset - Neanderthal or Pithecanthropus. It had been his favourite toy: they tried to tempt him with Meccano, but fate had struck. There is always one moment in childhood when the door opens and lets the future in. The hot wet river-port and the vultures lay in the wastepaper basket, and he picked them out. We should be thankful we cannot see the horrors and degradations lying around our childhood, in cupboards and bookshelves, everywhere.
Graham Greene. THE POWER AND THE GLORY, p12.

One marries..... and has children. One maintains them and rears them, teaching them to speak the truth, not to steal, not to use bad language and brush their teeth...... But in spite of it all, one knows that there is something else of importance that they ought to have, that one lacks a code to bring them up in, or to offer them, at least....... One wants to share something profound with them, something they will retain for life, something they will be able to return to and cherish when things are hard, something that will foster their love and their capacity to relate to people.
Ivan Klima. JUDGE ON TRIAL, p357.

"......Harry convinced me so. He says that the means a painter may employ he must take from his predecessors, such as a child learning a language, which he did not invent. At first he lisps childish things, then his syntax, his lexicon of words, become those of an adult, and he may speak naturally his own sentences and ideas without a thought for grammar and construction. Thus he grows out of a manner and prints according to his own lights.
Timothy Mo. AN INSULAR POSSESSION, p114.

And is not all the world like this? Gazing at this transfigured desert I remember the games of my childhood - the dark and golden park we peopled with gods; the limitless kingdom we made of this square mile never thoroughly explored, never thoroughly charted. We created a secret civilization where footfalls had a meaning and things a savour known in no other world.
And when we grow to be men and live under other laws, what remains of the park filled with shadows of childhood, magical, freezing, burning? What do we learn when we return to it and stroll with a sort of despair along the outside of its little wall of grey stone, marvelling that within a space so small we should have founded a kingdom that had seemed to us so infinite - what do we learn except that in this infinity we shall never again set foot, and that it is into the game and not the park that we have lost the power to enter?
Antoine de Sanit-Exupery. WIND, SAND and STARS, p111.

Children are vectors aimed at the future. All the doubts and anxieties about how they will turn out are balanced by the knowledge that their course and final destination are ultimately out of your hands. Whatever happens to them will happen when you are different, or dead, and the world an unrecognizable place.
Michael Dibdin. DARK SCEPTRE, p116.

The creative writer perceives his world once and for all in childhood and adolescence, and his whole career is an attempt to illustrate his personal world in terms of the great public world we all share.
Graham Greene. Intro. to THE HUMAN FACTOR, vi.

The difficulty for children trapped in the poverty-crime cycle is that they live their lives in which things are constantly being done to them. They are powerless because they are not adults but their parents are powerless too because someone else the DSS, loan-sharks, drug dealers - are always making decisions for them and they don't have enough money to give them the leeway to create any choices for themselves.
Linda Grant. "The Guardian". 17/3/98.

(re Gitta Sereny's book on Mary Bell) starts from the position that she believes in the innate goodness of human beings. I don't trust that belief. I think it is consoling but false to say that children are born good. A child is a bunch of inherited abilities and instincts - who it becomes will depend a lot on what society does to it, but to call it good or bad makes no sense.
Pat Barker. "The Guardian" 24/10/98.

CHOICE

I have a theory that every time you make an important choice, the part you left behind continues the other life you could have had.
Jeanette Winterson. ORANGES ARE NOT THE ONLY FRUIT, p215.

Choice from menus is a burden dressed up as a privilege. It is bondage with bells on. And, of course, it still makes us do all the work.
Lynn Truss. TALK TO THE HAND, p84.

In these days of relative affluence, people are persuaded to believe that more choice equals more happiness, and that life should be approached as a kind of happiness expedition to the shops. This attitude is not only paltry and degenerate, but it breeds misery and monsters.
Lynn Truss. TALK TO THE HAND, p85

"An ugly woman hopes to gain something from the lustre of her pretty friend; a pretty woman, for her part, hopes that she will stand out more lustrously against the background of the ugly woman; and for us it follows that our friendship is subjected to continuous trials. And it is precisely this that I value, that we will never leave the choice to the random development of events, nor even to some mutual struggle; choice for us is always a matter of courtesy...We'd offer each other the prettier girl like the two old-fashioned gentlemen who can never enter a room because neither wants to be the one who goes first."
Milan Kundera. LAUGHABLE LOVES. p107/8.

The idea that she was about to chose, not only a version of Lorin Jones's past, but her own unattractive future, made Polly giddy, as if she were standing on the top of a steep hill instead of looking out of an apartment window in a snowstorm. And what made it worse was the blurry knowledge that, once she had chosen, she would forget that there had ever been a choice. From the crossroads at the crest of the hill you can see in every direction; but after you start down one of the paths the view narrows, and other landscapes vanish.
Alison Lurie. THE TRUTH ABOUT LORIN JONES, p324.

CHRISTMAS & NEW YEAR

It's (Christmas Day) the worst day in the year and it brings out the bollocks in everybody.
Patrick Kavanagh in DEAD AS DOORNAILS, p74.

CITIES

The water of the fountain ran, the swift river ran, the day ran into evening, so much life in the city ran into death according to rule, time and tide waited for no man, the rats were sleeping close together in their dark holes again, the Fancy Ball was lighted up at supper, all things ran their course.
Charles Dickens. A TALE OF TWO CITIES, p70.

Stately Paris ignores the existence of these faces bleached by moral and physical suffering; but, then, Paris is in truth an ocean that no line can plumb. You may survey its surface and describe it; but no matter how numerous and painstaking the toilers in this sea, there will always be lonely and unexplored regions in its depths, caverns unknown, flowers and pearls and monsters of the deep overlooked or forgotten by the divers of literature. The Maison Vauquer is one of these curious monstrosities.
Honore de Balzac. OLD GORIOT, p10.

The great London dawn bled slowly into sight, a thin line of red blood leaking out between the rooftops, appearing at the windows of the building it had infiltrated, one at a time, as though in a soundless military coup.
Howard Jacobson. THE FINKLER QUESTION, p290.

The door to the balcony was open. The sky was the grayish-yellow night-blanket of a coal burning city, only marginally higher than our own yellow-grey ceiling.
Anna Funder. ALL THAT I AM, p193.

The city to which she was returning was inhuman in its indifference. It was a place of decaying brickwork and stinking waterways, a river that rose and fell with the tainted tide, and two canals of rotting lockgates and floating debris. It was a place of mindless despoliation where no building was sacred except the GPO.......
Patrick McGinley. THE FANTASIST, p61.

The city was a cold desert on a dark night. She walked between red-brick houses, past black iron railings, elegant street lamps, and doorways with semicircular fanlights; but when she looked for her reflection in them, all she could see were the images of childhood, motionless and unchanged - green winter wheat with patches of faded yellow, a tree reflected in a pool of water under a moire sky, gold cornfields on a misty morning with blackthorns like ghosts in the distance, a muddy pond like an evil eye in a meadow, driving rain like a thousand skivers on an unploughed field. She had come to the city with a thirst for experience, but so far her experience had been one of reservations
Patrick McGinley. THE FANTASIST, p 52.

"Do you like the city?"

"I do and I don't. It's like a rabbit warren, a maze of passages too complicated for any one person to get to know. When you arrive first, you're so excited you tell yourself that you won't rest till you know every inch of it, but after two weeks you're so overcome by the sameness of the burrows that you content yourself with two or three well-known runs. At first I thought the city was as mysterious as the country, but now I know I was wrong. The mystery of the country lanes, like the mystery of the best-loved nursery rhymes, makes you dream of greater mysteries, whereas the city in its indifference only breeds more indifference.

Patrick McGinley. THE FANTASIST, p200/1.

Is it merely its paintings, its palaces, the stones of its labyrinthine old quarter that draw us myriads of foreigners to Firenze like a magnet, despite the discomforts of the summer season? Or is it the odd combination of fanaticism and license, piety and cruelty, spirituality and sensual refinement, political corruption and intellectual daring, of its past that holds us in its sway in this stifling city deserted by its inhabitants?

Mario Vargas Llosa. THE STORYTELLER, p236.

Berlin. I used to love this old city. But that was before it caught sight of its own reflection and taken to wearing corsets laced so tight that it could hardly breathe. I loved the easy carefree philosophies, the cheap jazz, the vulgar cabarets and all the other cultural excesses that characterised the Weimar years and made Berlin seem like one of the most exciting cities in the world.

Philip Kerr. MARCH VIOLETS, p50.

Seattle was a pleasant place to live, but it was not a sexy city. No one dressed to impress, there was little eye-contact and street life was like her mother's cooking: bland, wholesome and homogenous.

Michael Dibdin. DARK SCEPTRE, p259.

CIVILIZATION

Why was K'ung-wen called cultured? The Master said, He was quick and loved learning; he was not ashamed to ask those beneath him: that is why he was called cultured.
Confucius. SAYINGS, p16.

If you were not ignorant and timid, civilization would be impossible.
Honore de Balzac. OLD GORIOT, p36.

'emotional knowledge' – people who had assimilated the idea that the Holocaust was a bad thing that should never be repeated, without knowing much about the details. Americans believed, as always, in a better future, in a morally better future. That was their civil religion. And if something called the Holocaust had denied familiar-sounding rights and freedoms, they were dutifully opposed.
Erna Paris. LONG SHADOWS: Truth, Lies and History', p327.

For a country is considered the more civilised the more the wisdom and efficiency of its laws hinder a weak man from becoming too weak or a powerful one too powerful.
Primo Levi. IF THIS IS A MAN, p94.

1960's - that golden age of high energy and low art........
All that remains of the Sixties guerilla is an unquenchable taste for anarchy: moral anarchy, artistic anarchy.
Martin Amis. THE MORONIC INFERNO, p88.

It would be a sad world if we all agreed and could not argue.
Hemingway to Bernard Berenson, 25/8/49.

Our culture is an arbitrary gadget and really not an intimate piece of our skin. Most people aren't aware how arbitrary it is.
Kurt Vonnegut.

Standards which would have shocked him in his own country seemed more like exciting indications of a different sense of values, here.
Doris Lessing. THE GRASS IS SINGING, p225.

In the trampled veldt where one area of Soweto ravelled into another the courts enclosed a quadrangle and their only access was from the verandah that ran along all four inner sides; red bricks and shrubs, hangover from the old colonial style when the forts of conquest became the administrative oases, ruled into geometrical lawn and flowerbeds that demarcated the gracious standards of the invader from the crude existence of his victims.
Nadine Gordimer. MY SON'S STORY, p225.

It is an age of exhausted whoredom groping for its god.
James Joyce. ULYSSES, p206.

One of the most elementary cultural skills is to know when (and how) to pretend not to know (or notice), how to go on and act as if something which has happened did not in fact happen.
Slavoj Zizek. LIVING IN THE END TIMES, p133

CLASS

Superiority is a two-way thing. If the people you feel superior to are suddenly removed, it can be quite devastating. The great thing about travelling business class or club class is not that you are being treated like a business man or a club member; it is that all that mob behind the curtain are being treated like tourists or economy class people. Your status is only defined by someone else's status.
Myles Kington. London INDEPENDENT. 5/89.

the leather jacket - symbol of free-thinking radicalism.
Sunday Times, Magazine, 30/7/89.

CLOTHES

Today he's wearing a white dress shirt with collar open, a navy blazer with a lining of brilliant scarlet, a black cashmere overcoat… This crossfire of dishevelment and suavity provides no end of fascination for Billy, and from it he infers a worldliness that could eat Bravo for breakfast and swallow the bones.
Ben Fountain, BILLY LYNN'S LONG HALFTIME WALK, p7.

CONFLICT

Germany's crime is the greatest crime the world has ever known, because it is not on a scale of History: it is on the scale of Evolution.
Lecomte du Nouy ('La Dignite Lumaine' 1944) in Diane Ackerman,
THE ZOOKEEPER'S WIFE, p92.

'...no means are criminal which are employed to obtain a sacred end'
Grachus Babeuf ('Conspiracy of Equals), quoted in Michael Burleigh's BLOOD AND RAGE: a Cultural History of Terrorism, p67

Conflict brings unhappiness, unhappiness poisons existence.
J M Coetzee. DUSKLANDS, p1.

The bullet is the hinge of history.
Mohammed Ali Agca.

(re Nazi atrocities) Perhaps one cannot, what is more one must not, understand what happened, because to understand is almost to justify.
Primo Levi. IF THIS IS A MAN & THE TRUCE, p395.

(re aerial duels) Above us, bare, helpless and unarmed, men of our time sought reciprocal death with the most refined of instruments.
Primo Levi. IF THIS IS A MAN, p178.

The Russian invasion (of Czechoslovakia) was not only a tragedy: it was a carnival of hate filled with a curious (and no longer explicable) euphoria.
Milan Kundera. THE UNBEARABLE LIGHTNESS OF BEING, p67.

(This reconciliation with Hitler) reveals the profound moral perversity of a world that rests essentially on the nonexistence of return, for in this world everything is pardoned in advance and therefore everything cynically permitted.
Milan Kundera. THE UNBEARABLE LIGHTNESS OF BEING, p4.

What is it like to be citizen of a superpower, to maintain democratically the means of planetary extinction?
Martin Amis. THE MORONIC INFERNO, ix.

The cost-benefit equation on this operation is already shot to shit!
Stephen Wright. MEDITATIONS IN GREEN, p186.

A Private knows intrinsically what a General must learn through experience. That is because a Private thinks with caution since he will be killed. A general can be daring when only the Private will die for his mistakes.
James Webb. FIELDS OF FIRE.

All the business or war, and indeed all the business of life, is an endeavour to find out what you don't know by what you do; that's what I call guessing what was at the other side of the hill.
Wellington.

The view that war is now to be won or lost by a magic button is a parochial delusion sustainable only in the relatively calm waters of Western Europe and the USA.
Dennis Barker. SOLDIERING ON.

In a war all is mental, and opinion makes up more than half of reality.
Napoleon.

Life, however, is like war: the more you experience it, the more terrifying it becomes.
Philip Caputo. THE HORN OF AFRICA.

A battlefield is, in a sense, a marketplace dedicated to the exchange of casualties.
Keegan & Holmes. SOLDIERS, p31.

War stories aren't really anything more than stories about people anyway.
Michael Herr. DISPATCHES, p196.

I think that Vietnam was what we had instead of happy childhoods.
Michael Herr. DISPATCHES, p195.

Conventional journalism could no more reveal this was than conventional firepower could win it, all it could do was take the most profound event of the American decade and turn it into a communications pudding, taking its most obvious, undeniable history and making it into a secret history.
Michael Herr. DISPATCHES, p175.

What is needed (for revolution) is the consciousness of poverty and the consciousness of oppression, and the conviction that poverty and oppression are not the natural order of this world.
Rysard Kapuscinski. SHAH OF SHAHS, p103.

And war, most of all, is a big confusion, on the field and in people's heads: half the time you can't even figure out who's won and who's lost. The generals decide that afterwards, and the people who write history books.
Primo Levi. IF NOT NOW, WHEN? p7.

Wars are fought by children. Conceived by their mad demonic elders and fought by boys.
Penelope Lively. MOON TIGER, p104.

The other great proletariat of the afterworld, of course, is the soldiery - those myriads of boy-faces beneath their tin hats, helmets, turbans, bearskins.......
Penelope Lively. MOON TIGER, p125.

War was a bracing current in the streams
Of a small country.
Frank Ormsby. THE EDGE OF WAR.

War endures......Before man was, war waited for him. The ultimate trade awaiting its ultimate practitioner.
.......(War) endures because young men love it and old men love it in them.
Cormac McCarthy. BLOOD MERIDIAN, p248.

War is the ultimate game because war is at last a forcing of the unity of existence.
Cormac McCarthy. BLOOD MERIDIAN, p249.

Conflicts between peoples, like conflicts between individuals, almost never end with the discovery of some redemptive formula. Rather, they gradually fade away, from weariness, from a steady erosion of ideological commitment, from fear of the escalating price of conflict, from a qualified willingness of the parties to make a half-conscious deal with their historical consciences.
Amos Oz. THE SLOPES OF LEBANON, p91.

Battle: nature's way of liquidating the weak and providing mates for the strong.
J.M. Coetzee. AGE OF IRON, p131.

A uniform is a sacerdotal vestment, a soldier is no longer a simple human being but a priest of death.
Hans Koningsberger. THE REVOLUTIONARY, p124.

It is well that war is so terrible, we should grow too fond of it.
Robert E Lee at Fredericksburg 1862-63.

The sorrow of war inside a soldier's heart was in a strange way similar to the sorrow of love. It was a kind of nostalgia, like the immense sadness of a world at dusk. It was a sadness, a misery, a pain which could send one soaring back into the past. The sorrow of the battlefield could not normally be pinpointed to one particular event, or even one person. If you focused on any one event it would soon become a tearing pain.
It was especially important, therefore, to avoid if possible focusing on the dead.
Bao Ninh. THE SORROW OF WAR, p86.

"Wonderful things can happen," Vincent said, "when you plant seeds of distrust in a garden of assholes."
Elmore Leonard. GLITZ, p161.

CONSCIENCE

I suppose that if one has no conscience one has no shame.
Henry James. THE PORTRAIT OF A LADY, p84.

(re Auschwitz) if we speak, they will not listen to us, and if they listen, they will not understand.
Primo Levi. IF THIS IS A MAN, p33.

If you believed that there was a fanlight in your mind, through which an old man with a beard was perpetually peering, taking down notes, you would think twice about throwing orgies in there.
David Lodge. GINGER, YOU'RE BARMY.

but whereas Christ speaks Hamlet is speech. He is the tormented empty sinful consciousness of man seared by the bright light of art, God's flayed victim dancing the dance of creation.
Iris Murdoch. THE BLACK PRINCE, p199.

"Ibergekumene tsores iz gut tsu dertseyln" - it's good to tell your past troubles.
Primo Levi. IF NOT NOW, WHEN? p239.

COURAGE

Courage – grace under pressure.
Hemingway.

CREATIVITY

Orthodoxy, whether of the right or of the left is the graveyard of creativity.
Chinua Achebe. ANTHILLS OF THE SAVANNAH, p100.

But however good you get at translating personality into line or print its no go if your personality isn't worth translating.
John Fowles. THE COLLECTOR, p169.

A picture is like a window straight through to your inmost heart.
John Fowles. THE COLLECTOR, p170.

When you draw something it lives, when you photograph it it dies.
John Fowles. THE COLLECTOR, p58.

That the discovery of the printing press led....to the spreading of knowledge, to propaganda, mendacity, contention and strife.
Graham Swift. WATERLAND, p118.

They say that genius lets grass and weeds and moss and rust grow on the fabric of ordinary existence while it concentrates, in blind and sublime exclusion, on the single burnished jewel it is in the process of creating.
H E Bates. LOVE FOR LYDIA, p299.

Having a mind is quite different from having a brain......a brain gets you on in the world, a mind lets you understand living.
Paul Potts. TO KEEP A PROMISE.

Talent is a dreadfully cheap commodity, cheaper than table salt....talent is a dull knife that will cut nothing unless it is wielded with great force - a force so great that the knife is not really cutting at all, but bludgeoning and breaking.....
Stephen King. INDEPENDENT, 11/11/89.

In the artist, there should be a strict separation between the man who suffers and the mind which creates.
T S Eliot.

The ability to find a mate, and with that mate make humans in your own image - if it didn't happen so often we'd be struck speechless by the grandeur of it.
Nuala O'Faolain. I.T. 7/1/91.

"Man is a minutely set, ingenious machine, for turning, with infinite artfulness, the red wine of Shiraz into urine."
Karen Blixen.

But that is only half the story, isn't it? We half perceive, but we also half create.
J.M. Coetzee. AGE OF IRON, p153.

With a beer and notebook on my desk, and concentrating for the first time since childhood on something that absorbed me, my thoughts raced: one idea pulled another behind it, like conjuror's handkerchiefs. I uncovered notions, connections, initiatives I didn't even know were present in my mind. I became more energetic and alive as I brushed in new colours and shades. I worked regularly and kept a journal: I saw that creation was an accretive process which couldn't be hurried, and which involved patience and, primarily, love.
Hanif Kureishi. THE BUDDHA OF SUBURBIA, p217.

CRIME

It shows the 31 year old star (Wynona Ryder) offering impromptu assistance to the fashion floor's inventory reduction programme.
Sunday Telegraph, 11/11/2012 describing Ryder in Saks in Beverley Hills where she stole a Gucci dress, St Laurent blouse, D&G handbag and 14 other items.

"Do not use," she said, "the possible crimes of one man to pay for the certain ones which you are about to commit!"
Thomas Keneally. THE PLAYMAKER, p277.

CRITICS & CRITICISM

We are culturally predisposed to sheltering criticism from criticism: we have enshrined the iconoclast.
Marilynne Robinson, WHEN I WAS A CHILD, p95.

There are hoards of critics eager to give birth. But it is a phantom pregnancy. Nothing is born.
Seamus O Sullivan. THE DUBLIN MAGAZINE, 10/87.

Besides, to distrust words, and indict them for the horrors that might slumber unobtrusively within them - isn't this, after all, the true vocation of the intellectual.
Vaclav Havel. INDEPENDENT, 9/12/89.

It is the critic's task, and there is hardly a more comical one, to coagulate an island of meaning upon a sea of negativity. (Kristeva)
Andre Brink. STATES OF EMERGENCY, p196.

While an author is yet living we estimate his powers by his worst performance, and when he is dead we rate him by his best.
Samuel Johnson. PREFACE TO SHAKESPEARE'S PLAYS.

There's no tension in "The Paradise Motel" (Eric McCormack) or in "The New York Trilogy" (Paul Auster) either: only a repertoire of well-rehearsed, deftly executed and quite familiar gestures of disillusionment. It's cocktail fiction: sophisticated, tiny and perfectly formed.
Colin Greenland. Sunday Times, 10/9/89.

CURIOSITY

Curiosity is a rash which men will scratch and scratch until it drives them frantic for the cure.
John Banville. DOCTOR COPERNICUS, p218.

DANGER

Those who find danger the salt of pleasure may visit Mecca; but if asked whether the results justify the risk, I should reply in the negative.
Sir Richard Burton.

Fame and power are aphrodisiacs......and so are courage and risk-taking. Most of us would not dare to tackle a high and remote mountain and yet we are drawn to those who do. They play out our fears and let us exercise our fascination with that edge between existence and death: we can read their articles and books or watch the films and slide shows, and be thrilled and horrified from the safety of our own unthreatened lives.
Maria Coffey. FRAGILE EDGE., p49.

DAWN

By the end of the day, the fate of the world would be decided; it began, like any other, with everyone waking and groaning and pulling the fragments of their consciousness together from wherever they had fallen in the course of the night.
Philip Hensher. THE MULBERRY EMPIRE, 210.s

Thus, while in the life the great whale's body may have been a real terror to his foes, in his death his ghost becomes a powerless panic to a world.
Herman Melville. MOBY DICK, p291.

He remembered the initial paraphenomena?
More active air, a matitutinal distant clock, ecclesiastical clocks at various points, avine music, the isolated thread of an early wayfarer, the visible diffusion of the light of an invisible luminous body, the first golden limb of the resurgent sun perceptible low on the horizon.
James Joyce. Ulysses, p626.

DEATH

Death is not an event in life; we do not live to experience death.
Wittgenstein.

Mary felt that the certainty of death and the uncertainty of both its timing and its meaning were fundamental facts of life.
Edward St Aubyn. AT LAST, p91.

I claim that the fact that we are strongly encouraged to identify with characters for whom death is not a significant creative possibility has real costs. We, the audience,.....lose any sense of eschatology, thus of teleology, and live in a moment that is, paradoxically, both emptied of intrinsic meaning or end and quite literally 'eternal'. If we're the only animals who know in advance we're going to die, we're also probably the only animals who would submit so cheerfully to the sustained denial of this undeniable and very important truth.
David Foster Wallace. BOTH FLESH AND NOT, p 51.

One death may explain itself, but it throws no light upon another.
E. M. Forster.

If we consider the entire Auschwitz universe, to its farthest reaches, as a youth I did not feel the acute, murderous, destructive discord and torment felt by every adult inmate who was uprooted and wrenched from his cultural world and its norms and hurled into a confrontation with norms of cruelty, of death. In my case, that discord, experienced by every adult inmate who remained alive, and which was almost always one of the elements of the shock that often felled them within a short time, did not exist, because this was the first world and the first order I had ever known: the order of selections, death as the sole certain perspective ruling the world..
Otto Dov Kulka, LANDSCAPES OF THE METROPOLIS OF DEATH, p23.

...and the wood of the coffin, struck by the pebbles, gave forth that dread sound that seems to us the reverberations of eternity.
Gustave Flaubert. MADAME BOVARY, p. 411.

The Five lived in a ferocious present because unlike the young, who entertain their finality in a remote, philosophical way, these women knew that death was not abstract.
Siri Hustvedt. THE SUMMER WITHOUT MEN, p11.

'When men die, they die in fear. They take everything they need from you, and as a doctor it is your job to give it, to comfort them, to hold their hand. But children die how they have been living – in hope. They don't know what's happening, so they expect nothing, they don't ask you to hold their hand – but you end up needing them to hold yours. With children, you're on your own..'
Tea Obreht. THE TIGER'S WIFE.

If you do not know how to die, don't worry yourself: Nature will inform you what to do on the spot, plainly and adequately.
Saul Frampton. WHEN I AM PLAYING WITH MY CAT, HOW DO I KNOW SHE IS NOT PLAYING WITH ME? p248

To a child, death is a story that is not quite believable.
Lloyd Jones. HERE AT THE END OF THE WORLD WE LEARN.

The British want so long for a funeral that people gather not so much to mourn, as to complain that the corpse is still hanging around.
Anne Enright. THE GATHERING, p182.

Everything was equal now. Only his own death came between him and his grave.
Gabriel Garcia Marquez. INNOCENT ERENDIRA, p82.

But life is never as we expect it to be. I recall an author reflecting that after death we may find ourselves not among choirs of angels but in some quite ordinary place, as for instance a bath-house on a hot afternoon, with spiders dozing in the corners; at the time it will seem like any Sunday in the country; only later will it come to us that we were in eternity.
J M Coetzee. FOE. p113/4.

His face remained closed, and I knew that in his eyes I was already dead, and that my present survival was no more than a brief administrative oversight.
J G Ballard. THE DAY OF CREATION, p132.

Violent deaths are natural deaths here. He died of his environment.
Graham Greene. THE COMEDIANS, p116.

The funeral aftermath - it was like a party from which the guest of honour had gone home early.
John Banville. MEFISTO, p107.

Self? It is the sum of everything we remember. Thus, what terrifies us about death is not the loss of the future but the loss of the past. Forgetting is a form of death ever present within life.
Milan Kundera. THE BOOK OF LAUGHTER & FORGETTING, p235.

People fascinated by the idea of progress never suspect that every step forward is also a step on the way to the end and that behind all the joyous "onward and up ward" slogans lurks the lascivious voice of death urging us to make haste.
Milan Kundera. THE BOOK OF LAUGHTER & FORGETTING, p179.

It is no coincidence that all poems about death depict it as a journey.
Milan Kundera. THE BOOK OF LAUGHTER & FORGETTING, p173.

If you wound the body of a dying man, the wound will begin to heal, even if the whole body dies within a day.
Primo Levi. IF THIS IS A MAN, p147.

What broke in a man when he could bring himself to kill another? If you wound the body of a dying man, the wound will begin to heal, even if the whole body dies within a day.
Alan Paton. CRY, THE BELOVED COUNTRY, p78.

(looking at a cancer victim) he saw how plausible it was to die, how death, far from invading earth like a meteor, occurs on the same plane as birth and marriage and the arrival of the daily mail.
John Updike. COUPLES, p473.

Images of death, dreamlike.
John Updike. COUPLES, p289.

For death.....produces a sudden nothingness in the world, a hole in the fabric of the world, with which the survivors must learn to live, and whether the lost one be loved or hated makes no difference, that learning still is difficult.
John Banville. DOCTOR COPERNICUS, p131.

There are situations in which consolation only threatens the equilibrium that time has instituted.
John Fowles. THE MAGUS, p309.

5 in red: five of ours dead. 7 in black: seven of theirs dead. More red and black digits in two columns at the bottom, without a line for totals, because death's account is always open.
Ryszard Kapuscinski. ANOTHER DAY OF LIFE, p80.

When you die, your awareness ceases, but, as long as there is awareness, then you participate in it. In other words, awareness belongs to the species, and the individual participates. You don't die, the individual "you" is simply transformed, forgetting all of your life, to the awareness of another. The dead see through the living......
So you participate in the pain, pleasure, and memory of some other individual. The nothingness we all fear doesn't exist, in fact cannot exist, unless awareness ceases to exist.....
Ian MacMillan. PROUD MONSTER, p92/3

(Someone dear to you has died) It is like travel. You journey from the event and as it becomes more distant it becomes less potent and more poignant, like a remembered home. As the weeks go by the knife turns differently.
Penelope Lively. MOON TIGER, p130.

Nothing resembles a person as much as the way he dies, and no death could resemble the man he was thinking about less than this one (death of Juvenal Urbino).
Gabriel Garcia Marquez. LOVE IN THE TIME OF CHOLERA, p256.

Death takes on reality only when it begins to penetrate through the crevices of old age.
Milan Kundera. LIFE IS ELSEWHERE, p104.

Philosophers say we own our deaths. I don't think so. Death contradicts ownership and self. If only one knew that all along.
Iris Murdoch. BRUNO'S DREAM, p130.

They're just decorating your death with the crepe-paper of love. If you don't make tracks now like an animal, they'll trick you into staying until you relax and forget that your life is your own.
Amos Oz. A PERFECT PEACE, p116.

What are all men's strivings, all that goes by the name of history, compared to his vain and ludicrous attempt to combat the absurdity of universal death, to give death a so-called meaning, as if it were possible to give death a meaning, to give it any other meaning than the one it has. The most cynical philosophers try to console the public by giving meaning, with the help of some higher logic or clever turns of phrase, to the meaninglessness of death. But what remains, to me at least, an inexplicable mystery is this: how has man been able, despite his knowledge of death, to go on living and acting, as though death were something outside him, as though it were a natural phenomenon.
Danilo Kis. HOURGLASS, p150.

Not even the devil can invent a vengeance for the blood of a small child.
Chaim Nachman Bialik.

I hung my head.....An old woman, sick and ugly, clawing on to what she has left. The living, impatient of long dyings; the dying, envious of the living.
J.M. Coetzee. AGE OF IRON, p50.

What is death after all, but an ascent into the final reaches of tiredness.
J.M. Coetzee. AGE OF IRON, p117.

Losing someone to AIDS - to anything, but especially to AIDS - is a university for the heart and an unwanted education in what really matters, how little anything else does.
Elgy Gillespie. I.T. 21/11/91.

Old people shroud themselves in the past during a war; that way they're ready to die when required.
Salman Rushdie. MIDNIGHT'S CHILDREN, p159.

'A railway accident is horrible for somebody who was on the train or who had a son there. But in news reports death means exactly the same thing as in the novels of Agatha Christie, who incidentally was the greatest magician of all time because she knew how to turn murder into amusement, and not just one murder but dozens of murders, hundreds of murders, an assembly-line of murders performed for our pleasure in the extermination camp of her novels. Auschwitz is forgotten, but from the crematorium of Agatha's novels the smoke is forever rising into the sky and only a very naive person could maintain that it is the smoke of tragedy.
Milan Kundera. IMMORTALITY, p133.

Do you realize what is the eternal precondition of tragedy? The existence of ideals which are considered more valuable than human life.
Milan Kundera. IMMORTALITY, p134.

"you can be a king or a street sweeper, but everybody dances with the grim reaper."
Last statement from condemned killer, Robert Alton Harris. 4/92.

Not only is death the one true arbiter of happiness (Solon's remark), it is the only measurement by which we can judge life itself.
Paul Auster. THE NEW YORK TRILOGY, p253.

".......What are you trying to prove down here? Why do you cut yourself off from everybody, everything?"
"It's just that I'm undergoing this very big change in my life called dying."
"Retirement isn't death."
"A distinction without a difference."
Toni Morrison. TAR BABY, p24.

(a baby dying) Her eyes were clear. She did not smile or cry. She did not turn away. She was watching me, listening to me. And I was remembering something I once heard: that right before children die, they become as they would have been had they lived a whole life. They understand their life, no matter how small it has been. And in her eyes I felt she was telling me, "This is my quick life, no worse, no better than a long one. I accept this, no blame."
Amy Tan. THE KITCHEN GOD'S WIFE, p267.

I held her hand, which could only muster a faint returning grip. If I had not known this was my mother, I would scarcely have recognised her. All the cheerful plumpness she had gained in middle age had gone. She was a bag of bones. Her eyes, little trapped pools in their sunken sockets, seemed the only living things about her. They looked at me, over the wall of her speechlessness, and I could not tell what their infinitesimal glints and dilations meant.
Graham Swift. EVER AFTER, p38.

... she put back her head and looked up at the sky, which was moonless and starless and black. She tried to imagine the baby in such a blackness, but this was not a void, and she could not properly imagine a soul beyond help, beyond time, beyond reach, for she could feel a light breeze upon her face and the ground under her feet was hard and cold; the leaves rustled in the orchard and she could hear the cries of the birds; when she breathed in, she could smell the earth's dampness. Then she knew she would never be able to take her own life, that it was a thing too terrible and too sacred. Death did not end life, it merely changed it. She knew that she would never be able to believe any thing other than this. The baby was still real, but it was a reality outside time.
Deirdre Madden. THE BIRDS OF THE INNOCENT WOOD, p100/101.

As Drew was leaving the cemetery, an army foot patrol was entering and spreading out among the gravestones. The dead too needed watching here. The dead above all needed watching here. Containing the dead, it could be said, was the beginning and end of policy in Northern Ireland. Containing the dead, it could even be said, was the whole rationale for the country's existence. But, whatever the policy or the rationale, the dead continued to leave their traces wherever you looked. They were there in the lilacs left annually on the platform of a suburban railway station, they were there in the small bunch of freesias tied to a bus-shelter on a quiet country road; they were there in the wreaths laid at the sides of disused barns and on the tops of hedgerows; they were there in the sudden efflorescence of nondescript city footpaths. They were everywhere nowhere, not to be sidestepped, no matter how far to the side you tried to step.
Glenn Patterson. FAT LAD, p 277.

Mirabeau announced that he would like a shave, since "my friend, I will die today. When one has come to that, all one can do is be perfumed, crowned with flowers, enveloped in music and wait comfortably for the sleep from which one will never wake."
Simon Schama. CITIZENS, p543.

But death is only part of life: one cannot see it, when recently bereaved; one sees only pain, waste, anger and humiliation, the worst and not the best. Only with time does the end sink back into proportion, become part of the whole. And that's another reason why the death of children is so particularly dreadful, and early deaths worse than later ones - there is less lived time available into which dying time can be swallowed up and incorporated.
Fay Weldon. LETTERS TO ALICE, p150.

She has left the house before, on two occasions: for the funeral of her father, and a year and a half later for that of her mother. At both she'd been reminded of the death of her cousin, not that reminding was necessary; but the words of farewell were the same, the repetition causing her to

reflect that the dead become nothing when you weary of doing their living for them. You pick and choose among the dead; the living are thrust upon you.
William Trevor. READING TURGENEV, p160.

The cemeteries were covered in snow, and they found it difficult to keep their sense of direction with only their maps to guide them. It was as though the snow was somehow averse to letting them remove the remains it was concealing in its depths. It had wrapped them in such delicate white, tranquil covering, and then as soon as the picks and shovels began their work everything became ugly: the glittering blanket was crushed and trampled. gashed open in places, to remain disfigured like that until a new fall of snow should come to dress its wounds.
Ismail Kadare. THE GENERAL OF THE DEAD ARMY, p186.

Death was the only absolute value in my world. Lose life and one would lose nothing again for ever. I envied those who could believe in a God and I distrusted them. I felt they were keeping their courage up with a fable of the changeless and the permanent. Death was far more certain than God, and with death there would be no longer the daily possibility of love dying. The nightmare of a future of boredom and indifference would lift. I could never have been a pacifist. To kill a man was surely to grant him an immeasurable benefit. Oh yes, people always, everywhere, loved their enemies. It was their friends they preserved for pain and vacuity.
Graham Greene. THE QUIET AMERICAN, p44.

...I like a good funeral...... more than I enjoy weddings. With funerals you know where you are, and also where, before long, you yourself will be. A funeral closes a chapter, gracefully or otherwise, according to the nature of the case. A wedding, on the other hand, opens up .... a train of awesome possibilities. At a funeral you meet people you know and may not have seen for a long time and are glad to see. At a wedding it is quite otherwise.
Maurice Craig.   THE ELEPHANT AND THE POLISH QUESTION, p59.

I wondered why it was that only black people seemed to treat death realistically in their art. White people wrote about it as an abstraction, used it as a poetic device, concerned themselves with it only when it was remote. Most of Shakespeare's and Frost's poems about death were written when both men were young. When Billy Holiday, Blind Loman Jefferson, or Leadbelly sang about it, you heard the cock of the prison guard's rifle, saw the black silhouette suspended from a tree against a dying red sun, smelled the hot pine box being lowered into the same Mississippi soil a sharecropper had laboured against all his life.
James Lee Burke.   THE NEON RAIN, p209.

Graveyards remind us of the vanity of all human endeavour.
Ivan Klima. WAITING FOR THE DARK, WAITING FOR THE LIGHT, p24.

...If he's waiting for anything it's waiting for death, and he's curious about what the face of death will look like. Will it be like an old woman who creeps about the world with a scythe, or will it be a beautiful young girl who approaches him with open arms?
Ivan Klima. WAITING FOR THE DARK, WAITING FOR THE LIGHT, p147.

When loved ones die, you have to live on their behalf. See things as though with their eyes. Remember how they used to say things, and use those words. Be thankful that you can do things that they cannot, and also feel the sadness of it.
Louis de Bernieres. CAPTAIN CORELLI'S MANDOLIN, p349.

Sometimes it seemed to me that children believed death occurred in different forms than adults did, in varying degrees, and that it intersected with life in all kinds of ways that were unofficial. It was adults who felt death exerted a lurid sameness over everyone. Why couldn't it be as varied as life was? Or at least have its lurid sameness similarly gussied up and disguised?

Lorrie Moore. A GATE AT THE STAIRS, p228.

DEFEAT

Defeat is a thing of weariness, of incoherence, of boredom and, above all, of futility.
Antoine de Saint-Exupery.

Moses never entered the Promised Land. He failed the test in the wilderness and died in the mountains.

DEFINITIONS

a philosopher is a blind man in a dark room looking for a black cat that isn't there, and a theologian is a man who has found it.
Letter to Irish Times, 30/6/88.

Graphomania - the desire to write books, to have a public of unkonown readers.
Milan Kundera. THE BOOK OF LAUGHTER & FORGETTING, p92.

M is for Marx and Movement of Masses
and Massing of Arses and Clashing of Classes.
Cyril Connolly.

It was doubtless an ingenious idea to call the camel the ship of the desert, but it would hardly lead one far in training that beast.
O Aristotle, if you had had the advantage of being "the freshest modern" instead of the greatest ancient, would you not have mingled your praise of metaphorical speech, with a lamentation that intelligence so rarely shows itself in speech without metaphor - that we can so seldom declare what a thing is, except by saying it is something else.
George Eliot. THE MILL ON THE FLOSS, p142.

A literary movement according to AE: "Five or six people who live in the same town and who hate each other cordially.

As soon as you have managed to define something in words, it has already slipped - crawled - away into a blurred shadowy twilight.
Amos Oz. TO KNOW A WOMAN, p91.

DREAMS

Dreams - simple elements, violent combinations.
Amos Oz. TOUCH THE WATER, TOUCH THE WIND.

Dreams are always different. That's what the word means: something real in another form, everything falsified.
Rachel Ingalls. BINSTEAD'S SAFARI, p133.

Our dreams prove that to imagine - to dream about things that have not happened - is among mankind's deepest needs. Herein lies the danger. If dreams were not beautiful, they would quickly be forgotten.
Milan Kundera. THE UNBEARABLE LIGHTNESS OF BEING, p59.

Dreaming must be fun. A way of telling a story to yourself without having to make sense, because there's no one else there. The story the dreamer dreams can be told in its own way, in its own order.
Jenni Diski. LIKE MOTHER, p30.

For even day-dreams need an element of hope to give satisfaction to the dreamer.
Doris Lessing. THE GRASS IS SINGING, p163.

The most beautiful thing about dreams is that fantastic meetings can take place, encounters between people and objects that could never happen in ordinary life. In a dream a boat could sail into a room through an open window, a woman dead for twenty years could rise from a bed, get into the boat and the boat could suddenly change into a coffin and the coffin could float by flower-strewn banks of a river. He cited the famous dictum of Lautreamont about beauty - the beauty to be found "in the random meeting of an umbrella and a sewing machine on an operating-room table".
Milan Kundera. LIFE IS ELSEWHERE, p42.

Dionysus is a mythological figure, but what makes his worshippers extraordinary is that they themselves developed myths.......Mythology is the dream-world language of society's unconscious: individuals dream, and try to interpret their dreams; myths try to make sense of those forces in the world which are beyond the reach of reason. Both dream and myth offer means of taking a symbolic hold, privately or collectively, on realities deeper and more literally unspeakable than those which our everyday lives will contain or represent.
Ronald Harwood. ALL THE WORLD'S A STAGE, p39.

Our dreams can be heavy with significance or at least emotion for us but are always pure nonsense for our interlocutor.
Primo Levi. THE MIRROR MAKER, p95.

A dream ran like a fuse towards the final deaths of the players of the dream, but the fuse in Mrs. Kempster's case might have run for forty or fifty years, since as everyone knows time was suspended in sleep.
Thomas Keneally. THE PLAYMAKER, p189.

"I have had a rich dream-life since I stopped taking sleeping tablets two years ago. Thank God for dreams! I think one needs to keep rooted in the mythic, symbolic dreamworld which is not accessible to consciousness; it is the grounding for all of us.
Dr. Oliver Sachs. Sunday Times Magazine. 30/6/91.

....in dreams we are always children.
J.M. Coetzee. AGE OF IRON, p152.

Is there any better way to pass these last days (waiting for the barbarians to arrive) than in dreaming of a saviour with a sword who will scatter the enemy hosts and forgive us the errors that have been committed by others in our name and grant us a second chance to build our earthly paradise? I lie on the bare mattress and concentrate on bringing into life the image of myself as a swimmer swimming with even, untiring strokes through the medium of time, a medium more inert than water, without ripples, persuasive, colourless, odourless, dry as paper.
J. M. Coetzee. WAITING FOR THE BARBARIANS, p143.

These (outbuildings) housed rusting machinery, the specific purpose of which was to remain obscure; no doubt something to do with husking nuts. The sight sobered me: corrupting iron, that was all that was left of a vision of the mind that had been perfect in its insubstantial state: the nightmare skeletons of someone else's dream. There's something about the tropics which seem to damn these schemes to perdition, to tempt men to such lush fantasies, extravagant declarations and beginnings which have this way of petering out into....nothing.
Timothy Mo. THE REDUNDANCY OF COURAGE, p48.

There's more truth in the chastity of dreams than in the kiss and steam of copulation.
Patrick McGinley. THE FANTASIST, p72.

DRUGS

They pulled their charpoys well away from my father's godown to avoid falling beams and showering sparks; and lying on their rope beds they sipped their tea and entered the bittersweet declensions of the drug. At first they became raucous, shouting the praises of their favourite whores in Pushtu; then they fell into wild giggling as the soft fluttering fingers of the drug tickled their ribs.......until the giggling gave way to dreams and they roamed in the frontier passes of the drug, riding the horses of the drug, and finally reached a dreamless oblivion from which nothing on earth could awaken them until the drug had run its course.
Salman Rushdie. MIDNIGHT'S CHILDREN, p89.

EDUCATION

The things they don't teach you at school. How to love. How to die. How to stage a dramatic comeback.
Shehan Karumatilaka. CHINAMAN, p4.

Education's about......the opposition of teacher and student. It's about what gets rubbed off between persistence of the one and the resistance of the other.
Graham Swift. WATERLAND, p207.

He continues to teach because it provides him with a livelihood; also because it teaches him humility, brings it home to him who he is in the world. The irony does not escape him: that the one who comes to teach learns the keenest lessons, while those who come to learn learn nothing.
J. M. Coetzee. DISGRACE, p5.

It is the manner of knowing that is important. We know the meaning of the singular thing only so long as we content ourselves with knowing it in the midst of other meanings; isolate it, and all meaning drains away. It is not the thing that counts, you see, only the interaction of things.
John Banville. DOCTOR COPERNICUS, p251.

stunning them with blunt classics.
John Updike. BECH, A BOOK, p87.

The greater the mind, the simpler the man.
Paul Potts on Swift.

A public school education cuts off a boy's retreat; he can no longer become a labourer or a mechanic, and these are the only people whose tenure of independence is not precarious.
Samuel Butler. THE WAY OF ALL FLESH, p35.

The skill of the master is lost in the pupil's lack of it.
Robert Bolt. A MAN FOR ALL SEASONS, act 1, p28.

If they are involved in communicating one particular ideology to young pupils in a context in which the pupils can hardly be expected to critically evaluate the supporting evidence; if the pupils are normally not exposed to alternative theories of similar scope; and if the manner of teaching relies on the innocent faith of the young rather than on their critical evaluation of the evidence available; then, whether they advert to it or not, teachers may well be involved in indoctrination.
Desmond M Clarke. OIDEAS 30, Spring 1987.

A schoolboy may be defined as one who can tell you what he knows in the order in which he has learned it.
Robert Frost. THE FIGURE A POEM MAKES.

Many of us stay away from school reunions because we don't want to be reminded how others saw us.
Blake Morrison. Independent on Sunday, 16/6/91.

The central question in teaching English is how to construct the relationship between the growth of knowledge and the critical practice of children as they read, write and speak.
Michael Armstrong. Times Educational Supplement, 28/5/93.

The difference between educated and uneducated people is perhaps largely that the educated can sometimes identify and allow for inherited elements in their ways of thinking and feeling, whereas to the less educated they appear to be part of nature and hence unquestionable.
Maurice Craig. THE ELEPHANT AND THE POLISH QUESTION, p56.

I think there are two important parts to education. One is to make sure you learn what you need to know whether you like it or not...... The other is to teach you how to organise knowledge and how to follow up any line of enquiry which happens to take your fancy.
Maurice Craig. THE ELEPHANT AND THE POLISH QUESTION, p73.

"I'd have thought you'd have been a good teacher."
"No....teachers need all sorts of large certainties."
Hilary Mantel. A CHANGE OF CLIMATE, p173.

Relationship between master and pupils: an intellect which has already actualised its own potentialities, with another intellect whose potentialities are still to be actualised by the teaching of the master.
Education is the art of leading from cocksure ignorance to thoughtful uncertainty.
Wilde.

ENDEAVOUR

"It is not the critic who counts: not the man who points out how the strong man stumbles or where the doer of deeds could have done better. The credit belongs to the man who is actually in the arena, whose face is marred by dust and sweat and blood, who strives valiantly, who errs and comes up short again and again, because there is no effort without error or shortcoming, but who knows the great enthusiasms, the great devotions, who spends himself for a worthy cause; who, at the best, knows, in the end, the triumph of high achievement, and who, at the worst, if he fails, at least he fails while daring greatly, so that his place shall never be with those cold and timid souls who knew neither victory nor defeat."

Theodore Roosevelt, 1910

EQUALITY

Fairness is not a province of the imagination. Fairness is the business of a tribunal, which is not the same animal.
Howard Jacobson. THE FINKLER QUESTION, p160.

EVIL

Her replies were kind and funny and perceptive - but above all pessimistic. She believed, and was entitled to believe, I must say, that all human beings were evil by nature, whether tormentors or victims, or idle standers-by. They could only create meaningless tragedies, she said, since they weren't nearly intelligent enough to accomplish all the good they meant to do. We were a disease, she said, which had evolved on one tiny cinder in the universe, but could spread and spread.
Kurt Vonnegut. JAILBIRD, p23.

EXCUSE

Jeffrey was a sad excuse for anything except an excuse.
Eric J Laing. CICADA, p105.

EXPECTATION

..but surely I shall see him before night; I feared the meeting in the morning; now I desire it, because expectation has been so long baffled that it is grown impatient.
Charlotte Bronte. JANE EYRE, p120.

FAME

Be sure of this, o young ambition, all mortal greatness is but a disease.
Herman Melville. MOBY DICK, p67 (K)

...for the common man the beings who are the most desired, and at the same time entirely real, are beings beyond reach. Everyone knows of the Queen of England, of her sister the Princess, of the former wife of the President of the United States, of the famous movie stars; that is to say, no one who is normal doubts for a minute the actual existence of such persons, even though he cannot directly (by touch) substantiate their existence. In turn, he who can boast of a direct acquaintance with such persons will no longer see in them phenomenal paragons of wealth, femininity, power, beauty, etc., because, in entering into contact with them, he experiences - by dint of everyday things - their completely ordinary, normal, human imperfection. For such persons, up close, are not in the least godlike beings or otherwise extraordinary. Beings that are truly at the pinnacle of perfection, that are therefore boundlessly desired, yearned for, longed after, must be remote even to full unattainability. It is their elevation above the masses that lends them their magnetic glamour; it is not qualities of body or soul but an unbridgeable social distance that accounts for their seductive halo.
Stanislaw Lem. A PERFECT VACUUM, p24.

FAMILY

(there are such unpleasant people in most families. Perhaps even in the highest aristocracy there are Brobdingnag specimens, gigantically in debt and bloated at greater expense)
George Eliot. MIDDLEMARCH, p181.

You'd think family would be the one sure thing in life, the gimme? Points you get just for being born? So much thick meaty, stuff bound you to these people, so many interlocking spirals of history, genetics, common cause, and struggle that it should be the most basic of all drives, that you would strive to protect and love one another, yet this bond that should be the big no-brainer was in fact the hardest thing.
Ben Fountain, BILLY LYNN'S LONG HALFTIME WALK, p100.

Creatures of habit, her husband and son. They shared a great love for the comfort of sameness.
Nathan Englander, THE MINISTRY OF SPECIAL CASES, p39.

Happy families are all alike; every unhappy family is unhappy in its own way.
Leo Tolstoy. ANNA KARENINA. (opening sentence).

There is perhaps nothing in family life, except a marriage of one of the daughters, so happily fingered-over as the aura which surrounds the first child sent up to university. Everyone from the servant to the grandmother must reach out to touch it; a faint nimbus of distinction, like a smear of phosphorescence rubbed on through contact, glimmers from them as well.
Nadine Gordimer. THE SOFT VOICE OF THE SERPENT, p76.

Television brought them the outer world. The little screen's icy brilliance implied a universe of profound cold beyond the warm encirclement of friends and family.
John Updike. COUPLES., p240.

We didn't have any particular sense of what we were - my sister and I. I mean, my father made of the circumscription of our life within the areas open to us a charmed circle.
Nadine Gordimer. MY SON'S STORY, p20.

It's not the fact that you're your father's son that's horrible, it's that you've started talking like your father... And my father. And my mother....All of us. As if one human being after another is nothing but a reject. One fresh draft is made after another, and each in turn is rejected and crumpled up and thrown in the wastepaper basket, to be replaced by a new, slightly improved version. How futile it all seems. How dull. What a pointless joke.
Amos Oz. MY MICHAEL, p198.

FANATICS

In that disputatious Province (Ulster) where the placing of a comma can mean a mass walk-out followed by riots, blazing busses and a half-dozen corpses, every nuance mattered.
Ferdinand Mount. COLD CREAM, p334.

There's no stopping a man in the pursuit of his own ambition, particularly if he's read God's mind and found that they think alike.
J Rizkalla. THE JERICHO GARDEN, cf Sunday Times, 10/4/88.

The most intolerable people are provincial celebrities.
Chekhov.

Recklessness is almost a man's revenge on his woman. He feels he is not valued, so he will risk destroying himself to deprive her altogether.
D H Lawrence. SONS AND LOVERS, p235.

Fear prophets, and those prepared to die for the truth, for as a rule they make many others die with them, often before them, at times instead of them.
Umberto Eco. THE NAME OF THE ROSE, p491.

The worst madman is the one who fails to consider the possibility of somebody else's being mad, too.
Vladimir Nabokov. CONVERSATION PIECE, 1945.

FATE & DESTINY

Pues no podemos haber aquello que queremos, queramos aquello que podremos.
Since we cannot get what we like, let us like what we can get.
Spanish proverb.   George Eliot. MIDDLEMARCH, p269.

It would all be so easy if all the things you meant to do were the things that happened.
H E Bates. LOVE FOR LYDIA, p240.

The heavier the burden (eternal return is the heaviest), the closer our lives come to the earth, the more real and truthful they become.
Milan Kundera. THE UNBEARABLE LIGHTNESS OF BEING, p5.

The goals we pursue are always veiled. A girl who longs for marriage longs for something she knows nothing about. The boy who hankers after fame has no idea what fame is. The thing that gives our every move its meaning is always totally unknown to us.
Milan Kundera. THE UNBEARABLE LIGHTNESS OF BEING, p122.

Fate holds terrible forfeits for those who gamble on certainties.
Winston Churchill.

Fear prophets, and those prepared to die for the truth, for as a rule they make many others die with them, often before them, at times instead of them.
Umberto Eco. THE NAME OF THE ROSE, p491.

For there are moments, out here in this place and at this time, when she feels that she is untethered, no longer hitched to past or future or to a known universe but adrift in the cosmos.
Penelope Lively. MOON TIGER, p90.

I have the feeling that deep inside every man there's something he is 'meant' to do. Something no one but he can achieve. And then it's a matter of discovering what your own personal something is. Some find it quite early in life. Others drive themselves to distraction trying to find it. And still others learn to be patient and prepare themselves for the day when, suddenly, they'll recognise it. Like an actor waiting for his cue.
Andre Brink. A DRY WHITE SEASON, p29.

.....And then you realise that all your life you've been hanging around waiting for something to happen, something special, something really worthwhile. But all that happens is that time passes.
Andre Brink. A DRY WHITE SEASON, p129

For each man's destiny is as large as the world he inhabits and contains within it all opposites as well......
Cormac McCarthy. BLOOD MERIDIAN, p330.

I hold the world but as the world, Gratiano;
A stage where every man must play his part,
And mine a sad one.
Antonio in THE MERCHANT OF VENICE, I,i 76.

Sometimes she seems to remind me of Browning's Pippa. You know: destined to wander through the world, and waking people with her little song, and going on again as lonely as before.
Andre Brink. LOOKING ON DARKNESS, p360.

Destiny is larger than facts or events. It is something to believe in the outside the ordinary borders of the senses, with God so distant from our lives.
Some people don't believe in God but they colour eggs at Easter just to change the pattern of their days.
Don De Lillo. LIBRA, p204.

.....I was rather gratified by the Met's good fortune. Their history was even more abominable than the Cubs', and to witness their sudden, wholly improbable surge from the depths seemed to prove that anything in this world was possible. There was consolation in that thought. Causality was no longer the hidden demiurge that ruled the universe: down was up, the last was the first, the end was the beginning. Heraclitus had been resurrected from his dung heap and what he had to show us was the simplest of truths: reality was a yo-yo, change was the only constant.
Paul Auster. MOON PALACE, p62.

When we meet those we fall in love with, there is an aspect of our spirit that is historian, a bit of a pedant, who imagines or remembers a meeting when the other has passed by innocently, just as Clifton might have opened a car door for you a year earlier and ignored the fate of his life. But all parts of the body must be ready for the other, all atoms must jump in one direction for desire to occur.
    I have lived in the desert for years and I have come to believe in such things. It is a place of pockets. The *tromp l'oeil* of time and water. The jackal with one eye that looks back and one that regards the path you consider taking. In his jaws are pieces of the past he delivers to you, and when all of that is fully discovered it will prove to have been already known.
Michael Ontaatje. THE ENGLISH PATIENT, p259.

FEAR

I was frightened, but I was even more frightened of showing my fear- that would unleash him. Like a savage dog he was safer while he barked.
Graham Greene. THE COMEDIANS, p226.

Vertigo is something other than the fear of falling. It is the voice of the emptiness below us which tempts and lures us, it is the desire to fall, against which, terrified, we defend ourselves.Milan Kundera. THE UNBEARABLE LIGHTNESS OF BEING, p60.

Cry, the beloved country, for the unborn child that is the inheritor of our fear. Let him not love the earth too deeply. Let him not laugh too gladly when the water runs through his fingers, nor stand too silent when the setting sun makes red the veldt with fire. Let him not be too much moved when the birds of his land are singing, not give too much of his heart to a mountain or a valley. For fear will rob him of all if he gives too much.
Alan Paton. CRY, THE BELOVED COUNTRY, p72.

and if charity does not move those who have everything to spare, fear will.
Nadine Gordimer. SOMETHING OUT THERE. p181.

When ignorance and superstition replace curiosity and information the result is fear.
Michael Longley.

The people too were changed in the evening, quieted. They seemed to be a part of an organisation of the unconscious. They obeyed impulses which registered only faintly in their thinking minds. Their eyes were inwards and quiet, and their eyes, too, were lucent in the evening, lucent in dusty faces.
John Steinbeck. THE GRAPES OF WRATH, p85.

FEELINGS

Those who use emotion to make other people feel lose it for themselves.
David Grossman. THE ZIGZAG KID, p300.

"We human beings, the crown of creation, make use of only twenty or thirty feelings in our entire life span! And in a regular and intensive way - ten or fifteen at most!
David Grossman. SEE UNDER: LOVE, p440.

Desire lies on the other side of repugnance.
A.S. Byatt. POSSESSION, p56.

"Why cry out against passions? Are they not the one beautiful thing on earth, the source of heroism, of enthusiasm, of poetry, music, the arts, of everything, in a word?"
Gustave Flaubert. MADAME BOVARY, p163.

(Emma's ecstasy) An azure of infinity encompasses her, the heights of sentiment sparkled under her thought, and ordinary existence appeared only afar off, down below in the shade, through the interspan of these heights.
Gustave Flaubert. MADAME BOVARY, p183.

She often longed to feel free and easy about her body.......She had even invented a special course in self-persuasion. She would repeat to herself that at birth every human being received one out of millions of available bodies, as one would receive an allotted room out of the millions of available rooms in an enormous hotel. Consequently, the body was fortuitous and impersonal, it was only a ready-made, borrowed thing. She would repeat this to herself in different ways, but she could never manage to feel it. This mind-body dualism was alien to her. She was too much one with her body; that is why she always felt such anxiety about it.
Milan Kundera. LAUGHABLE LOVES, p15.

But Charles was as yet only one-and-twenty years of age, an age when the freshness of life seems inseparable from the candor and purity of the soul; when the voice, the look, the countenance seem in harmony with the feelings.
Honore de Balzac. EUGENIE GRANDET, p161.

and made you gasp
into the awareness of my need.
John F Deane. ESTATE.

But the faithful don't commemorate the date of his death, they don't have to; sentiment is for those who don't know what to do next.
Nadine Gordimer. BURGER'S DAUGHTER, p130.

If we had kept them up, would he have opened his heart to me and allowed me to glimpse what his intentions were? Most likely not. The sort of decision arrived at by saints and madmen is not revealed to others. It is forged little by little, in the folds of the spirit, tangential to reason, shielded from indiscreet eyes, not seeking their approval of others - who would never grant it - until it is at last put into practice. I imagine that in the process - the conceiving of a project and its ripening into action - the saint, the visionary, or the madman isolates himself more and more, walling himself up in solitude, safe from the intrusion of others.
Mario Vargas Llosa. THE STORYTELLER, p34.

FOLLY

Nature, in her wisdom, seems to have arranged it so that men's stupidities should be ephemeral, and books make them immortal. A fool ought to be content with having exasperated everyone around him, but he insists on tormenting future generations; he wants his foolishness to overcome the oblivion which he might have enjoyed like a tomb; he wants posterity to be informed that he existed, and to be aware for ever that he was a fool.
Montesquieu. PERSIAN LETTERS, p134.

FOOD & DRINK

…insisted with the same urgency they once applied to snapping up the check at dinner: hospitality as ferocious force of nature.
Gillian Flynn. GONE GIRL.

'What are you trying to do?' Ottavio demanded indignantly. 'Put me out of business? Listen, the lamb is fabulous today. And when I say fabulous, I'm saying less than half the truth. Tender young sucklings, so sweet, so pretty it was a sin to kill them. But since they're dead already it would be a bigger sin not to eat them.'
Michael Dibdin. RATKING, p33.

When a man is properly drunk it is as though he is in a room by himself – there is a physical, impenetrable separation between him and his fellows.
Thomas de Witt. THE SISTERS BROTHERS, p60.

What you don't want is soup as warm as the champagne, the champagne as old as the chicken, and the chicken as fat as the waitress.
Sir Clement Freud, at a Graham Greene festival, quoted by Richard Green, Sunday Telegraph, 21/10/07.

Brandy - the mature man's consolation.
William Golding. THE PAPER MEN, p76.

Guy sat at the kitchen table and gazed, with steady incomprehension, at his veal: its pallor, its puddled beach juice. He had cooked the dinner himself, as usual, expressionlessly busying himself with meat-pounder, pasta-shredder, vegetable-slicer. The kitchen was a spotless laboratory of time-saving devices. Time was constantly being saved. But for what?
Martin Amis. LONDON FIELDS, p211.

For Quinn learned that eating did not necessarily solve the problem of food. A meal was no more than a fragile defence against the inevitability of the next meal. Food itself could never answer the question of food: it only delayed the moment when the question would have to be asked in earnest.
Paul Auster. THE NEW YORK TRILOGY, p114.

.......I found no end of nourishment around me. Pizza crusts, fragments of hot dogs, the butt ends of hero sandwiches, partially filled cans of soda - the meadows and rocks were strewn with them, the trash bins were fairly bursting with the abundance. To undercut my squeamishness, I began giving funny names to the garbage cans. I called them cylindrical restaurants, pot-luck dinners, municipal care packages - anything that could deflect me from saying what they really were.
Paul Auster. MOON PALACE, p60.

When the pint was first poured, it was a uniform creamy brown. Then the brown began falling in gentle waves to create the black while the same tiny bubbles rose to make a creamy collar on top. She could watch this simple phenomenon forever, not only because of the wonder of the goodness both rising and falling but because it reminded her of an hourglass and time passing pleasantly. Finally, when the black had separated from the white, the vigilant barman would put the tumbler under the tap until a thick, creamy top rose in a perfect convex over the rim. The separate black and white represented a world in which evil and good cohabited, in which the delights of evil are best tasted through the mollification of the good, as the black must be drunk through the white.
Patrick McGinley. THE FANTASIST, p36.

FORGIVENESS

Closing Schrab's door, I wondered if that was how forgiveness budded, not with the fanfare of epiphany, but with pain gathering its things, packing up and slipping away unannounced in the middle of the night.
Kallid Hosseini. THE KITE RUNER, p313.

FREEDOM

It can be atheism, not religion, that becomes a comforting illusion. We are free because there is no one to tell us what we may or may not do.
Jonathan Sacks. THE GREAT PARTNERSHIP, p210/211.

It was good to be moving, good to be free at times like this. The happy ache that came of knowing you were alive in a foreign place, and richly lost. Where none of your rules apply, where nothing you know is of any use.
Christopher Hope. MY MOTHER'S LOVERS, p163.

The charm of a liberal way of life is that it enables most people to renounce their freedom knowingly. Allowing the majority of humankind to imagine they are flying fish even as they pass their lives under the waves, liberal civilization rests on a dream.
John Gray. THE SILENCE OF ANIMALS, p62.

We have to use our freedom and privileges to see what respite we can give to those less equipped to deal with their challenges. (Andrew Boe, criminal lawyer)
Chloe Hooper, TALL MAN, p9.

(interest in books 'that had nothing Western about them'.) But I think it was in fact peculiarly western to feel no tie of particularity to any single past or history, to experience that much underrated thing called deracination, the meditative, free appreciation of whatever comes under one's eye, without any need to make such tedious judgments as 'mine' and 'not mine'.
Marilynne Robinson, WHEN I WAS A CHILD, p 85.

Freedom is a word, less than a word, a noise, one of the multitude of noises I make when I open my mouth.
J M Coetzee. FOE, p100.

(on returning from Auschwicz) We felt the weight of centuries on our shoulders, we felt oppressed by a year of ferocious memories; we felt emptied and defenceless. The months just past, although hard, of wandering on the margins of civilization, now seemed to us like a truce, a parenthesis of unlimited availability, a providential but unrepeatable gift of fate.
Primo Levi. THE TRUCE, p378.

"Arbeit Macht Frei" - work gives freedom, a sign at the entrance to Auschwitz.
Primo Levi. IF THIS IS A MAN.

To say what you think is always a luxury and often a curse.
Kenneth Roberts.

Liberty is not worth having without a belief that is strong enough to sustain it.
George Orwell.

You have a right to speak and a right to be wrong. And you exercise both rights extensively.
Neil Kinnock to Ken Livingstone.

Each man's freedom threatens that of all the others.
Andre Brink. A DRY WHITE SEASON, p222.

We're living in the wrong age. We've tasted a different forbidden fruit, so we have no choice but to go back.
Andre Brink. A DRY WHITE SEASON, p242.

Only through the water of one's body can one commune with solid earth. Not past or future was freedom, but this insignificant, tremendous moment. One always thinks of freedom as of something "out there", remote and separate, a territory to be reached by climbing a mountain or swimming a river or crossing some frontier. But is there, ever, anything "out there": freedom? truth? Can it ever be anywhere, or otherwise, than here, in here, inseparable from who you are, what you are, what you alone allow yourself to become?
Andre Brink. A CHAIN OF VOICES, p254.

The power of relinquishing
What one would keep; that is freedom.
Marianne Moore, quoted Independent Review, 20/5/90.

There is a rule that applies to every spell, namely, that it has to broken by someone from the outside; the person under the spell can never free himself.
Francesca Duranti. THE HOUSE ON MOON LAKE, p159.

Equality was not freedom, it had been only the mistaken yearning to become like the people of the town. And who wanted to become like the very ones feared and hated? Envy was not freedom.
Nadine Gordimer. MY SON'S STORY, p24.

When you are not a free man, time passes slowly: your soul is delayed and defeated along the way. You unconsciously moderate your actions and responses in order to be prepared for any evil. Any unexpected capriciousness of the occupier. Or the situation itself.
David Grossman. THE YELLOW WIND, p146.

It was there that I realised for the first time that lack of freedom harms people not only by blocking their path to knowledge and curtailing what they can say and where they can go, but also by damaging the very core of their being and enslaving them by switching their attention to themselves alone.
Ivan Klima. JUDGE ON TRIAL, p498.

He had indeed been fixated with freedom since his childhood, but had never proved capable of entering it. The war had shown it to him as a gate one might pass through to reach a world which had everything that people longed for and which he was denied: forests and home, bread and butter and warmth and a train you could get off anywhere. It was a gate that could not be opened from the inside - inside all one could do was to watch and wait until some more powerful force broke it down from the outside.
Ivan Klima. JUDGE ON TRIAL, p519.

FRIENDSHIP

I had friends – and they had me – just conventionally unconventional enough to perpetuate the belief that our existence might actually be exciting.
James Robertson. THE PROFESSOR OF TRUTH, p45.

Has anyone ever pinched into its pilulous smallness the cobweb of pre-matrimonial acquaintanceship?
George Eliot. MIDDLEMARCH, p14.

…passing each other for such a long time before constant recognition wore them down and they started to say hello.
Ann Patchett, RUN, p202.

But the disparaging of those we love always alienates us from them to some extent.. We must not touch our idols; the guilt sticks to our fingers.#
Gustave Flaubert. MADAME BOVARY, p. 344.

The moral lessons of friendship.

.....a conversation is like having a catch with someone. A good partner tosses the ball directly into your glove, making it almost impossible for you to miss it; when he is on the receiving end, he catches everything sent his way, even the most errant and incompetent throws.
Paul Auster. MOON PALACE, p92.

Popping in and out of each other's lives has left them better friends and more familiar than an unbroken association would have done. What they see again in the other confirms them in their opinion of themselves, and the increasing greyness of the hair and the furrowing of the brow, hardly noticeable to their families, merely confirm the workings of an ineluctable process.
Timothy Mo. AN INSULAR POSSESSION, p140.

Bit by bit.... it comes over to us that we shall never again hear the laughter of our friend, that this one garden is forever locked against us. And at that moment begins our true mourning, which, though it may not be heart-rending, is still slightly better. For nothing, in truth, can replace that companion. Old friends cannot be created out of hand. Nothing can match the treasure of common memories, of trials endured together, of quarrels and reconciliations and generous emotions. It is idle, having planted an acorn in the morning, to expect that afternoon to sit in the shade of the oak. So life goes on. For years we plant the seed, we feel ourselves rich; and then come other years when time does its work and our plantation is made sparse and thin. One by one our comrades slip away, deprive us of their shade.
Antoine de Sanit-Exupery. WIND, SAND and STARS, p26.

FUTURE

It is a far, far better thing that I do, than I have ever done; it is a far, far better rest that I go to than I have ever known.
Charles Dickens. A TALE OF TWO CITIES, p236.

Karl Popper, in 'The Poverty of Historicism', said that the future cannot be predicted because how it will happen depends on discoveries that cannot be predicted, because if they could be predicted they would already have been discovered.
Jonathan Sacks. THE GREAT PARTNERSHIP, p96.

Psychoanalysts are fond of pointing out that the past is alive in the present. But the future is alive in the present, too. The future is not some place we're going to but an idea in our mind. It is something we're creating, that in turn creates us. The future is a fantasy that shapes our present.
Stephen Grosz, THE EXAMINED LIFE, p157.

Once you hear something, you can never return to the time before you heard it.
Jonathan Safran Foer. EVERYTHING IS ILLUMINATED, p156.

How much of our existence seems to be taken up with preparation for the next generation - planning for the future, kids, looking after them. (RR)

The future is an apathetic void of no interest to anyone. The past is full of life, eager to irritate us, provoke and insult us, tempt us to destroy or repaint it. The only reason people want to be masters of the future is to change the past.
Milan Kundera. THE BOOK OF LAUGHTER & FORGETTING, p22.

The possession of money causes people to take a more favourable view of the world in comparison with the next.
J K Galbraith. AGE OF UNCERTAINTY, p43.

To get through to the future a man must march through the consequences of the past.
Ronald Lewin. SLIM: the Standard Bearer, in a comment on John Bunyon's SLOUGH OF DESPOND.

The Bantu language has no future tense; the concept of the future doesn't exist for the Bantu people, they are not tormented by the thought of what happens in a month, a year.......
Ryszard Kapuscinski. ANOTHER DAY OF LIFE, p111.

How can these men know that a man's need of slaves has nothing to do with oppression and wealth but with one's responsibility to the future?
Andre Brink. A CHAIN OF VOICES, p224.

the future comes disguised, if it came naked we would be petrified by what we saw.
J.M. Coetzee. AGE OF IRON, p149.

Professor Kouska sets an imaginary futurologist down at the threshold of the 20th century and endows him with all the knowledge that was then available, in order to put to this figure a series of questions. For instance: "Do you consider it probable that soon there will be discovered a silvery metal, similar to lead, capable of destroying life on Earth should two hemispheres composed of this

metal be brought together by a simple movement of the hands, to make of them something resembling a large orange? Do you consider it possible that this old carriage here, in which Karl Benz, Esq. has mounted a rattling one-and-a-half-horsepower engine, will before long multiply to such an extent that from its asphyxiating fumes and combustion exhausts day will turn into night in the great cities, and the problem of placing this vehicle somewhere, when the drive is finished, will grow into the main misfortune of the mightiest metropolises? Do you consider it probable that owing to the principle of fireworks and kicking, people will soon begin taking walks upon the Moon, while their perambulations will at the very same moment be visible to hundreds of millions of other people in their homes on Earth? Do you consider it possible that soon we will be able to make artificial heavenly bodies, equipped with instruments that enable one from cosmic space to keep track of the movement of any man in a field or on a city street? Do you think it likely that a machine will be built that plays chess better than you, compose music, translates from language to language, and performs in the space of a few minutes calculations which all the accountants, auditors, and bookkeepers in the world put together could not accomplish in a lifetime? Do you consider it possible that very shortly there will arise in the centre of Europe huge industrial plants in which living people will be burned in ovens, and that these unfortunates will number in the 'millions'?.......only a lunatic would have granted all these events even the remotest credibility.
Stanislaw Lem. A PERFECT VACUUM, p162-3.

To Seth, the future was a matter of keeping the past at bay.
Toni Morrison. BELOVED, p42.

GENERATION

......she idly constructed her own images, the accepted ways in which each generation sees its relationship to the next. They stand on our shoulders, she thought, and with the added height they can see farther. They can also, from up there, look back at the path we have taken and avoid making the mistakes we did. We are handing something on to them - a torch, a relay baton, a burden. As we weaken, they grow stronger; the young man carries the ancestor on his back and leads his own child by the hand.
Julian Barnes. STARING AT THE SUN, p106.

"...take a baby, for instance........Once I used to think that all the family dead, the uncles and the grandfathers and grandmothers and the cousins and even the distant ancestors, come to say goodbye to each baby before it's born, the way you say goodbye at the station to someone going on a long trip. And I'd imagine that each one of them asks it to take something of theirs along - a pair of eyes, or the colour of somebody's hair, or the shape of an ear or a foot, or a birthmark, or a forehead or a chin - because each of them wanted to send some little reminder or token of their affection to relatives still living. It's as if the baby were a lucky traveller who had received permission not just to go abroad but to cross an Iron Curtain that they knew they'll never be allowed to cross, which is why they load it with as much as they can so that people in the happy land it's going to will know that they haven't been forgotten.
Amos Oz. A PERFECT PEACE, p136.

In that book on human sacrifice in the Congo, it said that sleep is sent to us from the place where we were before we were born and will go back to after we die.
Amos Oz. A PERFECT PEACE, p163.

The son unborn mars beauty: born, he brings pain, divides affection, increases care. He is a male; his growth is his father's decline, his youth his father's envy his friend his father's enemy.
James Joyce. ULYSSES, p208.

GOD & PROVIDENCE

Some men spoke of God: His mysterious ways, the sins of the Jewish people, and the redemption to come. As for me, I ceased to pray. I concurred with Job! I was not denying His existence, but I doubted his absolute justice.
Elie Wiesel. NIGHT, p45.

(LBJ after a visit to WW2 war zone in New Guinea) 'I am happy to be here. How happy you don't know until you have been where I have been and seen what I have seen.' He told his audience that God had helped him return. 'There are no non-believers at 12,000 feet with Jap Zero fighters around!
Robert C Caro. MEANS OF ASCENT, p48.

Who was it said that coincidence was God's way of remaining anonymous?
Donna Tartt, THE GOLDFINCH, p758.

(on finding Auschwitz empty) Today I think that if for no other reason than that Auschwitz existed, no one in our age should speak of Providence. But without doubt in that hour the memory of biblical salvations in times of extreme adversity passed like a wind through all our minds.
Primo Levi. IF THIS IS A MAN, p164.

There's no stopping a man in the pursuit of his own ambition, particularly if he's read God's mind and found that they think alike.
J Rizkalla. THE JERICHO GARDEN, cf S.T. 10/4/88.

The Agency was the one subject in his life that could never be exhausted. Central Intelligence. Beryl saw it as the best organised church in the Christian world, a mission to collect and store everything that everyone ever said and reduce it to a microdot and call it God.
Don De Lillo. LIBRA, p260.

Heaven is a conception for people who die young: if you live long enough you want no part of it.
Joan Brady. THEORY OF WAR, p126.

GOOD

"That by desiring what is perfectly good, even when we don't quite know what it is and cannot do what we would, we are part of the divine power against evil – widening the skirts of light and making the struggle with darkness narrower."
George Eliot. MIDDLEMARCH, p231.

GOSSIP

Gossip is like water. It probes surfaces for their weak places, until it finds the breakthrough point.
Salman Rushdie. SHAME, p48.

and the way they talked about her was certain proof if proof was needed that nobody seriously believes in an after-life. They were sure they'd never hear the edge of her tongue again either in hell or heaven or the duck-arsed in-between.
John McGahern. NIGHTLINES, p20.

Gossip is simply the other name for judging. By means of gossip we overcome our natural instincts and gradually become better men. Gossip plays a powerful part in our lives, because our lives are exposed like a sun-drenched courtyard.
Amos Oz. ELSEWHERE, PERHAPS, p18.

Gossip is a liquor that must be poured in small doses into one ear, or possibly into more than one, but not into too many - otherwise its name changes.
Primo Levi, THE MIRROR MAKER, p146.

Tales of adulterous friars, cuckolded husbands and faithless wives were among the first productions of the printing press.
Ferdinand Mount. THE SUBVERSIVE FAMILY.

Another wife is noticeably missing from the tableau. So absent that her absence is a presence.
Joseph O'Connor. REDEMPTION FALLS, p155.

GRANDPARENTS

He was only a man, my grandfather. I could see that at moments like this when he first woke. His mouth open in a yawn of dental nightmare, dirty fingernails scratching at his white belly, leaving pink tracks, pulling on his boots and then his brown hunting shirt and jacket he always wore, shrinking in his clothing, his fringe of hair bent, digging a finger again into an ear. Only a man. But these moments never lasted.
David Vann. GOAT MOUNTAIN, p121.

HANDICAPPED

The handicapped person was at the heart of Vanier's vision. Put simply, he saw the essence of man as division. The world comprises rival countries, warring territories; each society is split into factions. Materialism, competitiveness and aggression ravage the human community. The 'normal' individual hides the wounds which society has inflicted upon him. He buries within himself the scars of his experience and thereby forms an unacknowledged area of himself which inevitably threatens to undermine the social self everyone strives to cultivate according to those values which society promotes. Society, like the individual, wishes to hide its scars.
Criminal offenders, the aged and the mentally ill are shut up in institutions. These people, especially the latter, must wear their scars on the front, on their very faces, and so they threaten the cosmetic order of society. In his community Vanier would attempt the reintegration of broken individuals through trust, concern, affection, commitment, routine, work, all the splendours of love - and especially by attention. For it is a witness, a pair of eyes, that such prisons forbid above all else.
Ronan Sheehan. "The Ark". BOY WITH AN INJURED EYE, p134.

HAPPENINGS

My God, that bloody casket has fallen on the floor! Some people were hammering in the next flat and it fell off its bracket. The lid has come off and whatever inside it has certainly got out. Upon the demon-riden pilgrimage of human life. What next I wonder?
Irish Murdoch. THE SEA, THE SEA. (final paragraph)

'If you're not prepared to look stupid, nothing great is ever going to happen.'
Hugh Laurie.

HAPPINESS & ENJOYMENT

And though in the clockless, temperature-controlled casino night, words like *day* and *Christmas* were fairly meaningless constructs, *happiness*, amidst the loudly clinked glasses, didn't seem quite such a doomed or fatal idea.
Donna Tartt, THE GOLDFINCH, p288.

When happiness is happening, it feels as if nothing else happened before it, it is a sensation that happens only in the present tense.
Deborah Levy. THINGS I DON'T WANT TO KNOW, p6

Happiness compresses time, makes it dense and bright, pocket-sized.
Ann Patchett, RUN, p14.

Someday you will find out that there is far more happiness in another's happiness than in your own.
Honore de Balzac. OLD GORIOT, p85.

Happiness, old man, depends on what lies between the sole of your foot and the crown of your head; and whether it cost a million or a hundred Louis, the actual amount of pleasure that you receive rests entirely with you, and is just exactly the same in any case.
Honore de Balzac. OLD GORIOT, p88.

The air of duty is less healthy to breathe than the air of innocent enjoyment.
John Wain. S.T. 11/9/88. G4.

Happy men don't ask questions.
Graham Swift. WATERLAND, p201.

stages of drunkenness: pleasure, satisfaction, well-being, elation, light-headedness, befuddlement, distraction, irascibility, pugnaciousness, imbalance, incapacity.
Graham Swift. WATERLAND, p149.

(on being told of their imminent return home from Auschwitz) We lit fires in the woods, and no one slept; we spent the rest of the night singing and dancing, recalling past adventures and remembering our lost companions - for it is not given to man to enjoy uncontaminated happiness.
Primo Levi. THE TRUCE, p349.

Human time does not turn in a circle; it runs ahead in a straight line. That is why man cannot be happy: happiness is the longing for repetition.
Milan Kundera. THE UNBEARABLE LIGHTNESS OF BEING, p298.

Happiness is a good conscience.
Tommy Ungerer.

the basis of comedy is showing persons with incomplete knowledge.
Kurt Vonnegut.

Happiness is like the pox. Catch it too soon and it ruins the constitution.
Flaubert.

Some must be defeated and driven down from the hills of their dreams so that the other ones, the deserving and the pious, may be given material for their reward of joy. That, Brennan, is the only happiness that ever descends upon the people of the valley. It may be said that they get their reward in this life.
Brindsley MacNamara. VALLEY OF THE SQUINTING WINDOWS p139.

Wine, women, mirth and laughter,
sermons and soda-water the day after.
Byron.

Your heart's desire is to be told some mystery. The mystery is that there is no mystery.
Cormac McCarthy. BLOOD MERIDIAN, p252.

By the time Maggie had to go back to London they had never felt closer in warmth, even happiness. The closeness was as strong as the pull of their own lives: they lost the pain of individuality within its protection.
John McGahern. AMONGST WOMEN, p85.

Rapid motion through space elates one; so does notoriety, so does the possession of money.
James Joyce. "After the Race" in DUBLINERS.

".......even those of us who call themselves happy feel the same gnawing sadness, the same worm of despair. For how well we know that happiness, transparent as a soap bubble and just as elusive, will be taken away and lost to us forever. Though ours by right and merit, we have been robbed of it by villains unknown. And that is why I say we are all disabled. Amputees of happiness, cripples of joy, paraplegics of significance......."
David Grossman. SEE UNDER: LOVE, p384.

In a paperback copy of "Tristam Shandy" bought in the second-hand bookstore in Alice, this was scribbled in the fly-leaf, "One of the few moments of happiness a man knows in Australia is that moment of meeting the eyes of another man over the tops of two beer glasses."
Bruce Chatwin. THE SONGLINES, p175.

The two men came in as he was collecting up his books to go to bed. They seemed wrapped in a web of warmth and companionship, the smell of beer and cigarette smoke clinging around them, the tail end of spoken words and other men's laughter was still with them.
Jennifer Johnston. SHADOWS ON OUR SKIN, p42.

The real geniuses of the comic are not those who make us laugh hardest but those who reveal some 'unknown realm of the comic'.
Milan Kundera. THE ART OF THE NOVEL, p126.

It seems to me that I will always be happy in the place where I am not.
Baudelaire.

If we lived in a world, he thought, which guaranteed a happy ending, should we be as long discovering it? Perhaps that's what the saints were at with their incomprehensible happiness - they had seen the end of the story when they came in and couldn't take the agonies seriously.
Graham Greene.   THE CONFIDENTIAL AGENT, p65/66.

HATE

The human heart may find here and there a resting place short of the highest height of affection, but we seldom stop in the steep downward slope of hatred.
Honore de Balzac. OLD GORIOT, p17.

Mrs Wagstaff's contempt for her young husband, if bottled, could have been vended as rat poison.
David Mitchell. CLOUD ATLAS, p170.

You cannot hate something so violently unless a part of you also loves it.
Paul Auster. THE NEW YORK TRILOGY, p98.

HOME

'Home is the place where, when you have to go there, they have to let you in.'
Robert Frost in 'Death of a Hired Man', BIRCHES AND OTHER POEMS.

Daphne tutted as she groped her way through the shadowy cupboard in which the wash-basin and lavatory were like surreal intrusions in a mountain of rubbish.
Allan Hollinghurst. THE STRANGER'S CHILD, p499 (Kindle)

Tom Wolfe is right. You can't go home again because home has ceased to exist except in the mothballs of memory.
John Steinbeck. TRAVELS WITH CHARLEY, p178.

As long as I remained among the hens and the barking dogs I too could belong, but each walk home from school by the new shopping arcades, each programme on television religiously switched on at half five in every terraced house, was thrusting me out into my own time. I began bringing home phrases that couldn't fit in that house when we still knelt for the family rosary. I hid photographs of rock stars beneath my mattress like pornographic pictures, wrote English soccer players' names on my copy book feeling I was committing an act of betrayal.
Dermot Bolger. THE JOURNEY HOME, p7.

Home was not the place where you were born but the place you created for yourself, where you did not need to explain, where you finally became what you were.
Dermot Bolger.   THE JOURNEY HOME, p264.

He felt he was entering a sensibility rather than a house.
Kiran Desai. THE INHERITANCE OF LOSS, p28.

HOPE

His birth brought indescribable happiness to his parents, who, from his cradle days, dreamed of a future for him as a prince of industry, a king of agriculture, a magus of diplomacy, or a Lucifer of politics.
Mario Vargas Llosa. AUNT JULIA AND THE SCRIPTWRITER, p280.

At this reply everything seemed to swim before Eugenie's eyes. The indistinct hopes in which, in the secret recesses of her heart, she had begun to indulge, seemed suddenly to burst into flower, to bloom, to converge towards each other and form a group of flowers, which she now beheld severed and lying on the ground.
Honore de Balzac. EUGENIE GRANDET, p91.

It is when our budding hopes are nipped beyond recovery by some rough wind that we are most disposed to picture to ourselves what flavours they might have borne, if they had flourished.
Charles Dickens. DOMBEY AND SON, ch.x.

HUMAN OBSERVATIONS

The smile trembling to be born at the corner of his mouth was even more active than usual.
Michael Dibdin. RATKING, p254.

...a man who stood so straight that he created a kind of architectural silence around him.
Howard Jacobson. THE FINKLER QUESTION,

In heavy traffic the car to watch is the one ahead of the one behind you.
Chinua Achebe. ANTHILLS OF THE SAVANNAH, p28.

(Crossing the road after loosing his child)....he tried to absorb the insult of the world's normality.
Ian McEwan. THE CHILD IN TIME, p20.

Mrs Touchett might do a great deal of good, but she never pleased.
Henry James. THE PORTRAIT OF A LADY, p17.

Living as he now lived was like reading a good book in a poor translation.
Henry James. PORTRAIT, p 36.

Disappointments were the only certainty he acknowledged.
Molly Keane. TIME AFTER TIME, p82.

You are like Sheraton joinery. You won't fall apart.
John Fowles. THE COLLECTOR, p185.

We admire the qualities which are beyond our reach.
Graham Greene. THE COMEDIANS, p96.

how defenceless we are in the face of flattery.
Milan Kundera. THE UNBEARABLE LIGHTNESS OF BEING, p185.

We are all exiles who need to bathe in the irrational.
John Updike. COUPLES, p485.

the basis of comedy is showing persons with incomplete knowledge.
Kurt Vonnegut.

The crises of individuals, like the crises of nations, are not realised until they are over.
Doris Lessing. THE GRASS IS SINGING, p162.

"That man's head was designed to keep his ears apart."
John McGahern. AMONGST WOMEN, p40.

"I wake to sleep, and take my waking slow."
Theodore Roethke. THE WAKING.

His voice seemed winnowed of vigour.
James Joyce. "Two Gallants" in DUBLINERS.

An attractive woman hurried towards a table, showing the happy exasperation that describes a journey through traffic snarls and personal drama to some island of prosperous calm.
Don De Lillo. LIBRA, p56.

We are all selfish. Sell up and go to the slums of Calcutta, work with lepers in the jungle....at my most cynical I ask whether even such things are not selfish, because it is easier for you to live with yourself having done that, knowing you have done all you could, rather than suffer the cramps of conscience.
Iain Banks. ESPEDAIR STREET, p242.

Valerian Street was mindful of their criticism, but completely indifferent to it. His grey eyes drifted over the face of such guests like a four o'clock shadow on its way to twilight.
Toni Morrison. TAR BABY, p9.

It was noting like the fear-shaped anger she had felt the morning he had held her from behind and pressed into her. Nothing like that. But he was bathed now, clipped and beautiful with spacious tender eyes and a woodsy voice. His smile was always a surprise like a sudden rustle of wind across the savanna of his face.
Toni Morrison. TAR BABY, p182.

Spectacles demonstrate conclusively that their owner is a man of consummate learning, so deeply buried in study that it has weakened his eyesight; any nose which they adorn, or encumber, undeniably qualifies as the nose of a scholar.
Montesquieu. PERSIAN LETTERS, p155.

'I suppose,' she said, 'it's the difference between fiction and life. Eyes are the first thing they tell you about in a book and the last thing you notice in a person. I never notice eyes.....
Frank Ronan. THE MEN WHO LOVED EVELYN COTTON, p124.

Human events display two faces, one of drama and the other of indifference. Everything changes according to whether the event concerns the individual or the species. In its migrations, in its imperious impulses, the species forgets its dead.... For man's greatness does not reside in the destiny of the species: each individual is an empire. When a mine caves in and closes over the head of a single miner, the life of the community is suspended... Inside the narrow skull of the miner pinned beneath the fallen timber, there lives a world. Parents, friends, a home, the hot soup of evening, songs sung on feast days, loving-kindness and anger, perhaps even a social consciousness and a great universal love inhabit that skull. By what are we to measure the value of man? His

ancestor once drew a reindeer on the wall of a cave; and two hundred thousand years later that gesture still radiates. It stirs us, prolongs itself in us. Man's gestures are an eternal spring. Though we die for it, we shall bring up that miner from his shaft. Solitary he may be; universal he surely is.
Antoine de Sanit-Exupery.   WIND, SAND and STARS, p168.

HUMOUR

Her sense of humour is really no more than an irritable suspicion that someone else might find something funny.
Alan Hollinghurst. THE STRANGER'S CHILD, p454 (Kindle version)

IDENTITY

In short, she is at once the embodiment and interpretation of her lodging-house, as surely as the lodging-house implies the existence of its mistress.
Honore de Balzac. OLD GORIOT, p10.

IGNORANCE

What ignorance, too, there was in their simple natures! Eugenie and her mother had not the slightest idea of Grandet's fortune. They valued the things of this life only in the light of their own feeble notions, and neither esteemed nor despised money; for they were well accustomed to dispense with it. Terrible condition of man's existence! There is not a single source of his enjoyment which does not proceed from ignorance of some kind or other.
Honore de Balzac. EUGENIE GRANDET, p43.

ILLUSIONS

Ardent souls, ready to construct their coming lives, are apt to commit themselves to the fulfillment of their own visions.
George Eliot. MIDDLEMARCH, p321.

People who share an illusion can never recognize it.
Freud, quoted   Sonke Neitzel & Harald Welzer. SOLDATEN: On Fighting, Killing and Dying, p28.

IMAGES

There was asbestos everywhere, like ashy snow. If you left a book for a few hours on the table and then picked it up, you found its profile in negative.
Primo Levi. THE PERIODIC TABLE, p66.

On the trolley with the Ajax box is a book of British Mesozoic Fossils with a shiny black cover, slightly curled, on which skeleton fish swim through the night of their own extinction.
Dai Vaughan. COTTAGE RUBBINGS.

...but, like Keasts in Yeats' image, I was like a child with his nose pressed to a sweetshop window, gazing from behind a barrier at the tempting mysteries beyond.
Seamus Heaney. GOVERNMENT OF THE TONGUE, p7.

The moon has nothing to be sad about,
Staring from her wood of bone.
Sylvia Plath. EDGE.

Now and then a car or lorry passed by, and a box of lighted geometry slid rapidly over the ceiling and down the walls and poured away in a corner.
John Banville. THE BOOK OF EVIDENCE, p91.

The next thing I recall is being on my knees in the lavatory, puking up a ferruginous torrent of wine mixed with fibrous strands of meat and carrot. The look of this stuff gushing out filled me with wonder, as if it were not vomit, but something rich and strange, a dark stream of ore from the deep mine of my innards. Then there is an impression of everything swaying, of glistening darkness and things in it spinning past me, as though I were being whirled round and round slowly on a wobbly carousel made of glass.
John Banville. THE BOOK OF EVIDENCE, p157.

The union building ......had...been designed in an appropriately depressing blind-cubist-with-a hangover style.
Iain Banks. ESPEDAIR STREET, p17.

The cleaning-woman was a jovial sort. She didn't stop to chat, though, because small groups of people had already gathered. She knew that she was too domestic an image; she would spoil the romance of her own carefully polished floor.
Thomas McCarthy. WITHOUT POWER, p243.

In those moments, as I stood watching him, an image presented itself and made me shiver. It had already, at that time, long been part of me. It would, in time, become as permanent a memory itself. But just at that moment, as if designed to underscore the thin ice of happiness, it forced its way into my consciousness.
Bruce Arnold. A SINGER AT THE WEDDING, p137.

From its sluice in Wood Quay wall under Tom Devan's office Poddle river hung out in fealty a tongue of liquid sewage.
James Joyce. Ulysses, p252.

At the edge of every experience is the refracted light of recollection, snagged there like an image in a beveled mirror.
Carol Shields. THE STONE DIARIES, p175.

IMAGINATION

The rest is history, they say. Bullshit, I say. It's imagination or it's nothing, and must be, because what is created in this world, or made, can be undone, unmade; the threads of a rope can be unwoven. And if that rope is needed as a guideline for a ferry to a farther shore, then one must invent a way to weave it back, or there will be drownings in the stream that cross our paths.
Kevin Powers. THE YELLOW BIRDS, p100.

She long ago realized that everyone has in the mind an ideal world which they think is their due.
Justin Cartwright. OTHER PEOPLES MONEY, p44

I call people rich when they're able to meet the requirements of their imagination.
Henry James. THE PORTRAIT OF A LADY, p176

The imagining was just like the whole summer, it throbbed with forbidden promise.
Neil Jordan. NIGHT IN TUNISIA, p21.

Isn't the most reliable form of pleasure, Flaubert implies, the pleasure of anticipation? Who needs to burst into fulfillment's desolate attic.
Julian Barnes. FLAUBERT'S PARROT.

Art is imagination. Imagination changes, fuses. Without imagination you have stupid details on one side and empty dreams on the other.
Iris Murdoch. THE BLACK PRINCE, p50.

.....and spent their nights depressed, and drunk, at the back of dancehalls, machine-gunning their imaginations to death with fantasies of girls in tight black skirts who tiptoed and jived across the dance floor in front of them.
Michael P Harding. PRIEST, p88.

"Nothing is so bad as having to imagine."
John McGahern. AMONGST WOMEN, p85.

"Your main problem, Herr Neigel, if I may say so, is that you never leave the confines of your own skin! After all, even the powers of the imagination need gymnastic exercise, else they wither and die, heaven forbid, like atrophied limbs."
David Grossman. SEE UNDER: LOVE, p232.

But whilst she wrote (love letters) it was another man she saw, a phantom fashioned out of her most ardent memories, of her finest reading, her most ardent desires, and at last he became so real, and tangible, that she panted in wonderment, without, however, having the power to imagine him clearly, so lost was he, like a god, beneath the abundance of his attributes. He dwelt in the azure land where silk ladders hang from balconies under breathing flowers, in the light of the moon.
Gustave Flaubert. MADAME BOVARY, p321.

The country of the imagination is rich and vast. Writers should surely not be tourists there but rather explorers and mountaineers.
Rose Tremain. Independent tribute to Angus Wilson 1990.

Any act or incident can carry within it the energy of the imagination.
Patrick Kavanagh. TARRY FLYNN, p21.

Imagination is a licensed trespasser. It has no fear of dogs, but may climb over walls and peep in at windows with impunity.
George Eliot. ADAM BEDE, ch 6.

INFORMATION

Paul knew already that information was a form of property – people who had it liked tom protect it, and enhance its value by hints and withholdings. Then, perhaps, they could move on to enjoying the glow of self-esteem and surrender in telling what they knew.
Alan Hollinghurst. THE STRANGER'S CHILD, p426 (Kindle version)

INNOCENCE

Our ignorance allowed us to live, as when you are in the mountains and your rope is frayed and about to break, but you don't know it and feel safe.
Primo Levi. THE PERIODIC TABLE, p129.

All you get from carrying a torch is sore fingers.
Alison Lurie. FOREIGN AFFAIRS, p31.

No innocent man buys a gun, and no happy man writes his memoirs.
Garrison Keillor. LAKE WOBEGON DAYS, p80.

If only the world outside could be shut out, and men could be made to forget what they knew.
V S Naipaul. cf STATES OF EMERGENCY by Andre Brink, p142.

(Looking at the photograph) I too could have fallen in love with that round-faced beauty with overtrained hair, the delighted, jaunty smile grazing the biceps of her loved one. It was the innocence that was so appealing, not only of the girl, or the couple, but of the time itself; even the blurred shoulder or head of a suited passer-by had a naive, unknowing quality, as did a frog-eyed saloon car parked in a street of pre-modern emptiness. The innocent time! Tens of millions dead, Europe in ruins, the extermination camps still a news story, not yet our universal reference point of human depravity. It is photography itself that creates the illusion of innocence. Its ironies of frozen narrative lend to its subjects an apparent unawareness that they will change or die. It is the future they are innocent of. Fifty years on we look at them with the godly knowledge of how they turned out after all - who they massacred, the date of their death - with no thought for who will one day be holding photographs of us.
Ian McEwan. BLACK DOGS, p37.

She could not explain to him that she felt that she already had new clothes, that with the loss of her virginity she had put on another skin. People say loss, she reflected, but they do not know what innocence is like. Innocence is a bleeding wound without a bandage, a wound that opens with every casual knock from casual passers-by. Experience is armour: and she felt already clad.
Hilary Mantel. FLUDD, p167.

IRELAND

For me, living in Ireland was like trying to breathe in through my nose and out through my mouth at the same time - it should be possible, but it isn't..
Philip Davison. TWIST AND SHOUT. p8.

Irish fury went into political nationalism.
Conor Cruise O'Brien.

'Irish' is both an identity and an allegiance. 'British' is only an allegiance, and one can be Northern Irish and British, Scottish and British, Welsh and British.
Edna Longley. Independent on Sunday, 12/1/92.

ISOLATION

Living on the extremity of a continent, facing two great simple spaces of the sea and sky, cultivates the sense that somehow you are less encumbered than those who live away from the shoreline. You feel less put upon by the fritter and mess of the quotidian. It is fifty yards from where I sit now to the foam and spume of the last breaker. There is not very much between here and there, you think, to distract you.
William Boyd. BRAZZAVILLE BEACH, p333.

JEALOUSY

Jealousy is never satisfied with anything short of omniscience that would detect the subtlest fold of the heart.
George Eliot. THE MILL ON THE FLOSS, p436.

I did not want to remember how he had loved other women before me, but the knowledge often teased me in the threadbare self-confidence of the small hours.
Angela Carter. THE BLOODY CHAMBER, p9.

JEWS

The Jews, a headstrong, moody, murmuring race
As ever tried the extent and stretch of grace;
God's pampered people, when, debauched with ease,
No king could govern nor no God could please;
John Dryden. ABSOLAM & ACHITOPHEL, lines 45-48.

A Jew is somebody who at Christmas does not have a tree, who should not eat salami but eats it all the same, who has learned a bit of Hebrew at thirteen but then has forgotten it.
Primo Levi. THE PERIODIC TABLE, p36.

(re Auschwitz) if we speak, they will not listen to us, and if they listen, they will not understand.
Primo Levi. IF THIS IS A MAN, p33.

"Jews, are you? It's all the same to me: Jews, Russians, Turks, Germans. One eats as much as the other when he's alive, and one stinks as much as the other when he's dead."
Primo Levi. IF NOT NOW, WHEN? p14.

We are a mob of the strangest individuals, thought Yolik, who ever pretended to be a people. To speak the same language. Exchanging old songs for new. Forever talking and writing of our hopes and longings as if mere longiloquence could still the promptings of one's inner voice.
Amos Oz. A PERFECT PEACE, p110.

....Israel is founded on so many contradictions, and on so many opposing forces, that its existence is always in great danger.
David Grossman. THE YELLOW WIND, p155.

We have lived for twenty years in a false and artificial situation, based on illusion, on a teetering centre of gravity between hate and fear, in a desert void of emotion and consciousness, and the passing time turns slowly into a separate, forbidding entity hanging above us like a suffocating layer of yellow dust.
David Grossman. THE YELLOW WIND, p216.

The slaughter and dispersion of Eastern Europe's Judaism have been an irreparable loss for all of humanity. It is not dead, but survives badly: gagged and unrecognised in the Soviet Union, hybridised in the two Americas, submerged and drowned in Israel by different traditions and profound sociological and historical transformations.
Primo Levi. OTHER PEOPLE'S TRADES, p74.

JOURNEYS

A disruptive minority of humankind regarded journeys, even short ones, as the occasion for pleasant encounters. There were people ready to inflict intimacies on strangers.
Ian McEwan. THE CHILD IN TIME, p49.

A sea-voyage will not give a man the nerve to put aside cheap pleasure; emigration has to be done before we climb the vessel; an aim in life is the only fortune worth finding; and it is not to be found in foreign lands but in the heart itself.
R L Stevenson. THE AMATEUR EMIGRANT, p35.

KNOWLEDGE

I realized that the question I had asked myself while writing this book was (as surgeons say) very close to the bone: 'What do we do with knowledge that we cannot bear to live with? What do we do with the things we do not want to know?
Deborah Levy. THINGS I DON'T WANT TO KNOW, p106.

A Private knows intrinsically what a General must learn through experience. That is because a Private thinks with caution since he will be killed. A general can be daring when only the Private will die for his mistakes.
James Webb. FIELDS OF FIRE.

An intellectual - that man who does not easily form categorical judgments.
Erasmus.

You don't need the weatherman to know which way the wind blows.
Bob Dylan.

We didn't know shit from Shinola.
Keith Richards. LIFE, p111.

The earth teaches us more about ourselves than all the books. Because it resists us. Man discovers himself when he measures himself against obstacles.
Antoine de Saint-Exupery. TERRES DES HOMMES.

Having acquired knowledge, we must now learn to live with that knowledge.
Andre Brink. THE AMBASSADOR, p216.

Maturity was not the result of time; it was the result of what you know.
Angela Carter. NIGHTS AT THE CIRCUS.

And it occurred to me that one is almost never where one is. Zeno's arrow. Part of you is always somewhere else. You seldom catch up with yourself. Language keeps you at a distance. And perhaps the only truly memorable moments in life are those rare, precious instants when you truly are where you are - knowing you are there- containing within yourself the whole of yourself and of your knowledge of yourself.
Andre Brink. STATES OF EMERGENCY, p133.

Man's vanity may well approach the infinite in capacity but his knowledge remains imperfect and howevermuch he comes to value his judgments ultimately he must submit them before a higher court.
Cormac McCarthy. BLOOD MERIDIAN, p250.

I believe that what we become depends on what our fathers teach us at odd moments, when they aren't trying to teach us.
Mark Twain.

LANGUAGE

He walked his restless suspicion in creaking shiny shoes, endlessly circling. He made us demonstrate the comic hopelessness of our understanding of the Irish language.
Niall Williams. FOUR LETTERS OF LOVE, p35

Human language is like a cracked kettle on which we beat out tunes for bears to dance to, when all the time we are longing to move the stars to pity.
Flaubert.

American is the language in which people say what they mean, as Italian is the language in which they say what they feel. English is the language in which what a character means or feels has to be deduced from what he or she says, which may be quite the opposite.
John Mortimer. MAIL ON SUNDAY, 26/3/89.

Tone is the inner life of a language, a secret spirit at play behind or at odds with what is being said and how it is being structured in syntax and figures of speech.
Seamus Heaney. GOVERNMENT OF THE TONGUE, p33.

You've got to make things new and the only way you can do that is with language......a writer can learn a lot about himself simply by the language he uses, by the sentences he forms.....You see yourself grow as an individual in the sentences you write.....I think a sentence that's properly made can have a moral force.
Don De Lillo. I.T. 16/9/89.

You have to know languages when you go to sell something. But when you go to buy, everyone does what he must to understand you.
Gabriel Garcia Marquez. LOVE IN THE TIME OF CHOLERA, p163.

There is a certain bliss in being surrounded by a language that no one expects you to know.
John Updike. Independent Review, 29/4/90.

(the language of some comics) onomatopoeic exclamations by supermen.
Nadine Gordimer. MY SON'S STORY, p20.

If we use language sloppily, we empty experience of meaning.
John Edgar Wideman's review of "Jump" by Nadine Gordimer, in New York Times Book Review, 29/9/91.

...a face is beautiful because it reveals the presence of thought, whereas at the moment of laughter man does not think.......Is not laughter a lightening thought that has just grasped the comical?..in the instant that he grasps the comical, man does not laugh; laughter follows 'afterwards' as a physical reaction, as a convulsion no longer containing any thought. Laughter is a convulsion of the face and a convulsed person does not rule himself, he is ruled by something that is neither will nor reason.
Milan Kundera. IMMORTALITY, p361.

Torrid.... Interesting how our vocabulary responds providing us with words we have never needed before, words stacked away for us, neatly folded into our brain and there for our use: like a bride's lifetime supply of lines, or a ducal trove of monogrammed china. Death will overtake us before a fraction of those words are used
Hilary Mantel. A CHANGE OF CLIMATE, p12.

LAWS

'Cops contain explosive contradictions within themselves. Supposed to be law enforcers, they tend to conceive of themselves as the law... They are attached umbilically to the concept of honesty, they are profoundly corrupt. They possess more physical courage than the average man, they are unconscionable bullies.'
Norman Mailer, ARMIES OF THE NIGHT, p148

"Laws are made for one purpose only," he told me; "to hold us in check when our desires grow immoderate. As long as our desires are moderate we have no need of laws."
J M Coetzee. FOE, p36.

I rejected absolutes the day I rejected Father Christmas. But you cannot hope to fight for justice unless you know injustice very well. You've got to know your enemy first.
Andre Brink. A DRY WHITE SEASON, p122.

Even as a young man he would interrupt his reading of poetry in the park to observe elderly couples who helped each other across the street, and they were lessons in life that had aided him in detecting the laws of his own aging.
Gabriel Garcia Marquez. LOVE IN THE TIME OF CHOLERA, p256

No juridical system absolves one murderer because other murderers exist in the house across the street.
Primo Levi. THE MIRROR MAKER., p164.

LIFE

My brother Zahid was born at the normal time. Life is full of such decisions, and turns that come to no harm; moments of normality, where no story springs and nothing goes wrong.
Philip Hensher. SCENES FROM EARLY LIFE, p138.

"…And if the proposal came from you, I am sure Mrs Vincy would say that we wanted Fred for Mary."
"Life is a poor tale, if it is to be settled by nonsense of that sort," said Caleb, with disgust.
George Eliot. MIDDLEMARCH, p242.

The meaning of life (according to Tolstoy) is the realization that you are held in the arms of a vast presence; that you are not abandoned; that you are here because you were wanted to be. It is the sense that life is something you have been given, so that you live with a feeling of gratitude and you seek to give it back, to 'pay it forward'. To be a blessing to others.
Jonathan Sacks. THE GREAT PARTNERSHIP, p188.

There are certain queer times and occasions in this strange mixed affair we call life when a man takes this whole universe for a vast practical joke, though the wit thereof he but dimly discerns, and more than suspects that the joke is at nobody's expense but his own.
Herman Melville. MOBY DICK, p210 (Kindle)

Early in life, the world divides crudely into those who have had sex and those who haven't. Later, into those who have known love, and those who haven't. Later still – at least, if we are lucky (or, on the other hand, unlucky) – it divides into those who have endured grief, and those who haven't. These divisions are absolute; they are tropics we cross.
Julian Barnes. LEVELS OF LIFE, p68.

Life is "a tale / Told by an idiot, full of sound and fury, / Signifying nothing".
Macbeth.

Destiny. My destiny! Droll thing life is – that mysterious arrangement of merciless logic for a futile purpose.
Joseph Conrad. HEART OF DARKNESS, p72.

I saw on that ivory face the expression of somber pride, of ruthless power, of craven terror – of an intense and hopeless despair. Did he live his life again in every detail of desire, temptation, and surrender during that supreme moment of complete knowledge?
Joseph Conrad. HEART OF DARKNESS, p71.

It is impossible to convey the life-sensation of any given epoch of one's existence – that which makes its truth, its meaning – its subtle and penetrating essence. It is impossible. We live, as we dream, alone.
Joseph Conrad. HEART OF DARKNESS, p28.

'Beyond that, Olunda views life in general as a regrettable contract.'
Barbara Kingsolver. THE LACUNA, p142.

But at my age it's difficult to change the way you see the world. We take on a certain view when we are young then spend the rest of our lives gathering the evidence.
Andrew Millar. OXYGENE, p104.

No one passes through life unnoticed.
Lloyd Jones. HERE AT THE END OF THE WORLD WE LEARN, p14.

The things that will destroy us are: politics without principle; pleasure without conscience; wealth without work; knowledge without character; business without morality; science without humanity; and worship without sacrifice.
Mahatma Gandhi

Life has to be lived forward but can only be understood backwards.
Soren Kirkegaard.

For her, cigarettes were as necessary to life as the breathing they interfered with.
Molly Keane. TIME AFTER TIME, p23.

There is a point of no return unremarked at the time in most lives.
Graham Greene. THE COMEDIANS, p1.

Life is like a box of chocolates; you never know what you're gonna get.
Forrest Gump (1994, Zemakis)

She believes that talking about what's gone wrong in one's life is dangerous; that it sets up a magnetic force field which repels good luck and attracts bad.
Alison Lurie. FOREIGN AFFAIRS, p237.

But the self, whatever its age, is subject to the usual laws of optics, However peripheral we may be in the lives of others, each of us is always a central point around which the entire world whirls in radiating perspective.
Alison Lurie. FOREIGN AFFAIRS, p199.

She has tried for years to accustom herself to the idea that the rest of her life will be a mere epilogue to what was never a very exciting novel.
Alison Lurie. FOREIGN AFFAIRS, p199.

Life plays us so many jokes.
Lewis Nkosi. MATING BIRDS, p38.

......and the odd melancholy of the adulthood they were about to straddle, to ride like a Honda down a road with one white line, pointless and inevitable.
Neil Jordan. NIGHT IN TUNISIA, p53.

Even though man is mortal, he cannot conceive of the end of space or time, of history, or a nation: he lives in an illusory infinity.
Milan Kundera. THE BOOK OF LAUGHTER & FORGETTING, p179.

The conviction that life has a purpose is rooted in every fibre of man, it is a property of human substance.
Primo Levi. IF THIS IS A MAN, p77.

No matter how brutal life becomes, peace always reigns in the cemetery.
Milan Kundera. THE UNBEARABLE LIGHTNESS OF BEING, p104.

Crossing the Shadow Line - an imaginary line between youth and maturity, sanity and insanity.

Life is such a daily thing, so no boredom!
John Updike. COUPLES, p289.

"Our lives, brother, are a little journey through God's guts."
John Banville. DOCTOR COPERNICUS, p115.

Life is a comedy for him who thinks and a tragedy for him who feels.
Jonathan Swift.

But in itself the physical drama only touches us if it shows us its spiritual sense.
Antoine de Saint-Exupery.

Most of what matters in our lives takes place in our absence.
Salman Rushdie. MIDNIGHT'S CHILDREN.

Life, however, is like war: the more you experience it, the more terrifying it becomes.
Philip Caputo. THE HORN OF AFRICA.

Life was like a long and costly mortgage to them: they were debtors in relation to existence, slowly paying off their souls.
Judith Thurman. ISAK DINESEN, ch1.

There are times when we see the small events we look forward to - a visit, a wedding, a new day - as having no existence but in the expectation. They are to be, they will happen, and before they do they almost are not: minute replicas of expectation that we call the rest of our life.
John McGahern. "Doorways", GETTING THROUGH.

Living is an eternal wanting more, in the coarsest grocer and in the sublimest mystic.
John Fowles. THE MAGUS, p309.

We too are so dazzled by power and money as to forget our essential fragility, forget that all of us are in the ghetto, that the ghetto is fenced in, that beyond the fence stand the lords of death, and not far away the train is waiting.
Primo Levi. MOMENTS OF REPRIEVE, p172.

It is wrong to write about people without living through at least a little of what they are living through.
Ryszard Kapuscinski. ANOTHER DAY OF LIFE, p66.

The world's much too interesting a place to let oneself get stuck with one aspect of it.
Penelope Lively. MOON TIGER, p19.

You do things, and only later do you see why you did them, if ever you do. Most of life is passive, the present a pinprick between the invented past and the imagined future.
Julian Barnes. STARING AT THE SUN, p182.

Usually one lives like a man walking with a candle in the dark. Behind him, where a moment ago it was light, darkness closes in. Ahead, where it will soon be light, darkness still lies undisturbed. Only where he is right now is there light enough to see by, for a moment; and then he moves on. But in a night like this it is different: then the darkness that was and the darkness that is to be merge in the light of what is now. I can close my eyes and see inside. Everything is alive in the heart of the flame. Within the falling of the stone lies the silence of before and after.
Andre Brink. A CHAIN OF VOICES, p490.

And the days are not full enough
And the nights are not full enough
And life slips by like a field-mouse.
                    Not shaking the grass.
Ezra Pound.

It can be no coincidence that Ovid's *Metamorphoses* is one of the seminal writings of the West.(Cf. Harry Mulisch in "The Assault": 'It was as if he were saying that life is a metaphor for another story, and that it is our business to discover that other story'.)
Andre Brink. STATES OF EMERGENCY, p158.

"The issue may be no more than symbolic. But only fools refuse to recognise that life is made up of symbols."
Amos Oz. ELSEWHERE, PERHAPS, p173.

Life is a game, at once frivolous and serious, played on several levels, a game in which there are no given rules; the game consists precisely in trying to discover the rules according to which it should be played.
Review of "La Regle du Jeu" (Magazine) in THE EUROPEAN 5/8/90.

She believed no message she could send a friend was more intimate and telling than a story in the paper about a violent act. a crazed man, a bombed Negro home, a Buddhist monk who sets himself on fire. Because these are the things that tell us how we live.
Don De Lillo. LIBRA, p261.

The gong is ringing. Here comes your ice-cream.
There's more to mind than raising heads of steam.
Richard Murphy. LINER.

......all of life is a free ticket, but in the end we are returned against our will to the domain of some invisible force, grave and inevitable, which collects its rightful debt, without mercy or solace.
David Grossman. SEE UNDER: LOVE, p429.

What is the point in worrying oneself too much about what one could or could not have done to control the course one's life took? Surely it is enough that the likes of you and I at least try to make our small contribution count for something true and worthy. And if some of us are prepared to sacrifice much in life in order to pursue such aspirations, surely that is in itself, whatever the outcome, cause for pride and contentment.
Kazuo Ishiguro. THE REMAINS OF THE DAY, p244.

Forgetfulness is an essential part of survival.
Ted Hughes, quoted Independent on Sunday, 23/6/91.

On the other hand, the vision of the bald spot was transubstantiated into quasi-philosophical maxims to the effect that time passes more quickly than any man is able to live, and that life is terrible, because everything in it is necessarily doomed to extinction.
Milan Kundera. LAUGHABLE LOVES, p37.

But this is the way life goes: a man imagines that he is playing his role in a particular play, and does not suspect that in the meantime they have changed the scenery without his noticing, and he unknowingly finds himself in the middle of a rather different performance.
Milan Kundera. LAUGHABLE LOVES, p229

a man lives a sad life when he cannot take anything or anyone seriously.
Milan Kundera. LAUGHABLE LOVES, p242.

"Do you know what Madame Campan told us: - 'So long, my children, as a man has any political power, bend your knee to him; but as soon as he falls, help to drag him down still lower.' Powerful, he is a kind of deity; overthrown, he is lower than was Marat in his meanest state, because he lives, and Marat is dead. Life is a long course of combinations, which require to be studied and followed closely, in order to succeed in maintaining one's-self constantly in a good position."
Honore de Balzac. EUGENIE GRANDET, p161.

As a physicist he had learned that of the 70 years of complete human life at least 2/7th, viz, 20 years passed in sleep. As a philosopher he knew that at the termination of any allotted life only an infinitesimal part of any person's desires has been realized. As a physiologist he believed in the artificial placation of malignant agencies chiefly operative during somnolence.
James Joyce. Ulysses, p641.

School, home, university, friends - all in their different ways offered a consensus of values, ambitions, approved styles of failure.
Julian Barnes. METROLAND, p85.

The dial of life: Up to a certain moment our death seems too distant for us to occupy ourselves with it. It is unseen and invisible. That is the first, happy period of life.
        But then we suddenly begin to see our death ahead of us and we can no longer keep ourselves from thinking about it. It is with us. And because immortality sticks to death tightly as Laurel to Hardy, we can say that our immortality is with us, too. And the moment we know it is with us we feverishly begin to look after it.
        ....followed by still another period, the shortest and most mysterious, about which little is known and little is said. Strength is ebbing, and a person is seized by disarming fatigue. Fatigue: a silent bridge leading from the shore of life to the shore of death. At that stage death is so close that looking at it has already become boring ....Immortality no longer interests the weary old man at all.
Milan Kundera. IMMORTALITY, p80.

Inexperience.......We are born one time only, we can never start a new life equipped with the experience we've gained from the previous one. We leave childhood without knowing what youth is, we marry without knowing what it is to be married, and even when we enter old age, we don't know what it is we're heading for: the old are innocent children of their old age.
Milan Kundera. THE ART OF THE NOVEL, p132.

If life was a story, as Uncle Victor had often told me, and each man was the author of his own story, then I was making it up as I went along. I was working without a plot, writing each sentence as it came to me and refusing to think about the next. All well and good, perhaps, but the question was no longer whether I could write the story off the top of my head. I had already done that. The question was what I was supposed to do when the pen ran out of ink.
Paul Auster. MOON PALACE, p42.

Name, age, marital status, former occupation, last permanent address, and so on. That never took more than a couple of minutes, but it was the rare interview that stopped at that point. They all wanted to tell me their stories and I had no choice but to listen. It was a different story every time, and yet each story was finally the same. The string of bad luck, the miscalculations, the growing width of circumstances. Our lives are no more than the sum of manifold contingencies and no matter how diverse they might be in their details they all share an essential randomness in their design: this then that, and because of that, this. One day I woke up and saw. I'd hurt my leg and so I couldn't run fast enough. My wife said, my mother fell, my husband forgot.
Paul Auster. IN THE COUNTRY OF LAST THINGS, p143.

I stood on the platform by the hour; and as I saw, one after another, pleasant villages, carts upon the highway and fishers by the stream, and heard cockcrows and cheery voices in the distance, and beheld the sun no longer shining blankly on the plains of ocean, but striking among shapely hills, and his light dispersed and coloured by a thousand accidents of form and surface, I began to exult with myself upon this rise in life like a man who had come into a rich estate. For we are creatures of the shore; and it is only on the shore that our senses are supplied with a variety of matter, or that the heart can find her proper business.
R L Stevenson. THE AMATEUR EMIGRANT, p101/2.

> The aim of all is but to nurse the life
> With honour, wealth and ease, in waning age;
> And in this aim there is such thwarting strife
> That one for all or all for one we gaze:
> As life for honour in fell battle's rage;
> Honour for wealth; and oft that wealth doth cost
> The death of all, and all together lost.
>
> So that in vent'ring ill we leave to be
> The things we are for that which we expect;
> And this ambitious foul infirmity,
> In having much, torments us with defect
> Of that we have; so then we do neglect
> The thing we have, and, all for want of wit,
> Make something nothing by augmenting it.

William Shakespeare. THE RAPE OF LUCRECE. 1141-154.

Life is an endless recruiting of witnesses. It seems we need to be observed in our postures of extravagance or shame, we need attention paid to us. Our own memory is altogether too cherishing, which is the kindest thing I can say for it. Other accounts are required, other perspectives, but even so our most important ceremonies - birth, love, and death - are secured by whomever and whatever is available. What chance, what caprice!
Carol Shields. THE STONE DIARIES, p36.

Stephen Crane once suggested that few people are nouns; instead, most of us are adverbs, modifying a long and weary sequence of events in which the clearly defined culprit, with black heart and demonic intent, seldom makes himself available for the headsman.
James Lee Burke. DIXY CITY JAM, p302.

The fury of life is always stronger than the compulsion of death.
Brian Keenan. AN EVIL CRADLING, p171.

But who will I be? What will I be? Maybe somewhere in this world a baby girl has just been born who will be my wife in twenty years. Maybe she's in school already and she has no idea that I'm opening a savings account for us, she has a boyfriend and doesn't realize its only a phase, that someday fate will bring us together. He smiles and shivers with anticipation, with secret joy, could it be that he's already living his fate? Mama didn't know anything about Papa either, she was busy raising her brothers and sisters in Jerusalem while he was slaving away in the taiga, in the ice, and little by little their paths converged, until suddenly, boom, like colliding stars, they knew they were made for each other.
David Grossman. THE BOOK OF INTIMATE GRAMMAR, p38.

(Hanna X finds the slough of a snake nearby)When she squats down to pick it up it disintegrates into dust more insubstantial than ash at the touch of her finger. It leaves her unsettled. Once this skin was inhabited by something alive and quick, a feared shiver of lightning rippling through the scrub and stones. Now that life has moved on, leaving only this trace behind; and even the trace dissolves. There will be nothing left, nothing at all.
Andre Brink. THE OTHER SIDE OF SILENCE, p177.

After a certain age, a life exists not for what it really was, but for its mythological qualities.
Justin Cartwright. THE SONG BEFORE IT IS SUNG, p122.

Life has become an exercise in what one can get away with.
Simon Heffer. The Telegraph.

Why is it that the intellectual apparatus that has evolved for human beings seems to be incapable of comprehending in any degree of detail its own complexity?
J M Coetzee. DIARY OF A BAD YEAR, p85.

Why does the world have to be a kill-or-be-killed gladiatorial amphitheatre rather than, say, a busily collaborative beehive or anthill?
J M Coetzee. DIARY OF A BAD YEAR, p119.

LITERATURE

In literature we move through a blest world in which we know nothing except by style, but in which also everything is saved by it.
Henry James.

Literature is mostly about having sex and not much about having children. Life is the other way round.
David Lodge. THE BRITISH MUSEUM IS FALLING DOWN, p56.

A literary movement according to AE: "Five or six people who live in the same town and who hate each other cordially.

There are two distinct strains of Irish literature, indeed world literature, a sort of ego and id. One comes from Joyce. Joyce looked at the world and accepted it in all its chaos and folly. Beckett, on the other hand, can't accept the world. He stands aghast at it. Even the moments of lightness only make it all the worse. I would belong to that strain that can't accept the world.
John Banville, Irish Times,. 21/10/89.

Kavanagh referred to the romantic nationalist revival of Synge and Yeats as 'a thorough-going English-bred lie.'
Quoted by Seamus Heany in PREOCCUPATIONS, p126.

One could not write a sinless literature about sinful man.
Cardinal Newman.

I admit that if you stop at such a view you hardly leave the way for those lengthy critical discussions and erudite commentaries which are the mainstay of the professional study of literature. I admit it is stating the obvious. But why shirk the obvious? Literature doesn't, after all. A great deal of literature - why not be frank? - only states the obvious. A great deal of literature is only (only!) the obvious transformed into the sublime.
Graham Swift. EVER AFTER, p70.

LONELINESS

He distrusted her affection; and what loneliness is more lonely than distrust?
George Eliot. MIDDLEMARCH, p259.

I was living alone for the first time in my life; without a stake of responsibility in that of anyone else. For us - coming from that house - that was the real definition of loneliness: to live without social responsibility.
Nadine Gordimer. BURGER'S DAUGHTER, p77.

LOVE

Nuptial love maketh mankind; friendly love perfecteth it; but wanton love corrupteth, and embasseth it.
Francis Bacon. ESSAYS, p30.

What is love? The Master said, To rank the effort above the prize may be called love.
Confucius. SAYINGS, p20.

Whenever she smiled at me Heaven blew in.
Donna Tartt, THE GOLDFINCH, p460.

Her mother's face was serious, her big green eyes like snake skin. 'If there's one thing you can be sure about in this life, it's that you won't always be kissing the right person.'
Liza Klaussmann. TIGERS IN RED WEATHER, p159.

Love may not lead where we think or hope, but regardless of outcome it should be a call to seriousness and truth. If it is not that – if it is not moral in its effects – then love is no more that an exaggerated form of pleasure.
Julian Barnes. LEVELS OF LIFE, p82.

So why do we constantl;y aspire to love? Because love is the meeting point of truth and magic. Truth, as in photography; magic, as in ballooning.
Julian Barnes. LEVELS OF LIFE, p36.

Love in Paris is a thing distinct and apart; for in Paris neither men nor women are the dupes of the commonplaces by which people seek to throw a veil over their motives, or to parade a fine affectation or disinterestedness in their sentiments. In this country within a country it is not merely required of a woman that she should satisfy the senses and the soul; she knows perfectly well that she has still greater obligations to discharge, that she must fulfill the countless demands of a vanity that enters into every fibre of that living organism called society.
Honore de Balzac. OLD GORIOT, p139.

Emma was like all his mistresses, and the charm of novelty, gradually falling away like a garment laid bare the eternal monotony of passion, that has always the same forms and the same language. He did not distinguish, this man of so much experience, the difference of sentiment beneath the sameness of expression.
Gustave Flaubert. MADAME BOVARY, p234.

She confused in her desire the sensualities of luxury with the delights of the heart, elegance of manners with delicacy of sentiment. Did not love, like Indian plants, need a special soil, a particular temperature?
Gustave Flaubert. MADAME BOVARY, p76.

Love does not consist in gazing at each other but in looking together in the same direction.
Saint-Exupery.

Love is the beginning of violence and betrayal. Something in yourself or in the other is killed or betrayed.
Andre Brink. AN INSTANT IN THE WIND, p101.

If M is unfaithful she is so much the dearer to me, for if strangers prize her she must be valuable, and I am reassured.
J M Coetzee. DUSKLANDS, p11.

Love? Who knows what love is? A dog loves his master. A man takes care of his woman and children. Then he is happy. But love? Such talk smacks too much of the kind of weak sentimentality so beloved by our European masters.
Lewis Nkosi. MATING BIRDS, p44.

The real love of one human being for another is the most important thing in the world, it is as important to life as the Missippi is to Huckleberry Finn.
Paul Potts. TO KEEP A PROMISE.

We assemble love as we assemble our life and grow so absorbed in the assembling that we wake in terror at the knowledge that all we have built is terminal, that in our pain we must do it again.
John McGahern. "Along the Edges", in GETTING THROUGH, p113.

Once he had promised her that he would love her forever. But forever at that time seemed to her like a small circle bathed in pleasant light, and love like a game of tennis on a clear blue Sunday morning.
Amos Oz. THE HILL OF EVIL COUNSEL, p26.

Love is - or at any rate, the love of a place is - the way a rock feels when a wave has broken over it and has not yet dried in the hot sun with that swift, radial erasure which is the converse of the spread of a stain: in other words it is a modality of time's articulation.
Dai Vaughan. COTTAGE RUBBINGS.

He told himself that it was not too difficult to love somebody sophisticated, lovely, elegantly dressed: such a love was a meaningless reflex automatically stimulated by the accident of beauty. But a great love seeks to create a beloved being out of an imperfect creature, a creature all the more human for her imperfections.
Milan Kundera. LIFE IS ELSEWHERE, p208.

The passion of lovers to trade recollections, even at moments when they appear to be concerned only with being together here, now. The past not as an escape from the urgency of the present but as a manifestation and confirmation of it.
Andre Brink. STATES OF EMERGENCY, p63.

At each moment, when we are in love, we cannot but live fully the presentness of all our past selves, all our past certainties and vacillations, attempts, failures, delusions, sufferings, victories. It is no good simply to exist on the surface of love: that is infatuation. We must know where we come from and where our earth comes from. The archaeology of love.
Andre Brink. STATES OF EMERGENCY, p69.

And I would not have you think either that love is all sweet desire and gratification, and thereafter peace. The essence of love is pain; deep in the heart of love is a terrible wound. Yes, and though a

man should grow wise and quiet at last, yet if he hath trafficked in love but once, he shall be borne to his grave with the stigma of suffering on him. His monument shall bleed.
George Mackay Brown. GREENVOE, p205.

And moreover who knoweth where the one jewel of love is to be found? For let a man travel far in search of it, and trade in every bazaar and market, and bear off the best treasures that are offered there; yet receiveth his soul no satisfaction therefrom; and many there be that after a lifetime of lust and liking and amorous dalliance descend disappointed to the dust. Yet on a day set apart and hallowed it may chance, once in many generations, that a knight cometh to a certain place, a tower or a chancel or a stone in the desert, and knoweth of a surety that there, guarded by ghost or dragon, abideth his heart's desire, the one pearl that all his life he hath sought.
George Mackay Brown. GREENVOE, p207.

Love is worth nothing until it has been tested by its own defeat.....Love is to enable you to transcend defeat.
Rian Malan. MY TRAITOR'S HEART, review in Indepdent 29/4/90.

"Perhaps one can only really love a person if one knows there'll be an end. If that end is already part of it all."
"How can one live in such a negative way?"
"Negative? Perhaps that is the most positive form of love there is...."
Andre Brink. LOOKING ON DARKNESS, p332.

He neither liked nor trusted words. Yet he was well aware that most people were in need of more love than they ever received and that this sometimes made them try to make friends with total strangers in the most ludicrous ways, including talking too much.
Amos Oz. A PERFECT PEACE, p81.

Love looks not with the eyes, but with the mind,
And therefore is winged Cupid painted blind...
And therefore is Love said to be a child,
Because in choice he is so oft beguiled.
Shakespeare. A MIDSUMMER NIGHT'S DREAM, I,i, 235.

People are eager to fascinate or charm others so as to fill some void in themselves. A widespread void that Yoel inwardly termed love.
Amos Oz. TO KNOW A WOMAN, p38.

(making love) For the first time......I realised how great is the anguish in the small sound men and women alike make at such intimate times, moments of carnal joy....the moaning of despair, steeped in torment, the groaning of a secret intelligence, ejaculated in a spasm and instantly forgotten...
David Grossman. SEE UNDER :LOVE, p416.

'Falling in love', characteristically, combs the appearances of the world, and of the particular lover's history, out of a random tangle and into a coherent plot.
A.S. Byatt. POSSESSION, p422.

I fell in love at the first lecture I attended. She was sitting in the row beneath mine in Theatre L, her black hair falling across the collar of her sheepskin coat. When the lecture was over and she was out of sight part of me went with her, part of her stayed with me.
Ronan Sheehan. "Universitas" in BOY WITH AN INJURED EYE, p7.

At last, bored and weary, Rodolphe took back the box (of love letters) to the cupboard, saying to himself, 'What a lot of rubbish!' Which summed up his opinion: for pleasures, like schoolboys in a school courtyard, had so trampled upon his heart that no green thing grew there, and that which passed through it, more heedless than children, did not even, like them, leave a name carved upon the wall.
Gustave Flaubert. MADAME BOVARY, p226.

Heartbreak is a necessary mile-stone in a girl's life, like your first husband. Now I was a little worried about this, because I had seen the popular Spanish resorts where the locals regard the holiday girls rather like library books: they return a brown one to Departures, and then immediately go round to Arrivals to pick up a white one.
Colin Dunne. GOOD HOUSEKEEPING, Aug. 1991.

....Eugenie dreamed of love.
In the pure and monotonous life which young girls lead, a blissful hour at last arrives when the sun expands its warm rays in the soul, when the restless throbbings of the heart communicate the fervour of their teeming fancies to the brain, and fuse its ideas in one vague desire; the period of innocent melancholy and sweet sensations of delight, when infants begin to observe objects, they smile; when a young girl begins to discover feeling and sentiment in nature around her, she smiles as she was wont to smile as a child. If light be the first object of attachment and regard in life, is not love the light of the heart?
Honore de Balzac. EUGENIE GRANDET, p76.

For the twenty-five-year-old Leonard who had not seen her for five days, who struggled all day with cardboard and wood shavings, and whose only token was the smaller piece of cardboard bearing her address, the face was elusive. The more intensely he summoned it, the more provocative was its disintegration. In fantasy he had only an outline to play with, and even that wavered in the heart of his scrutiny.
Ian McEwan. THE INNOCENT, p47.

If you ask me.....love - or whatever people call love - is just a system for getting people to call you Darling after sex.
Julian Barnes. TALKING IT OVER, p225.

Love and money are two great holograms that glitter before us, turning and twisting like real 3-D things. Then you reach out and your hand goes straight through them.
Julian Barnes. TALKING IT OVER, p233.

Physical love only rarely merges with the soul's love. What does the soul actually do when the body unites (in that age-old, universal, immutable motion) with another body? What a wealth of invention it finds in those moments, thus reaffirming its superiority over the monotony of corporeal life! How it scorns the body, and uses it (together with its partner) as a pretext for insane fantasies a thousand times more carnal than the two coupled bodies! Or conversely: how it belittles the body by leaving it to its pendular to-and-fro while the soul (already wearied by the caprices of the body) turns its thoughts entirely elsewhere: to a game of chess, to recollections of dinner, to a book....
Milan Kundera. THE JOKE, p194.

You fall in love with someone you think that everything about her is wonderful and unique to her. You are amazed by the beauty of her every small gesture, and in your love you isolate everything that you take to be an individual trait of hers. These are your treasures. The things you can recall to make yourself happy or miserable from time to time.
Frank Ronan. THE MEN WHO LOVED EVELYN COTTON, p83/4.

Her dilemma was something that is common enough among those of us who have the misfortune to be capable of falling in love, because we never fall in love with a reality. We fall in love before we have the chance to study the other person properly, and by the time we could know them well, we are so blinded by love that we cannot know them at all. And so love makes a misery of our lives as the daily evidence of the real person contradicts the person we believe them to be.
Frank Ronan. PICNIC IN EDEN, p9.

The love of the Sahara, like love itself, is born of a face perceived but never really seen. Even after this first sight of your new love, an indefinable bond is established between you and the veneer of gold on the sand in the late sun.
Antoine de Sanit-Exupery. WIND, SAND and STARS, p88.

He was thirty-six when he met Sarah. For most of us the intensities that come with first love are well in the past by that time, something that happens at sixteen, seventeen - even younger. What you feel then is so powerful that it lays waste everything around it and, even in the midst of your transports, you come to realise that if you're going to survive you'll have to do without feelings like it. So you grow up a little. You lose your intensity. You learn to manage with dignity but with a more shadowy product altogether.
Joan Brady. THEORY OF WAR, p148.

The erotic realm is our nearest approach to the wild half of our nature..... There is a part of the human self that is unclassifiable. That is what he (Barker Flett) must learn to accept. And to be open to visitations of ardour without the thought of shame stealing in through every window. Why must everything be flattened by the iron of goodness and badness? Why?
Carol Shields.THE STONE DIARIES, p153.

The French knew that love is a form of metaphysical enquiry; the English think it has something to do with plumbing.
Lawrence Durrell.

LOYALTY

Loyalty has to be earned. There's too much made of loyalty. All too often men talk of loyalty and follow blindly. I for one have no wish to lead my life like that.
Kazuo Ishiguro. AN ARTIST OF THE FLOATING WORLD, p72.

But today loyalty is simply given brutal explanations which are even more horrifying that the brutalities.
Joseph Roth. LONDON MAGAZINE 25 YEARS, p129.

LUCK

To me luck was something you either earned or invented through strength of character. You had to come by it honestly; you could not trick or bluff your way into it.
Thomas de Witt. THE SISTERS BROTHERS, p50

"Then what is luck, mother?"
"It's what causes you to have money. If you're lucky you have money. That's when it's better to be born lucky than rich. If you're rich, you may loose your money. But if you're lucky, you will always get more money."
D H Lawrence. THE ROCKING-HORSE WINNER, p94.

Airmen say that you start with a full pot of luck and an empty one of experience, and hope that the latter fills up before the former has run out.
Michael Burleigh. MORAL COMBAT, p478.

MACHINES

He has chosen the most rational mode of transport in the world for his trip round the Carpathians. To ride a bicycle is in itself some protection against superstitious fears, since the bicycle is the product of pure reason applied to motion. Geometry at the service of man! Give me two spheres and a straight line and I will show you how far I can take them. Voltaire himself might have invented the bicycle, since it contributes so much to man's welfare and nothing at all to his bane. Beneficial to the health, it emits no harmful fumes and permits only the most decorous of speeds. How can the bicycle ever be an implement of harm.
Angela Carter. "The Lady of the House of Love" in THE BLOODY CHAMBER.

MANNERS

Wrench did not take it at all well. Lydgate was as polite as he could be in his offhand way, but politeness in a man who has placed you at a disadvantage is only an additional exasperation, especially if he happens to have been an object of dislike beforehand. Country practitioners used to be an irritable species, susceptible on the point of honor.
George Eliot. MIDDLEMARCH, p156.

Rudeness is an art form best characterised by that famous New Yorker cartoon of an out-of-towner asking a gruff-looking local, 'Can you tell me where Fifth Avenue is, or should I just go screw myself?'
New Woman magazine, 8/88.

The redundancy of the question was made more comical by the relish of its delivery.
Dennis Potter. TICKET TO RIDE, p12.

No act is so private it does not seek applause.
John Updike. COUPLES, p132.

...there is no element of the metaphysical about pissing, not, at least, in our culture.
Angela Carter. NIGHTS AT THE CIRCUS, p52.

MARRIAGE

A woman dictates before marriage in order that she may have an appetite for submission afterwards. And certainly, the mistakes that we make and female mortals make when we have our own way might fairly raise some wonder that we are so fond of it.
George Eliot. MIDDLEMARCH, p44.

My wife had a brilliant, popping brain, a greedy curiosity.
Gillian Flynn. GONE GIRL, p30.

People go to endless trouble to divorce one person and then marry someone who is exactly the same, except probably a bit poorer and a bit nastier. I don't think anybody learns anything.
John Mortimer, quoted by Allison Pearson in The Telegraphy 16/1/14

He is a slow starter in the morning; neither of us likes to talk. These are the commonalities that glue a long marriage – it isn't whether you are each other's soul mate or intellectual equal: it's whether you are both happy with no more than an exchange of grunts over breakfast.
Louise Doughty. APPLE TREE YARD, p31.

My mother told me: 'Before you are married keep both eyes open and after you are married close one eye.'
Aminatta Forna. ANCESTRAL STONES, p109.

As Romeo and Juliet found to their cost, marriage is never just about two people falling in love, it is about families.
Marina Lewycka. A SHORT HISTORY OF TRACTORS IN UKRAINIAN.

She has a deep distrust of marriage, which in her observation has an almost irresistible tendency to turn friends and lovers into relatives, if not into foes.
Alison Lurie. FOREIGN AFFAIRS, p273.

Marriage is a long journey at close quarters.
Iris Murdoch. THE BLACK PRINCE.

Look, marriage is marvellous for people who are prepared to become an indispensible habit to one another. If you're prepared to accept your mate as a key to your own existence.
Andre Brink. RUMOURS OF RAIN.

What is marriage if not a voluntary exclusion of other alternatives? For better or for worse? Even if other possibilities do arise later - more beautiful ones, younger ones, easier ones, more adventurous ones - they don't exist as alternatives, they're irrelevant. Because you've made your choice. Unless that choice is exclusive there can never be trust.
Andre Brink. STATES OF EMERGENCY, p191.

Jerry married? Don't be silly. He's too sorry for all the women who'll have to do without him if he got married.
Andre Brink. LOOKING ON DARKNESS, p227.

Marriage is fate. What we marry we become. We who marry South Africa become South Africans: ugly, sullen, torpid, the only sign of life in us a quick flash of fangs when we are crossed. South Africa: a bad-tempered old hound snoozing in the doorway, taking its time to die.
J.M. Coetzee. AGE OF IRON, p64.

....then as you go on living with someone, you slowly lose the power to make them happy, while your capacity to hurt them remains undiminished.
Julian Barnes. TALKING IT OVER, p224.

As the Preacher said, there is nothing in this world that is new, and white weddings, Theresa thought, like the popular press and much television, are greatly dependent upon unoriginality and repetition for their ultimate success.
Deirdre Madden. HIDDEN SYMPTOMS, p67.

MATHEMATICS

It is said that there are two types of mathematician. 90 per cent see in figures. 10 per cent see in pictures. The most brilliant, the most profound come from that 10 per cent. In my own case I think that I had the gift up to the age of two and then, for some reason, it faded into mere proficient numeracy. But the great mathematicians never lose that facility. Perhaps that is why infant prodigies only occur in the world of maths, music and chess. These regions can be surveyed pictorially, patterns and shapes can be perceived there.
William Boyd. THE NEW CONFESSIONS, p53.

MEDICINE

Drugs are more often a symptom of failure than an aid to success.
Simon Jenkins Sunday Times, 2/10/88.

My boy, the first and foremost work of a doctor is to inspire confidence in his being one. So long as the public has faith in him, then any man can be a doctor.
Garrison Keillor. LAKE WOBEGON DAYS, p34.

The Great Barbiturate in the Sky!

MEMORY

For, as I draw closer and closer to the end, I travel in the circle, nearer and nearer to the beginning. It seems to be one of the kind smoothings and partings of the way. My heart is touched now, by many remembrances that had long fallen asleep, of my pretty young mother (and I so old!), and by many associations of the days when what we call the World was not so real with me, and my faults were not confirmed in me.
Charles Dickens. A TALE OF TWO CITIES, p194.

She was the golden thread that united him to a Past beyond his misery, and to a Present beyond his misery: and the sound of her voice, the light of her face, the touch of her hand, had a strong beneficial influence with him almost always.
Charles Dickens. A TALE OF TWO CITIES, p50.

There's something disturbing about recalling a warm memory and feeling utterly cold.
Gillian Flynn. GONE GIRL, p7.

Old lovers go the way of old photographs, bleaching out gradually as in a slow bath of acid: first the moles and the pimples, then the shadings, then the faces themselves, until nothing remains but the general outlines. What will be left of them when I'm seventy? None of the baroque ecstasy, none of the grotesque compulsion. A word or two, hovering in the inner emptiness. Maybe a toe here, a nostril there, or a moustache, floating like a little curl of seaweed among the other flotsam.
Margaret Atwood, CAT'S EYE, p266.

He was asking for memories, too young himself to know that memories were only memories of memories. It was diamond-rare to remember something fresh.
Alan Hollinghurst. THE STRANGER'S CHILD, p496 (K)

I felt an obligation to remember him correctly, because all remembrances are assignations of significance, and no one else would ever know what happened to him.
Kevin Powers. THE YELLOW BIRDS, p61.

How many forgotten heroes sleep in history's great cemetery?.. Memory is of no use to the remembered, only to those who remember. We build ourselves with memory and console ourselves with memory.
Laurent Binet. HHhH, P151.

What are we, if not an accumulation of our memories? How will I feel, when I look in a mirror and see the reflection of my grandmother?
S J Watson. BEFORE I GO TO SLEEP, Kindle 2824.

The problem with life is that you can only live it blindly, in one direction. Memory has its own ideas; it matches elements of story from wherever, tries to put them together. It comes back at you from all angles, with all that you later knew, and it gives you the news.
Anna Funder. ALL THAT I AM, p259.

We may be immune to typhoid, tetanus, chickenpox, diphtheria, but never memory. There is no inoculation against that.
Sebastian Barry. ON CANAAN'S SIDE, p83.

He had been gone for years, but his memory was still alive and, as often happens, had acquired a gilded patina of legend.
Primo Levi. THE PERIODIC TABLE, p67.

.......as long as there is memory for them to happen in......
Graham Swift. WATERLAND, p238.

History is a succession of ephemeral changes. Eternal values exist outside history. They are immutable and have no need of memory.
Milan Kundera. THE BOOK OF LAUGHTER & FORGETTING, p187.

We imagine that we remember things as they were, while in fact all we carry into the future are fragments which reconstruct a wholly illusory past.
John Banville. BIRCHWOOD, p4.

Freud doubted if we ever deal with a memory from childhood. Perhaps we may possess memories relating to childhood.

She is both mother of my ancestors, and the child waiting in the seeds of my lovemaking. Memory, more than anything else, makes nonsense of history.
Michael P Harding. PRIEST, p99.

It has been observed by psychologists that survivors of traumatic events are divided into two well-defined groups: those who repress their past en bloc, and those whose memory of the offense persists, as though carved in stone, prevailing over all previous or subsequent experience.
Primo Levi. MOMENTS OF REPRIEVE, p11.

......and then over long distances human memory is an erratic instrument especially if it is not reinforced by material mementoes and is instead spiced by the desire that the story be a good one.
Primo Levi. MOMENTS OF REPRIEVE, p144.

What is it this young man reminds me of? A piece of music composed for one instrument and played on another. An oil sketch for a great canvas.
Angela Carter. NIGHTS AT THE CIRCUS, p264.

Men's memories are uncertain and the past that was differs little from the past that was not.
Cormac McCarthy. BLOOD MERIDIAN, p330.

(On making a musical instrument out of tin cans and tabbed rings from beer cans) He didn't know Charles was reminded of the ingenuity of objects displayed in the concentration camps of Europe, now museums. There were made by inmates out of nothing, effigies of the beautiful possibilities of a life to be lived.
Nadine Gordimer. SOMETHING OUT THERE, p163.

There are things you have to put out of your mind, parts of yourself, parts of your life. Memory management.
Hugo Hamilton. THE KISSOGRAM GIRL (short story).

Time and memory favour trivial words. They treat them with particular kindness. They surround them with the tender glow of twilight.
I cling to memory and to words as one clings to a railing in a high place.
Amos Oz. MY MICHAEL, p63.

"But I would guess that most of the time your marriage - like mine - is marked by delicacy, consideration and a certain ceremony."
Thomas Keneally. THE PLAYMAKER, p214.

Real memories are a muddle of overlooked experience; odd and irrelevant facts lurk in the mind, stubbornly unforgotten after a period of years; snatches of forgotten times appear unsummoned in the head; strange associations exist, a smell will evoke a particular event, a colour will be an inexplicable reminder of a place visited long ago.
Christopher Priest. THE GLAMOUR, p173.

These and hundred other memories I strove to hold on to, but the fabrics vanished at the very moment of their bodying forth on the looms of sickness.
George Mackay Brown. THE SUN'S NET, p180.

(re the assassination of both Kennedys and Martin Luther King)
All of us who lived through these moments remember precisely where we were and what we were doing. We suddenly stopped in our tracks, and in the face of the enormity of the event we felt bound to everyone around us. For a few instants we ceased to see one another through our roles and perceived ourselves as equals, stripped down to the core of our common humanity.
Robert Darnton. S.T. Mag. on "French Revolution." 9/7/89.

Before he had a chance to absorb the woman's presence, to describe her to himself and form his impressions, she was talking to him, forcing him to respond. Therefore, even in those first moments, he had lost ground, was starting to fall behind himself. Later, when he had time to reflect on these events, he would manage to piece together his encounter with the woman. But that was the work of memory, and remembered things, he knew, had a tendency to subvert the things remembered. As a consequence, he could never be sure of any of it.
Paul Auster. THE NEW YORK TRILOGY, p13.

Memory is an act of the will, and so is forgetting. I think I have sufficiently erased most of my first eighteen years, pureed them into harmless baby food. What could be worse than to be dogged by all that stuff? The first bicycle, the first tears, that old teddy with the chewed-off ear. It's not just an aesthetic matter, it's practical as well. If you remember your past too well you start blaming your present for it.......
They say that as you get older, you remember your earliest years better. One of the many tank-traps that lie ahead: senility's revenge.... Life is like invading Russia. A blitz start, massed shakos, plumes dancing like a flustered henhouse; a period of svelte progress recorded in ebullient dispatches as the evening falls back; the beginning of a long, morale-sapping trudge with rations getting shorter and the first snowflakes on your face. The enemy burn Moscow and you yield to General January, whose fingernails are very icicles. The bitter retreat. Harrying Cossacks. Eventually you fall beneath a boy-gunner's grapeshot while crossing some Polish river not even marked on your general's map.
Julian Barnes. TALKING IT OVER, p15.

The struggle for daily survival, the routine of patrolling and foraging, dulled the reflective edge; you were kind of so shoved down into the minutiae of everyday life that you didn't get your head above water for long enough to do anything other than gasp. Remembering is what gives significance; the shape is never there at the time.
Timothy Mo. THE REDUNDANCY OF COURAGE, p299.

For no word can be written without first having been seen, and before it finds its way to the page it must first have been part of the body, a physical presence that one has lived with in the same way

one lives with one's heart, one's stomach, and one's brain. Memory, then, not so much as the past contained within us, but as proof of our own life in the present. If a man is to be truly present among his surroundings, he must be thinking not of himself, but of what he sees. He must forget himself in order to be there. And from that forgetfulness arises the power of memory. It is a way of living one's life so that nothing is ever lost.
Paul Auster. THE INVENTION OF SOLITUDE, p138.

They seemed to be sniggering at him from the threshold of his memory, slipping between his fingers like playful kittens just when he had almost caught them. Then he remembered, and opened his mouth to reply, but they escaped from under his tongue and vanished into the darkness.
Amos Oz. FIMA, p42.

Who we are is thread of memory. A thread of clear memory if we are lucky, of distorted memory if we are not.
Pat Barker. "The Guardian", 24/10/98.

Levade had told her one day that there was no such thing as a coherent human personality. When you are forty you have no cell in your body that you had at eighteen. It was the same, he said, with your character. Memory is the only thing that binds you to earlier selves; for the rest, you become an entirely different being every decade or so, sloughing off the old persona, renewing and moving on. You are not what you were, he told her, nor who you will be.
Sebastian Faulks. CHARLOTTE GREY, p374.

You forget what you want to remember and you remember what you want to forget.
Cormac McCarthy. THE ROAD, p11.

Memory is social: people remember collectively, they remember publicly, and they remember interactively.
Holger Hoock, EMPIRES OF THE IMAGINATION, p40.

MEN & WOMEN

..you cannot control the mincing vanities and giddiness of empty-headed girls; you must not expect to do it, or you will always disappoint.
Charles Dickens. A TALE OF TWO CITIES, p93.

Wives are young men's mistresses; companions for middle age; and old men's nurses.
Francis Bacon. ESSAYS, p22.

Wives create their husbands. They begin with that rough raw material, that blundering, well-meaning and handsome youthfulness they have fallen in love with, and then commence the forty years of unstinting labour it takes to make the man with whom they can live.
Niall Williams. FOUR LETTERS OF LOVE, p55.

'What about the women question?'
'Not everything can be about everything!'
Gertrude Stein in her Oxford lecture on contemporary literature.

Spinster women – they are the possessors of nothing but their own souls.
Rose Tremain. RESTORATION, p67

He'd go for models and married women, working, as so many men did, on the well-tried and tested principle that a slice off a cut cake won't be missed.
Pat Barker. TOBY'S ROOM, p23.

Men are modeled on the fruit machine. Sometimes you can feed them all night and all you get is flashing lights.
New Woman magazine, 9/88.

But Vinnie has been brought up to believe that though a man may work for wealth or fame, a woman must labour for love.
Alison Lurie. FOREIGN AFFAIRS, p111.

In this culture, where energy and egotism are rewarded in young and good-looking, plain women are supposed to be self-effacing, uncomplaining.
Alison Lurie. FOREIGN AFFAIRS, p3.

.....in the hope that she would cease to be a private woman whose charity was half a sop to her own indignation, half a relief to her own curiosity.....
Virginia Woolf. TO THE LIGHTHOUSE, p20.

Recklessness is almost a man's revenge on his woman. He feels he is not valued, so he will risk destroying himself to deprive her altogether.
D H Lawrence. SONS AND LOVERS, p235.

The effect produced by a beautiful woman is visual.....touching her does not bring you any closer to her beauty than touching the paint of a Botticelli brings you any closer to the beauty of his painting. It might even be argued that the closer you get to this painting or this woman the less you are able to appreciate its or her beauty, or even what makes each different from others of its kind.
J G Farrell. THE SINGAPORE GRIP, p294.

Women, it seemed, had no easily acquired mental map of cities........(they) never folded maps up properly: because the overall conception of the city was unimportant to them, so that there was no 'right order' from which to start. All of Ami's maps had been put away as if they'd been interrupted in mid-use.......A map, for him, once folded back into its proper order, lost its user's stamp: it could be lent or given away without touching on any feelings or attachments.
Julian Barnes. BEFORE SHE MET ME, p57.

But when a woman decides to sleep with a man, there is no wall she will not scale, no fortress she will not destroy, no moral consideration she will not ignore at its very root: there is no God worth worrying about.
Gabriel Garcia Marquez. LOVE IN THE TIME OF CHOLERA, p229.

But newspapermen - they sniff out the perfume of a woman the way certain creatures.....can detect the presence of truffles under the ground.
Nadine Gordimer. MY SON'S STORY, p158.

She hoped for a son......A man, at least, is free; he may travel over passions and over countries, overcome obstacles, taste of the most far-away pleasures.
But a woman is always hampered. At once inert and flexible, she has against her the weakness of the flesh and legal dependence. Her will, like a veil of her bonnet, held by a string, flutters in every wind; there is always some desire pulling at her, some conventionality holding her back.
Gustave Flaubert. MADAME BOVARY, p103.

Do women work harder than men?
Jon Ronson, T.V. journalist: Yes, but they're no good at lifting weights, interrupting conversations, reading maps and being terrorists. Pull up your socks, girls.
Independent on Sunday, 19/9/93.

'How long will you be putting on your bonnet, Fancy?...
'Only a minute'
'How long is that?'
'Well, dear, five.'
'Ah, sonnies!' said the tranter, as Dick retired, "tis a talent of the female race that low numbers should stand for high, more especially in matters of waiting, matters of age, and matters of money.'
Thomas Hardy. UNDER THE GREENWOOD TREE, p169.

But sometimes a vague jealousy stirred inside him, a sense of deprivation or loss, as though he had been cheated of some secret gift that enabled them to relate to the world in a way that was barred to him forever. The more he thought about it, the less he was able to distinguish between his pity and his envy. The womb, conception, pregnancy, childbirth, motherhood, breast feeding, even menstruation, even miscarriage and abortion - he tried to imagine them all, struggling over and over again to feel what he was not meant to feel. Sometimes, while he was thinking, he absently fingered his own nipples. They seemed a hollow joke, a sad relic. Then he was swept by a wave of profound pity for all men and women, as though the separation of the sexes was nothing but a cruel prank. He felt that the time had come to rise up and with sympathy and reason do something to put an end to it.
Amos Oz. FIMA, p31.

MEN

Men are modeled on the fruit machine. Sometimes you can feed them all night and all you get is flashing lights.
New Woman magazine, 9/88.

We must judge men not so much by what they do, as by what they make us feel that they have it in them to do.
Samuel Butler. THE WAY OF ALL FLESH, p13.

A man, on the contrary, should he not know everything, excel in manifold activities, initiate you into the energies of passion, the refinements of life, all mysteries? But this one taught nothing, knew nothing, wished nothing. He thought her happy; and she resented this easy calm, this serene heaviness, the very happiness she gave him.
Gustave Flaubert. MADAME BOVARY, p52.

They had the complexion of wealth - that clear complexion that is heightened by the pallor of porcelain, the shimmer of satin, the veneer of old furniture, and that an ordered regimen of exquisite nurture maintains at its best.
Gustave Flaubert. MADAME BOVARY, p63.

(Humpty Dumpty......a man?)....For all men are eggs, in a manner of speaking. We exist, but we have not yet achieved the form that is our destiny. We are pure potential, an example of the not-yet-arrived. For man is a fallen creature - we know that from Genesis. Humpty Dumpty is also a fallen creature. He falls from his wall, and no one can put him together again - neither the king, nor his horses, nor his men. But that is what we must all strive to do. It is our duty as human beings: to put the egg back together again. For each of us, sir, is Humpty Dumpty. And to help him is to help ourselves.
Paul Auster. THE NEW YORK TRILOGY, p82.

Jeanne, unlike Polly, had no sympathy with male homosexuals. She regarded them as, if possible, worse than so-called normal men, because they were cut off from the sensitizing and civilizing influence of women.
Alison Lurie. THE TRUTH ABOUT LORIN JONES, p70.

MONEY

Mind you, what is there to do with money except spend it when you've got it or be bitter about it when you haven't? It's a very limited commodity in which people invest the most extraordinary emotions. What I suppose I really mean is *do* be bitter about money: it's one of the few things it can do: siphon off some bitterness.
Edward St Aubyn. AT LAST, p8.

The best thing about the money was being freed from all the ways in which money is boring. 'Hurry up, we've got to make the 4 o'clock matinee so that we don't spend twice as much money to see the same film,' she says. 'That's a boring conversation I don't have any more. I've never been interested in stuff like Ferraris, or a villa in the south of France, but it's wonderful to be financially safe.'
Ann Patchett, in an interview with The Telegraph Magazine, 9/11/2013, p43.

Many skills, as every successful entrepreneur knows, cannot be taught at school. They require doing. Sometimes a lifetime of doing. And where money-making is concerned, nothing compresses the time frame needed to leap from my-shit-just-sits-there-until-it-rains poverty to which-of-my-toilets-shall-I-use affluence like an apprenticeship with someone who already has the angles figured out.
Mohsin Hamid, HOW TO GET FILTHY RICH IN RISING ASIA, p78.

If you want to become filthy rich in rising Asia… then sooner or later you must work for yourself. The fruits of labour are delicious, but individually they're not particularly fattening. So don't share yours, and munch on those of others whenever you can.
Mohsin Hamid, HOW TO GET FILTHY RICH IN RISING ASIA, p98.

Money you spend on necessities was boring: the money that was amusing to spend was the money you spent on luxuries.
Somerset Maugham. THE ANT AND THE GRASSHOPPER.

Money and fame are not necessarily bad things, yet Brendan (Behan) paid the highest price for them and put them to appalling use.
A J Cronin. DEAD AS DOORNAILS, p44.

The possession of money causes people to take a more favourable view of the world in comparison with the next.
J K Galbraith. AGE OF UNCERTAINTY, p43.

Schumpeter once accused J M Keynes of being subject to the curse of usefulness.
J K Galbraith. AGE OF UNCERTAINTY, p27.

Money is indeed not everything, but there is nothing to beat it for paying the bills.
Frederick Raphael. THINK OF ENGLAND, p144.

For money is the token of civilized self-preservation.
Max Plowman. MONEY AND THE MERCHANT.

(Money) is the shore to which every human craft is anchored, and will remain anchored until mankind has learnt the greatest lesson history can teach it - how to live by a more spiritual means of exchange.
Max Plowman.

Where any view of money exists art cannot be carried on.
Blake.

MORALITY

We are all of us born in moral stupidity, taking the world as an udder to feed our supreme selves.
George Eliot. MIDDLEMARCH, p127.

For much of what they took to be morality proved to be merely consciousness of the other couples watching them.
John Updike. COUPLES, p179.

It is not difficult to deceive the first time, for the deceived possess no antibodies.....
unvaccinated by suspicion, she overlooks lateness, accepts absurd excuses, permits the flimsiest patchings to repair great rents in the quotidian.
John Updike. COUPLES, p132.

Moral law is an invention of mankind for the disenfranchisement of the powerful in favour of the weak.
Cormac McCarthy. BLOOD MERIDIAN, p250.

....it is impossible to be occupiers and remain moral. Even people with moral intentions are led slowly into an immoral situation. The situation turns into a sort of monster with a life of its own, which can no longer be controlled. An unjust and immoral monster.
David Grossman. THE YELLOW WIND, p148.

Why had the greedy, arrogant and ego-bloated members of the Academy voted en masse for 'Ghandi'? Ghandi was everything Hollywood moguls wanted to be but aren't – thin, tan and moral.
Joe Morgenstern, film critic. Telegraph, 30/1/10.

Machiavelli says that if, as a ruler, you accept that your every action must pass moral scrutiny, you will without fail be defeated by an opponent who submits to no such moral test.
J M Coetzee. DIARY OF A BAD YEAR, p17.

MOTHERS

All mothers feel judged by their daughters: it is unavoidable. As they are coming into sexual maturity, emerging from the chrysalis of childhood, we are at the other end of the reproductive cycle, sagging and desiccating. What teenage girl would want to turn into her middle-aged mother?
Louise Doughty. APPLE TREE YARD, p220.

MUSIC

Music: a pump for inflating the soul.......
Mahler is the last great European composer who still appeals, naively and directly, to *homo sentimentalis*. After Mahler, feeling in music starts to become suspicious; Debussy wants to enchant us, not to move us, and Stravinsky is ashamed of emotion.
Milan Kundera. IMMORTALITY, p229.

Years ago, in Alabama at Christmas, the radio played 'Holy Night', the most glorious of carols - that soaring high note (especially sung full force by a pure, clean soprano) and gooseflesh all over: it's one of the few places left where you can sense the mystery and beauty of the idea that it's possible to save mankind.
Joan Brady. THEORY OF WAR, p87.

NATURE, HUMAN

The Bible is interested not in Homo Sapiens the biological species, but in the moral animal who, communing with the source of his and all being, discovers for the first time that although, like everything else that lives, we have desires, like nothing else that lives, we are able to pass judgment on our desires. That is when humans first heard the voice of God.
Jonathan Sacks. THE GREAT PARTNERSHIP, p231.

We are culture-producing, information-sharing, meaning-learning animals. Nature built us for culture.
Jonathan Sacks. THE GREAT PARTNERSHIP, p230.

Many besides Angel have learnt that the magnitude of lives is not as to their external displacements, but as to their subjective experiences. The impressionable peasant leads a larger, fuller, more dramatic life than the pachydermatous king.
Thomas Hardy. TESS OF THE D'URBERVILLES, p152.

The mould in which the human form is cast is exceedingly fragile. Give it the slightest tap with your fingers and it breaks.
Angela Carter. NIGHTS AT THE CIRCUS, p61.

She ventures out to earn her living every day, but no longer is one of those truly out there, driven by adrenalin and sex hormones, surging along, black skins, white skins, inhaling toxic ambitions, the stress of solving, of becoming - what? The five-thirty to six-thirty hour is an illusion of peace in middle age just as the innocence of Cape thrush calls and the freshness of leaves spattered by water from the municipal supply is an illusion of undetected nature.
Nadine Gordimer, "A Correspondence Course" in SOMETHING OUT THERE, p109.

Everyone here judges, everyone is judged, and no weakness can succeed for long in escaping judgment. There are no secret corners. You are being judged every minute of your life. That is why each and every one of us is forced to wage war against his nature. To purify himself. We polish each other as a river polishes its pebbles. Our nature notwithstanding. What is nature, but blind, selfish instinct, deprived of free choice?
Amos Oz. ELSEWHERE, PERHAPS, p17.

...Man is a builder of receptacles; a species that does not build any is not human by definition........Two qualities which are exclusively human....the ability to think about tomorrow....the capacity to foresee the behaviour of matter.
Primo Levi. OTHER PEOPLE'S TRADES, p19.

Why we like to watch nature programmes – they provide a glimpse into a utopian world where no language or training are needed .. a harmonious society in which everyone spontaneously knows his or her role.
Slavoj Zizek. LIVING IN THE END TIMES, p83.

NATURE

Jewish laws of kashrut dictated how the fruit of a tree could not be harvested until the third year – that before its cycles can be interfered with the tree must know about ripeness and withering, until it becomes so adamant in its growth and so voluptuous with fruit that no amount of picking will disturb it. And for the harveser's part, the virtue of patience must be learned. The virtue of waiting for one's pleasure until the waiting itself doubles or triples the joy.
Samantha Harvey, THE WILDERNESS, p40

The sky looks lacquered; clouds there are none; the horizon floats; and this nakedness of the unrelieved radiance is as the insufferable splendors of God's throne.
Herman Melville. MOBY DICK, p470.

But my father passed without stopping, and I was still gazing back at the tree. A refusal of scale, a rupturing of normal form into this giant, an indication of what was always there lurking behind all that we believe. Any part of our world capable of this at any moment.
David Vann. GOAT MOUNTAIN, p124.

'Mature is what we were put on earth to rise above!
Katherine Hepburn to Humphrey Bogart in *The African Queen*.

The similarity of nature patterns: the shape of a snowflake - the vertebrae of a rocky hill - erosion ditches - a fern frond - the skeleton of a reptile.
Andre Brink. AN INSTANT IN THE WIND, p206.

The harder the bargain men must strike with nature to survive, the more rules they're likely to have amongst themselves to keep them all in order.
Angela Carter. NIGHTS AT THE CIRCUS, p281.

The developers will always win as they have a higher motivation than we have: we only want to enjoy the scenery but they want lots of money.
Stan Gebler Davies. THE INDEPENDENT, 16/9/89.

Every material of man grows at last mellow and beautiful, except concrete - as the years passed the site stared out of the heather like scabs of blindness. A concrete foundation is never sweetened by weeds and grass. It looks hot and hurt in sunlight; it resents the gentle or the resounding kisses of the rain.
George Mackay Brown. GREENVOE, p245.

He tore the flower gravely from its pinhold smelt its almost no smell and placed it in his heart pocket. Language of flowers. They like it because no one can hear. Or a poison bouquet to strike him down. Then, walking slowly forward, he read the letter again, murmuring here and there a word. Angry tulips will you darling manflower punish your cactus if you don't please poor forgetmenot how I long violets to dear roses when we soon anemone meet all naughty night-stalk wife Martha's perfume.
James Joyce. ULYSSES, p77.

The flies, poor things, were a mine of observations: the wings, a delicate labyrinth of veins set in the transparent and iridescent membrane; the eyes, a crimson mosaic of miraculous regularity; the legs, an arsenal of talons, rigid hairs, and rubbery pads - slippers, foam-rubber soles and hobnail all in one.
Primo Levi. OTHER PEOPLE'S TRADES, p49.

In the spring or warmer weather when the snow thaws in the woods the tracks of winter reappear on slender pedestals and the snow reveals in palimpsest old buried wanderings, struggles, scenes of death. Tales of winter brought to light again like time turned back upon itself.
Cormac McCarthy. SON OF GOD, p138.

We travelled in a small hydroplane, and in some places in native canoes, along narrow river channels so choked with tangled vegetation overhead that in bright daylight it seemed dark as night. The strength and solitude of Nature - the tall trees, the mirror-smooth lagoons, the immutable rivers - brought to mind a newly created world, untouched by man, a paradise of plants and animals. When we reached the tribes, by contrast, there before us was prehistory, the elemental, primeval existence of our distant ancestors: hunters, gatherers, bushmen, nomads, shamans, irrational and animistic.
Mario Vargas Llosa. THE STORYTELLER, p72.

Down in the parlour cupboard, there is a delft bowl with soil, in which are planted five tulip bulbs and Catherine thinks of them now. She knows that they have reached the point of being five short yellow spikes, but they will continue to grow, and when they are in the light they will grow further. They will be like stiff green flames unfurling, hard and vibrantly green, and then the green flower will come and grow and the colour will blush into it; in her mind's eye the flower grows and gains colour, and she finds this promise of spring a comfort, the same comfort she feels when, on a summer evening, she sees the late light slant thick through the window and fall upon the wall in a broad gold bar; gilding the air through which it passes.
Deirdre Madden. THE BIRDS OF THE INNOCENT WOOD, p92.

NEWS & REPORTING

Think, for instance, about the way prolonged exposure to broadcast drama makes each one of us at once more self conscious and less reflective. A culture more and more about *seeing* eventually perverts the relation of seer and seen. We watch various actors who play various characters involved in various relations and events. Seldom do we think about the fact that the single deep feature the characters share, with each other and with the actors who portray them, is that they are *watched*.... We, the audience, receive unconscious reinforcement of the thesis that the most significant feature of persons is 'watchableness', and that contemporary human worth is not just isomorphic with but rooted in the phenomena of watching. Precious distinctions between truly being and merely appearing get obfuscated.
David Foster Wallace. BOTH FLESH AND NOT, p 49.

Those whose work it is to sustain the endless palaver of radio and television increasingly stimulate these excitements. No great wonder if they are bored, or if they suspect their audience might be. But the effect of this marketing of rancor has unquestionably been to turn debate or controversy increasingly into a form of tribal warfare, harming the national community and risking always greater harm.
Marilynne Robinson, WHEN I WAS A CHILD, p 27.

Editor: A person employed on a newspaper, whose business it is to separate the wheat from the chaff, and to see that the chaff gets printed.
Elbert Hubbard. THE ROYCROFT DICTIONARY (1914)

Reportage, taking religion's place, endlessly feeds its reader with accounts of deaths of other people, and therefore places him continually in the position of survivor.
John Carey. FABER BOOK OF REPORTAGE, xxxv

American Sunday supplements - brain candy (Tom Wolfe).

To convey the problems of one part of the world to people living in another part, it is vital to know very well both those areas.
Review of THE USES OF ADVERSITY by T Garton Ash. Indpendent, 16/9/89.

I think the appetite for news is a function of Western consumerism.
Don De Lillo. IrishTimes, 16/9/89.

In my view newspapers have one extenuating attribute: they make no noise. Their tediousness is silent; they can be put aside, thrown into the wastebasket. The tediousness of radio lacks that extenuating attribute; it persecutes us in cafes, restaurants, trains, even during our visits to people who have become incapable of living without nonstop feeding of the ears.
Milan Kundera. THE JOKE, p175.

Reflecting on noted Democratic gains at his expense in the autumn State and Senate congressional elections, Lincoln was asked for his reaction to all the bad news. He felt like the boy who had stubbed his toe - he was too big to cry, and it hurt too much to laugh.

A newsreel: A series of catastrophes, ended by a fashion show!
Oscar Levant.

Trying to determine what is going on in the world by reading newspapers is like trying to tell the time by watching the second hand of a clock.
Comment in the Guardian, 13/9/2006.

NOSTALGIA & SADNESS

I kept the grey plastic clip on my desk, in a little wooden bowl… A memory occurs, or perhaps there is something on the news, and it is there for me to pick up and hold. To recollect. It never wears out, it never changes. It has a kind of permanently renewable energy. It warms quickly to my touch and that is all it does. I like its banality, its uselessness, the way its utility was removed forever by the destruction of the aircraft. It became something different then, something useful only to me.
James Robertson. THE PROFESSOR OF TRUTH, p39.

Light griefs can speak: deep sorrows are dumb.
Seneca. HIPPOLYTUS, act ii sc 3.

The longer and more carefully we look at a funny story, the sadder it becomes.
Gogol.

The area around the station (in Kuala Lumpur) was electric with the static left behind by the great imperial star, long since exploded; it crackled with currents of an improbable past. The ghosts of the old imperialists didn't just walk around the old railway station, they held fucking demonstrations.
Christopher Hope. MY MOTHER'S LOVERS, p163.

Nostalgia is a limpid and clean pain, but demanding; it permeates every minute of the day, permits no other thoughts and induces a need for escape.
Primo Levi. THE TRUCE, p316.

NOVELS & NOVELISTS

It is difficult to be a fiction writer in America because reality often outdoes the novelist's imagination. (Philip Roth)
Robert Dallek, NIXON AND KISSINGER, p204.

...to discuss the moralist Jane Austen, author of Persuasion, ironic observer, precise dissector of human feeling, stylist from heaven, and an author who died away with perverted monks but retained her own version of virtue rewarded.
Siri Hustvedt. THE SUMMER WITHOUT MEN, p173.

Fine novels, like all women and some mountains, deserve their remoteness.
Patrick Gallagher on Salman Rushdie, Sunday Independent, 23/10/88.

Any novel in itself is an enormous lie (you are constantly selecting evidence) but even within the context of that lie you are presenting doctored and selected versions.
Penelope Lively. Good Book Guide, 10/88.

Clever people will always write books about what is known as "the human condition" and that is about as far as it goes.
D J Taylor. Sunday Time, 2/10/88. G4.

All the Victorian novelist could offer as a solution to the problems of industrial capitalism were: a legacy, a marriage, emigration or death.
David Lodge. NICE WORK.

The stupidity of people comes from having a question for everything. The wisdom of the novel comes from having a question for everything.
Milan Kundera. THE BOOK OF LAUGHTER & FORGETTING, p237.

Novels are the fruit of the human illusion that we can understand our fellow men.
Milan Kundera. THE BOOK OF LAUGHTER & FORGETTING, p89.

(Someone commenting to Beckett on the fact that such a small country like Ireland produced so many great writers since the end of the 19th century) It's the priests and the British. They have buggered us into existence. After all, when you are in the last bloody ditch, there is nothing left but to sing.
Deirdre Bair. BECKETT.

But young novelists are imitative; they must be for they have not lived long enough to know who they are or - perhaps more to the point - who those others in the world are.
Gore Vidal. WILLIWAW, p9.

Most novels are written off the top of the head, that is, with the top tenth or so of the mind, because depth requires the kind of expenditure of concentration which most novelists cannot manage or do not care to attempt.
John Banville. Irish Times, 31/10/87.

When I am inside a text I can say what I like.
John Fowles. Writer's Monthly, 1/89.

(re Bruce Chatwin who died 1/89) working in New York and London, brilliantly poised for a fat and fashionable career in that seductive world where rivulets of art meet reservoirs of loot.
Melvyn Bragg, MAIL ON SUNDAY, 22/1/89.

Some writers are only born to help another writer to write one sentence.
Ernest Hemingway. GREEN HILLS OF AFRICA, p25.

Writers should work alone. They should see each other only after their work is done, and not too often then. Otherwise they become like writers in New York. All angleworms in a bottle, trying to derive knowledge and nourishment from their own contact and from the bottle. Sometimes the bottle is shaped art, sometimes economics, sometimes economic-religion. But once they are in the bottle they stay there.
Ernest Hemingway. GREEN HILLS OF AFRICA, p25.

Half a writer's work.....is the discovery of his subject.
V S Naipaul. FINDING THE CENTRE, p26.

Life under a totalitarian regime - a hidden opportunity for writers.

Long novels written today are perhaps a contradiction: the dimension of time has been shattered, we cannot love or think except in fragments of time each of which goes off along its own trajectory and immediately disappears. We can rediscover the continuity of time only in the novels of that period when time no longer seemed stopped and did not yet seem to have exploded, a period that lasted no more than a hundred years.
Italo Calvino. IF ON A WINTER'S NIGHT A TRAVELLER, p13.

"The present era grabs everything that was ever written in order to transform it into films, T.V. programmes....What is essential in a novel is precisely what can only be exposed in a novel, and so every adaptation contains nothing but the non-essential. If a person is still crazy enough to write novels nowadays and wants to protect them, he has to write them in such a way that they cannot be adapted, in other words, in such a way that they cannot be retold.'
Milan Kundera. IMMORTALITY, p266.

In the age of excessive division of labour, of runaway specialization, the novel is one of the last outposts where man can still maintain connections with life in its entirety.
Milan Kundera. THE ART OF THE NOVEL, p67.

The novel is a meditation on existence as seen through the medium of imaginary characters.
Milan Kundera. THE ART OF THE NOVEL, p83.

A theme is an existential inquiry. And increasingly I realize that such an enquiry is, finally, the examination of certain words, theme-words. Which leads me to emphasise: A novel is based primarily on certain fundamental words.
Milan Kundera. THE ART OF THE NOVEL, p84.

A novel is often, it seems to me, nothing but a long quest for some elusive definitions.
Milan Kundera. THE ART OF THE NOVEL, p127.

We can't bear to know people as imperfectly as we invariably do, which is why we invent whole lives and histories for our friends without realising it. We can't help it. In our separate ways we are all would-be novelists. Otherwise real novelists would have no readers.
Patrick McGinley. THE FANTASIST, p107.

A novel is a mirror which passes over a highway. Sometimes it reflects the blue of the skies, others the churned up mud of the road.
Stendhal.

OLD AGE

As we get older we reflect more on the past; there are fewer days ahead of us than behind.

The torrent of an old man's water may no longer smash into the bole of the roadside tree a full stride away as it once did but fall around his feet like a woman's; but in return the eye of his mind is given to fly away beyond the familiar sights of the homestead.
Chinua Achebe. ANTHILLS OF THE SAVANNAH, p124.

I like old men. They can be wonderful bastards because they have nothing to lose. The only people who can be themselves are babies and old bastards.
John Updike. COUPLES, p42.

In old age we live under the shadow of Death, which, like a Sword of Damocles, may descend at any moment, but we have so long found life to be an affair of being rather frightened than hurt that we have become like people who live under Vesuvius, and chance it without much misgiving.
Samuel Butler. THE WAY OF ALL FLESH, p37.

The middle-aged, who have lived through their strongest emotions, but are yet in the time when memory is still half passionate and not merely contemplative, should surely be a sort of natural priesthood, whom life has disciplined and consecrated to be the refuge and rescue of early stumblers and victims of self-despair.
George Eliot. THE MILL ON THE FLOSS, p247.

There is nothing like the proximity of elderly people, and of their suffering, to make us doubt the value of all we do.
Dai Vaughan. COTTEGE RUBBINGS.

Perhaps being old is having lighted rooms
Inside your head, and people in them, acting.
Philip Larkin. THE OLD RODS.

I will be 77 soon and at this age you live more with the dead than the living.
Jorge Amado. THE INDEPENDENT, 5/8/89.

The old scholar was watching the noisy young people around him and it suddenly occurred to him that he was the only one in the whole audience who had the privilege of freedom, for he was old. Only when a person reaches old age can he stop caring about the opinions of his fellows, or of the public, or of the future. He is alone with approaching death and death has no ears and does not need to be pleased. In the face of death a man can do and say what pleases his own self.
Milan Kundera. LIFE IS ELSEWHERE, p172.

When the old meet as strangers......they are at their best. They may be direct and need not pretend.....The middle-aged are most susceptible, are easily hurt and most in need of reassurance. They are strait-laced in their different ways, serious and intent. They have lost what they have always been thought to value: youth and a vigour for living. They suspect their health, scared to lose it too. The prime of life is a euphemism... Everything happens in middle age. One is old and young at the same time. One bids farewell and prepares. One's children begin the command they later take over completely.
William Trevor. THE OLD BOYS, p98.

Yes, it is possible that we do not grow up, that even as we grow old, we remain the children we always were. We remember ourselves as we were then, and we feel ourselves into what we are now, and we remain what we were, in spite of the years. We do not change for ourselves. Time makes us grow old, but we do not change.
Paul Auster. THE INVENTION OF SOLITUDE, p145.

All Jonathan had to do was wait, and he'd have had the pleasure of wathching Alvah and Wify suffer the tortures of the damned: this is what old age and the far edges of life are all about. But what could he have known of things like this? What do any of the young know? Death for them - when they think of it at all - is a box-office hit of a tragedy, elegantly plotted, somberly choreographed, with the world weeping in the stalls. No wonder we worship them; they're so magically blind.
Joan Brady. THEORY OF WAR, p40.

It's the habit of old men to look back on their youth with regret.
Brian Keenan. TURLOUGH, p65.

OPPORTUNISM

George Eliot said: Cruelty, like every other vice, requires no motive outside of itself; it only requires opportunity.
Amir Gutfreund. OUR HOLOCAUST.

OPTIMISM

It is lucky that it is not windy today. Strange, how in some way one always has the impression of being fortunate, how some chance happening, perhaps infinitesimal, stops us crossing the threshold of despair and allows us to live. It is raining, but it is not windy.
Primo Levi. IF THIS IS A MAN, p137.

The telephone worked. The concept of totality exists in theory, but never in life. In even the best-built wall there is always a chink (or we hope there is, and that means something). Even when we have the feeling that nothing works anymore, something works and makes a minimal existence possible. Even if there's an ocean of evil around us, green and fertile islets will poke above the water.
Ryszard Kapuscinski. ANOTHER DAY OF LIFE, p92.

(re American optimism) The optimism was surreal, objectionable in an undefined, ominous way.
Robert Fisk. Irish Times, 13/8/90.

Let us defy the cautious whose eyes are like frosted lavatory windows. Charles Lahr was a man who kept the beliefs which made youth possible when others, after the first enthusiasms of life, find that only habits make life endurable.
David Goodway. LONDON MAGAZINE 25 YEARS, p189.

ORDER & CHAOS

Disorder is the condition of the mind's fertility.
Paul Valery.

The first line of defense for any corrupt dysfunctional system is an ignoramus guarding the door.
Nathan Englander, THE MINISTRY OF SPECIAL CASES, p128.

oases of order in a desert of randomness.
John Banville. MEFISTO, p170.

Chaos is nothing but an infinite number of ordered things.
John Banville. MEFISTO, p183.

Yet almost every revolution contains within it an opposite if less obvious tendency: the idea of a return. A redemption, a restoration. A reaffirmation of what is pure and fundamental against what is decadent and false. A return to a new beginning.
Graham Swift. WATERLAND, p119.

This, I think, is the strangest thing of all: not that we have so few words left in this deep, desolate region we've reached, but that the few we have left are so meaningless.
Andre Brink. THE AMBASSADOR, p218.

If a way to the Better there be, it exacts a full look at the Worst.
Thomas Hardy.

There is a kind of order in the world, as the philosophers say, a kind of logic: intelligence doesn't go with kindness, and kindness and good works do not walk together. Otherwise, one person would be perfect in every way, and another would be a swine's snout, as they say. That's why it is ordained that a beautiful woman should be vulgar.
Amos Oz. ELSEWHERE, PERHAPS, p31.

"Why is Thekla's construction taking such a long time?"
"So that its destruction cannot begin."
Italo Calvino. INVISIBLE CITIES.

She (Phuong) had stuck a telegram for me up among the cosmetics - some message or other from the London office. I wasn't in the mood to open it. Everything was as it had been before Pyle came. Rooms don't change, ornaments stand where you place them; only the heart decays.
Graham Greene. THE QUIET AMERICAN, p168.

I sincerely believe that we're attracted to films about the Mafia because the violence and evil portrayed in them seems to have an explanation and a beginning and an end. It's confined to one group of people, who in their fictional portrayal even have tragic proportions, and we're made to believe the problem is not endemic to the species.
James Lee Burke. DIXY CITY JAM, p303.

OSTENTATION

Zinc - It has been known to humanity for two or three centuries, so it is not a veteran covered with glory like copper, nor even one of those newly minted elements which are still surrounded with the glamour of their discovery.
Primo Levi. THE PERIODIC TABLE, p33.

No act is so private it does not seek applause.
John Updike. COUPLES, p132.

OWNERSHIP

Sure, cried the tenant men, but it's our land. We measured it and broke it up. We were born on it, and we got killed on it, died on it. Even if it's no good, it's still ours. That's what makes it ours - being born on it, working it, dying on it. That makes ownership, not a paper with numbers on it.
John Steinbeck. THE GRAPES OF WRATH, p27.

PARENTS

I want my father to be just my father, the way he has always been, not a separate person with an earlier, mythological life of their own. Knowing too much about other people puts you in their power, they have a claim on you, you are forced to understand their reasons for doing things and then you are weakened.
Margaret Atwood. CAT'S EYE, p217.

Strange how things turn round: we become like our parents when we get older but we don't get older till they're dead.
Christopher Hope. MY MOTHER'S LOVERS, p235.

Some terrible parents before the war were great parents during it, said Anne Frank. The convenience of an enemy, Mr Krugel; no nation has more enemies abroad than the one failing at home; no father yells more loudly at the Little League coach – he was safe! – than the father of the child who is utterly unsafe at home.
Shalom Auslander. HOPE – A TRAGEDY, p209/10

The way you think about your parents and their meaning to you changes all the time. It's not a monument, it's not done.... Memory is a river.
Hanif Kureishi, 'Sunday Telegraph' *Seven*, 9/12/2012, p14.

How fortunate, Merivel. For it is one of my beliefs that we cannot truly live until the debts we owe our parents have been paid. For they and their debts can never be forgotten.
Rose Tremain. RESTORATION, p368.

I would rather have been with one parent who was genuinely happy than with two who had so many axes to grind you could almost hear them being sharpened.
Rachel Abbott. ONLY THE INNOCENT.

Dying parents.... exercise a power over you that they never had before. And when your father dies you will pick him up and carry him inside you all your life like an unborn child or a malignant growth, he will accompany you through all your rebellions, he will never again be angry or punish you but only laugh quietly inside you. All your life.
Amos Oz. TOUCH THE WATER, TOUCH THE WIND, p145.

His (his father) presence, diffident and fleeting, lent a mysterious weight to the most trivial occasion.
John Banville. MEFISTO, p13.

They reckon being a parent makes you grow up; if that's so we'd all chose to remain children forever.

Daddy was small and sickly, and when he walked along the street with Tamina, he looked so proud he seemed to be presenting the entire world with a monument to the heroic night when he created her.
Milan Kundera. THE BOOK OF LAUGHTER & FORGETTING, p100.

Like everything else in his life, he saw me only through the mists of solitude, as if at several removes from himself. The world was a distant place for him, I think, a place he was never truly able to enter, and out there in the distance, among all the shadows that flittered past him, I was

born, became his son, and grew up, as if I were just one more shadow, appearing and disappearing in a half-lit realm of his consciousness.
Paul Auster. THE INVENTION OF SOLITUDE, p24.

Many men live to find their mothers a nuisance. So many mothers live to become a nuisance. A mother who dies before that happens is with you always.
Patrick McGinley. THE FANTASIST, p 48.

PAST & HISTORY

History isn't history unless you show the effects of power.
Robert Caro.

The interpretation of what people perceived within a process that later turned into a catastrophe is a very tricky enterprise – not least because we pose our questions of what people knew with our own hindsight as to how things turned out. We view history from the end to the beginning and are forced to suspend our own historical knowledge in order to say what people knew at any specific historical juncture.
Sonke Neitzel & Harald Welzer. SOLDATEN: On Fighting, Killing and Dying, p13.

'History? We don't have a history really,' I remembered her telling one of my many uncles. 'Just a police record.'
Christopher Hope. MY MOTHER'S LOVERS, p36.

Historians – of all the clichés about 'history', the one that appealed to me was the assertion that we were but philosophers teaching with examples.
Tony Judt, THE MEMORY CHALET, p11.

The illusion that we understand the past fosters overconfidence in our ability to predict the future.
Daniel Kahnman, THINKING FAST AND SLOW, p 218.

'Historians rarely do justice to the psychological stress on a policy maker. What they have available are documents written for a variety of purposes – under contemporary rules of disclosure, increasingly to dress up the record – and not always relevant to the moment of decision.' (Kissinger).
Robert Dallek, NIXON AND KISSINGER, p197.

There is no future without a past because what is to be cannot be imagined except as a form of repetition. I had begun to expect calamities.
Siri Hustvedt. THE SUMMER WITHOUT MEN, p111.

'And history is nothing but a cemetery,' I said to Mrs Brown…
'That's exactly right. For us to visit when we have a mind, or just not go at all. Let the weeds grow up.'
Barbara Kingsolver. THE LACUNA, p 400.

"The past becomes dreamy because its symbols have all vanished, and the present too is dreamy because it is linked with no memories."
George Eliot, SILAS MARNER.

'History is a raw onion sandwich, sir.'
'For what reason?'
'It just repeats, sir. It burps…
Julian Barnes. THE SENSE OF AN ENDING, p16.

History is that certainty produced at the point where imperfections of memory meet the inadequacies of documentation.
Patrick Lagrange, quoted in Julian Barnes, THE SENSE OF AN ENDING, p17.

I have long had a weakness for that transparent fabulist (Herodotus), since invented history is always more appealing than the wearisome tyranny of fact.
Cees Nooteboom. THE FOLLOWING STORY, p25.

History is like an ocean into which rivers of individual histories flow. Everything that has gone before underpins the present; we continue those stories just as those who come after us continue ours.
Marcelo Figueras. KAMCHATKA, p273/4

The past was precious because it was different, not better.
Tessa Hadley. THE LONDON TRAIN, p4.

There are as many interpretations of an event as there are voices to give on.
Penelope Lively. Good Book Guide, 10/88.

To live in such a place was, for Isabel, to hold to her ear all day a shell of the sea of the past.
Henry James. PORTRAIT OF A LADY, p239.

If history (the past) had something to teach us then history would be the record of inexorable progress.....The future would be an ever more glowing prospect.
Graham Swift. WATERLAND, p133.

That history is a record of decline. What we wish upon the future is very often the image of some lost, imagined past.
Graham Swift. WATERLAND, p122.

There are times (they come round really quite often) when good, dry textbook history takes a plunge into the old swamps of myth and has to be retrieved with empirical fishing lines.
Graham Swift. WATERLAND, p74.

History is a thin garment, easily punctured by a knife blade called NOW.
Graham Swift. WATERLAND, p31.

History is a succession of ephemeral changes. Eternal values exist outside history. They are immutable and have no need of memory.
Milan Kundera. THE BOOK OF LAUGHTER & FORGETTING, p187.

The future is an apathetic void of no interest to anyone. The past is full of life, eager to irritate us, provoke and insult us, tempt us to destroy or repaint it. The only reason people want to be masters of the future is to change the past.
Milan Kundera. THE BOOK OF LAUGHTER & FORGETTING, p22.

History is written by the winners.
George Orwell. AS I PLEASE.

An old man is gunned down in the street and within a couple of days this senseless act is both normal and inevitable. It was as if these newspaper articles were poultices placed on sudden inflammations of violence. In a day or two all the poison has been drawn out of them. They become random events of the year 1919, inevitable, without malice, part of history.
J G Farrell. TROUBLES, p102.

Is history to be considered the property of the participant solely?
Salman Rushdie. SHAME, p28.

History is lived forward but it is written in retrospect.
Veronica Wedgewood.

The past has the clarity of memories. It is clear, paradoxically, precisely because it is vague: because it cannot contradict us with any confidence.
Dai Vaughan. COTTAGE RUBBINGS.

Mythology is much better stuff than history. It has form; logic; a message.
Penelope Lively. MOON TIGER, p7.

It was an old-fashioned house, so much so that, in those years, it had a way of seeming almost too modern for its own good, as the past so often does when it outruns the present.
Angela Carter. NIGHTS AT THE CIRCUS, p26.

You come out of 'Gone with the Wind' feeling that history isn't so disturbing after all. One can always make a dress out of a curtain.
Dilys Powell. Independent Review, 29/4/90.

"This is what history consists of. It's the sum total of all the things they aren't telling us."
Don De Lillo. LIBRA, p321.

She took particular delight in showing visitors the small plaque which marks the spot where the gallows had once stood: 'They were hanged for a sixpence,' she used to say, 'and now there's no such coin! What strange tricks history plays on our pockets.'
Peter Ackroyd. CHATTERTON, p28.

(re the Emergency) Our dreary Eden of grey piety.
Kevin Myers. Irish Times, Jan '92.

History is the essence of innumerable biographies.
Carlyle.

How can we live without our lives? How will we know it's us without our past.
John Steinbeck. THE GRAPES OF WRATH, p75.

Myths are versions of the past which people believe in for irrational motives - usually because they feel good or find their prejudices confirmed.
F. Fernandez-Armesto. HISTORY TODAY, Vol 42, 5/92.

The past is hidden, beyond the reach of intellect, in some material object (in the sensation which that material object will give us) which we do not suspect. And as for that object, it depends on chance whether we come upon it or not before we ourselves must die.
Proust.

I accept my whole history, of course: even my inventions. I am ashamed of nothing. Only by acknowledging it can one hope to go beyond it. But the point is, surely, that one is not simply the result of one's history. One is also a reaction to it, a rebellion against it; in the process of amplifying or testing it, trying to corroborate it, one also rejects and replaces it.
Andre Brink. AN ACT OF TERROR, p826.

And history is terrible because it so often ends up a playground for the immature; a playground for the young Nero, a playground for the young Bonaparte, a playground for easily aroused mobs of

children whose simulated passions and simplistic poses suddenly metamorphose into a catastrophically real reality.
Milan Kundera. THE JOKE, p87

Today history is no more than a thin thread of the remembered stretching over an ocean of the forgotten, but time moves on, and an epoch of millennia will come which the inextensible memory of the individual will be unable to encompass; whole centuries and millennia will therefore fall away, centuries of paintings and music, centuries of discoveries, of battles, of books, and this will be dire, because man will lose the notion of his self and his history, unfathomable, will shrivel into a few schematic signs destitute of all sense.
Milan Kundera. THE JOKE, p293/4.

I think it was Utz who first convinced me that history is always our guide for the future, and always full of capricious surprises. The future itself is a dead land because it does not yet exist.
Bruce Chatwin. UTZ, p119.

I lower the camera without taking a picture, remembering how Kate used to tell Rose and me about the Bardons and the war. It seemed so exciting. Life stretched ahead like a road unfurling to bright light. The past was already written up, a definite adventure story told by people who had infinite freedom to do what they wished, whose function was to entertain the young and provide skeins of information on the world and its ways.
Mary O'Donnell.   THE LIGHT-MAKERS, p170.

....I reflected upon the ambiguous importance of the past in our lives. In order to free ourselves from it, we treat it as a decaying memory. At the same time, it's the only measure of identity we have. There is no mystery to the self; we are what we do and where we have been. So we have to resurrect the past constantly, erect monuments to it, and keep it alive in order to remember who we are.
James Lee Burke. THE NEON RAIN, p132.

What is historical opportunity?
Merely a moment when people believed they had managed to disrupt the flow of history and thus open up room for maneuver. Whether they had actually done so, or whether they had actually closed something off is a judgment that could only be passed by history itself.
Ivan Klima. WAITING FOR THE DARK, WAITING FOR THE LIGHT, p144.

And if you should ever doubt the proximity of the past, you only had to look over your shoulder at the rain slanting on the fields, like now, the smoke rising in wet plumes out of the stubble, the mist blowing off the lake, and you can see and hear with the clarity of a dream the columns marching four abreast out of the trees, emaciated as scarecrows, their perforated, sun-faded colours popping above them in the wind, their officers cantering their horses in the field, everyone dressing it up now, the clatter of muskets shifting in unison to the right shoulder, yes, just a careless wink of the eye, just that quick, and you're among them, wending your way with liege lord and serf and angel, in step with the great armies of the dead.
James Lee Burke. BURNING ANGEL, p340.

It is in the nature of betrayal, she thought, that it not only changes the present, but that it reaches back with its dirty hands and changes the past.
Hilary Mantel. A CHANGES OF CLIMATE, p304.

The past doesn't change, of course, it lies behind you, petrified, immutable. What changes is the way you see it. Perception is everything. It turns villains into heroes and victims into collaborators.
Hilary Mantel. A CHANGES OF CLIMATE, p337.

History is a body of knowledge that we agree to regard as important.
Pat Barker. "The Guardian", 24/10/98.

Isn't it wonderful how people only remember the history that suits them?
Brian Keenan. TURLOUGH, p191.

We are what the past has made us.

PATRIOTISM

Oh, one doesn't give up one's country any more than one gives up one's grandmother. They're both antecedent to choice - elements of one's composition that are not to be eliminated.
Henry James. THE PORTRAIT OF A LADY, p84.

An Englishman's never so natural as when he's holding his tongue.
Henry James. THE PORTRAIT OF A LADY, p82.

Winding caravan of Irish nationalism - its poets, assassins, scholars, crackpots, parlour revolutionaries, windbags, mythopoeic essayists, traitors, orators from the scaffold, men of action.......
Irish Times, 1/7/88, review of THE GREEN FLAG by Robert Kee.

There's no stopping a man in the pursuit of his own ambition, particularly if he's read God's mind and found that they think alike.
J Rizkalla. THE JERICHO GARDEN. cf Sunday Times, 10/4/88.

Scratch every Irishman deeply enough and you'll find a windy patriot.
Benedict Kiely. NOTHING HAPPENS IN CARMINCROSS, p239.

Nationalism.....is driven by nostalgia, a desire to return home, to recover an original state of nature which has been effaced or overlaid with the alien and artificial landscape of colonialism.
Eamon Halpin. Canadian Journal of Irish Studies, 12/91.

PEOPLE

"He is a good neighbour, Brian, but a man of small and constant calculation."
James Robertson. THE PROFESSOR OF TRUTH, p146.

'God must have loved the common people – he made so many of them!'
Richard Nixon in 1952 Election campaign, quoted by Robert Dallek,
NIXON AND KISSINGER, p24.

But people are never more interesting than when they are sinning or acting bizarrely.
Brian Walden. Sunday Times, 6/11/88.

JFK - a cleverly manufactured politician who happened to catch a nobody's bullet.
John Updike. COUPLES, p343.

You come into the world alone, you go out alone. In between it's nice to know a few people, but being alone is a fundamental quality of human life, depressing as that is.........
Helen Mirren. Sunday Independent, 29/1/89.

One thing to remember, Americans got the shortest memories of any citizen who ever took a shit on this planet.
James Robison. THE ILLUSTRATOR, p24.

Kafka....endlessly unravels the hallucination that he draws from incredibly profound layers, and he never filters them. The reader feels them swarm with germs and spoors: they are gravid with burning significances, but he never receives any help in tearing through the veil or circumventing it to go and see what it conceals. Kafka never touches ground, he never condescends to giving you the end of Ariadne's thread.
Primo Levi. THE MIRROR MAKER, p107.

The cleaning-woman was a jovial sort. She didn't stop to chat, though, because small groups of people had already gathered. She knew that she was too domestic an image; she would spoil the romance of her own carefully polished floor.
Thomas McCarthy. WITHOUT POWER, p243.

Dire Straits - menopausal rock gods.

The British deserve to be examined in haste and judged without pity: for centuries they have applied that treatment to others in Europe and elsewhere.
Beppe Severgnini. Sunday Times, 18/8/1991.

The French! says the citizen. Set of dancing masters! Do you know what it is? They were never worth a roasted fart to Ireland. Aren't they trying to make 'Entente Cordiale' now at Tay Pay's dinner party with perfidious Albion? Firebrands of Europe and they always were?
James Joyce. ULYSSES, p328.

Actually Father Duryea, our contact, our man, always saw us right away; but that didn't stop Hamilton hanging around for hours afterwards, in the waiting room. Tense, silent, on the chair by the table with its flower bowl and its dish of cracked apples. Fr. Duryea was an Irishman. His rampant facial heat had set up its headquarters in his nose; from there, strong tendrils of blood seemed to leak into his remorseful grey eyes. His mouth, too, was a scene of pain.
Martin Amis. TIME'S ARROW, p118/119.

PERSONALITY

One thing love and death have in common, more than those vague resemblances people are always talking about, is that they make us question more deeply, for fear that its reality might slip away from us, the mystery of personality.
Proust. SWANN'S WAY.

PHILOSOPHERS & THEOLOGIANS

a philosopher is a blind man in a dark room looking for a black cat that isn't there, and a theologian is a man who has found it.
Letter to Irish Times, 30/6/88.

"Philosophy! Empty thinking by ignorant conceited men who think they can digest without eating! They fancy their substanceless thought can lead to deep conclusions."
Iris Murdoch. THE BOOK AND THE BROTHERHOOD, p22.

PHOTOGRAPHY

To photograph is to confer importance. There is probably no subject that cannot be beautified; moreover, there is no way to suppress the tendency inherent in all photographs to accord value to their subjects.
Susan Sontag. ON PHOTOGRAPHY, chapter 2.

PLACES

"T he Middle East isn't a place. It's a cauldron of oil and creeds."
James Robertson. THE PROFESSOR OF TRUTH, p63.

'Af-ri-ca.'
Those must be the emptiest three syllables ever coined. A menacing prayer that passed for patriotism from Cape to Cairo, the sort that said: if you love the place, reach out and hit some one.
Christopher Hope. MY MOTHER'S LOVERS, p189.

I have always been more interested in the relationship between landscape and individual lives, and how the places we inhabit shape the people we are.
Robert Macfarlane, THE OLD WAYS, p187.

Two questions we should ask of any strong landscape: firstly, what do I know when I am in this place that I can know nowhere else? And then, vainly, what does this place know of me that I cannot know of myself?
Robert Macfarlane, THE OLD WAYS, p27.

We are adept, if occasionally embarrassed, at saying what we make of places – but we are far less good at saying what places make of us.
Robert Macfarlane, THE OLD WAYS, p29.

It was the inn that is in every provincial faubourg, with large stables and small bedrooms, where one sees in the middle of the court chickens pilfering the oats under the muddy gigs of the commercial travelers – a good old house, with worm-eaten balconies that creak in the wind on winter nights, always full of people, noise and feeding, whose blank tables are sticky with coffee and brandy, the thick windows made yellow by the flies, the damp napkins stained with cheap wine, and that always smells of the village, like ploughboys dressed in Sunday clothes, has a café on the street...
Gustave Flaubert. MADAME BOVARY, p344.

I have demonstrated that I can't describe Deer Isle. There is something about it that opens no door to words.
John Steinbeck. TRAVELS WITH CHARLEY, p45.

Marshall Foch, visiting the Grand Canyon: the perfect place to drop one's mother-in-law.

The commercial station is cold and anonymous and ultra contemporary; its glass-fronted lobby is decorated in Madison Avenue minimalism.
Alison Lurie. FOREIGN AFFAIRS, p191.

Kavanagh on Dublin: Dublin was the cruellest city on the face of the earth because Dublin led you on. A city should ignore you, like London did...... A city should be impersonal, but Dublin was full of warm promise, like the worst kind of woman.
A J Cronin. DEAD AS DOORNAILS, p76.

One of the pleasures of life in Africa was the hardness of its edges, the uncertainty at its centre and the extravagance of human energy that was its 'leavening'.
Judith Thurman. ISAK DINESEN.

Roots, I sometimes think, are a conservative myth, designed to keep us in our places.
Salman Rushdie. SHAME, p86.

London stretched away on all sides, modulating towards colourness with distance. The streets below were coloured stone, cement, rooftiles. And it was difficult to believe that all those people down there had nothing in common but accidents of location.
Christopher Barnes. DEALING IN FICTION.

To the Europeans, South America is a man with a moustache, and guitar and a gun.
Gabriel Garcia Marquez. NO ONE WRITES TO THE COLONEL, p21.

Destinations that are not ours always seem romantic. I was in Finland, but was sitting on it like a raindrop that, unlike the raindrops on my scalp and raincoat, had not begun to soak in.
John Updike. Independent Review, 29/4/90.

They can print statistics and count the populations in hundreds of thousands, but to each man a city consists of no more than a few streets, a few houses, a few people. Remove those few and a city exists no longer except as a pain in the memory, like the pain of an amputated leg no longer there.
Graham Greene. OUR MAN IN HAVANA, p183.

You are never at the mercy of the elements in London, where the huddled warmth of humanity melts the snow before it has time to settle.
Angela Carter. "The Courtship of Mr Lyon" in THE BLOODY CHAMBER, p48.

South Africa is a centripetal force that draws people, in the region, not only out of economic necessity, but also out of the fascination of commitment to political struggle.
Nadine Gordimer. MY SON'S STORY, p88.

Castro's Cuba - the moonlit fixation in the emerald sea.
Don De Lillo. LIBRA, p22.

Dublin in the morning was a great place for a walk - you looked and stepped to the sound of everyone else's thoughts; that is if you had nothing to think about yourself.
Evelyn Conlon. "Transition" from MY HEAD IS OPENING, p46.

And, although, on a public level, one would like Ireland to be run in a reasonable, pluralist, modern way, there is more to living here than being a citizen. There is a capaciousness not so much of belief as of endlessly suspended judgement, which to my mind is precious.
Nuala O Faolain. Irish Times, 2/9/91.

California, the fun state, the rich state, America's frontier with the future.
Independent on Sunday, 26/4/92.

I have come to New York because it is the most forlorn of places, the most abject. The brokenness is everywhere, the disarray is universal. You have only to open your eyes to see it. The broken people, the broken things, the broken thoughts. The whole city is a heap of junk....I find the streets an endless source of material, an inexhaustible storehouse of shattered things.
Paul Auster. THE NEW YORK TRILOGY, p78.

The Slaney north of Enniscorthy and south of Bunclody. This was the land the English had taken over and tilled. They had cut down trees, they had given new names to each thing, as though they were the first to live there. In the beginning she had been trying to paint the land as though it had no history, only colours and contours. Had the light changed as the owners changed? How could it matter? At dawn and dusk she walked along the river. In the morning there was a mist along the Slaney, palpable, grey, lingering. In the evening at four, when the light faded, an intense calm descended on the river, a dark blue stillness as though glass were moving from Wicklow to the sea, even the sounds then were muted, a few crows in the trees, cattle in the distance and the faint noise of water.

Colm Tobin. THE SOUTH, p220.

To hear them talk about the place (Ireland) now, even to traduce it, you'd have thought it was somewhere, the centre of the significant universe. Not a misshapen little jug of a country teetering on the brink of a continental shelf: one ten-thousandth of the earth's surface.

Glenn Patterson. FAT LAD, p216.

The political tragedy in Spain was rehearsed in full dress twenty years earlier on Mexican soil. For those with eyes to see. Nothing was the same and yet everything. In the Spaniard's heart is a great yearning for freedom but only his own. A great love for truth and honor in all its forms but not in its substance. And a deep conviction that nothing can be proven except that it can be made to bleed. Virgins, bulls men. Ultimately God himself.

Cormac McCarthy ALL THE PRETTY HORSES, p231.

England, what could he see in it? The villages were overcrowded and the fields between them too enormous. There seemed to be nothing natural or old about it. There were ancient houses, but they were all double-glazed and over-pointed and restored to within inches of newness. Every barn that might have once been nice had a family of burgeoning stockbrokers living within its converted walls. What wasn't frozen by the preservers was destroyed by the developers.

Frank Ronan. THE MEN WHO LOVED EVELYN COTTON, p68.

Room 999 was ten feet from the highway, fronted by a plate glass window. Every set of headlights veered into the parking lot, the glare sliding over the walls of the room like raw eggs in oil.

E Annie Proulx. THE SHIPPING NEWS, p52.

Skerries in the 1960's was probably like any other Irish seaside resort. But in the sepia glow of memory, the ordinariness of pebble-dash and honky tonk of plastic palaces and tacky variety shows is transformed into something special.

Aodhan Madden. "Halcyon Holidays", Irish Times, 23/8/97.

POETRY

It is no coincidence that all poems about death depict it as a journey.
Milan Kundera. THE BOOK OF LAUGHTER & FORGETTING, p173.

To be a poet and not know the trade,
To be a lover and repel all women,
Twin ironies by which great saints are made,
The agonising pincer-jaws of heaven.
Patrick Kavanagh.

being a poet is all, being known as a poet is nothing.
John Fowles. THE MAGUS, p57.

Poetry is more a threshold than a path, one constantly approached and constantly departed from, at which reader and writer undergo in their different ways the experience of being at the same time summonsed and released.
Seamus Heaney. GOVERNMENT OF THE TONGUE, p108.

The purpose of poetry is to remind us how difficult it is to remain just one person, for our house is open, there are no keys in the doors, and invisible guests come in and out at will.
Czeslaw Milosz. ARS POETICA?

......a poet must go with his or her own flow, ignoring to a large extent all praise as much as all blame. A useful type of criticism is analysic. It should explain what's going on without smearing it with a marmalade of approval or sprinkling it with a vinegar of dismissal.
George MacBeth. Writer's Monthly, 12/87.

In rhyme and rhythm resides a certain magic power. An amorphous world becomes at once orderly, lucid, clear, and beautiful when squeezed into regular meters. If a woman "weary of breath" has "gone to her death", dying becomes harmoniously integrated into the cosmic order. Even if such a poem were intended as a bitter protest against mortality, death becomes justified as an occasion for beautiful protest. Bones, funeral wreaths, gravestones, coffins - everything in a poem becomes transmuted into a ballet in which both the reader and the poet perform their dance. The dancers, of course, cannot disagree with the dance. Through poetry, man realizes his agreement with existence, and rhyme and rhythm are the crudest means of gaining consent.
Milan Kundera. LIFE IS ELSEWHERE, p193.

Lyric poetry is the realm in which any statement immediately becomes truth........The lyrical poet does not have to prove anything. The only proof is in the intensity of his own emotion. The genius of lyrical poetry is the genius of inexperience. The poet does not know much about the world, but he arranges the words that stream out of his being into structures as formal as crystals. The poet himself is immature, yet his verse has the finality of a prophecy before which he stands in awe.
Milan Kundera. LIFE IS ELSEWHERE, p212.

...but there is a conversation above grossness and below refinement, where propriety resides, and where this poet seems to have gathered his comic dialogue.
Samuel Johnson. PREFACE TO SHAKESPEARE'S PLAYS, p129.

No question can be more innocently discussed than a dead poet's pretensions to renown; and little regard is due to that bigotry which sets candour higher than truth.
Samuel Johnson. PREFACE TO SHAKESPEARE'S PLAYS, p129.

Governments pretend to be based on reason and argument alone; poetry is a better model of human reality because it is the body and mind, dancing and dreams, acting in concert.
Les A Murray. Independent Review, 15/4/90.

Kenneth White talks of his work as a triple literary activity. He compares it to an arrow: "The essays, maintaining direction, are the feathers; the prose, ongoing autobiography, or what I like to call 'way-books' (alias transcendental travelogues) is the arrows shaft; and the poem is the arrow head."
Article by Sean Dunne, POETRY IRELAND No. 29.

Since poetry is intrinsic violence done to everyday language, it is understandable that every true poet feels the drive to become a violator, that is, an innovator, in his own right: to invent his own poetics, which stands in relation to the reigning poetics as the latter stands in prose.
Primo Levi. THE MIRROE MAKER, p111.

For the difference between poets and novelists is this - that the former write for the life of the language - and the latter for the betterment of the world.
A.S. Byatt. POSSESSION, p132.

Every baby is born a poet, but first parents and then teachers made him see the world in prose.
Patrick McGinley. THE FANTASIST, p66.

A conversation about poetry is only less pleasurable than poetry itself. Poetry is a pure white cloud painted on a windowpane. You look at the window and you think you're looking at a sky in summer, but when you open the casement you see that outside all is blackest night. The knack is to enjoy the painted clouds and keep the window tightly shut.
Patrick McGinley. THE FANTASIST, p236.

It gave him a sense of victory and triumph that Nur had so effectively stopped the raucous babble around him and placed the whole argument in perspective. That, he saw, was the glory of poets - that they could distance events and emotions, place them where perspective made it possible to view things clearly and calmly. He realised that he loved poetry not because it made things immediate but because it removed them to a position where they became bearable. That was what Nur's verse did - placed frightening and inexplicable experiences like time and death at a point where they could be seen and studied, in safety.
Anita Desai. IN CUSTODY, p54.

Very sensibly, he began at the right end, with the incantatory mode which lies at the very origin of poetry. Learn and enjoy the sound first, and afterwards the meaning will unfold itself.
Maurice Craig. THE ELEPHANT AND THE POLISH QUESTION, p75.

POLITICS

We're given no raw facts to base our votes upon; everything washes up on the shores of our consciousness rinsed and planed by the media. To ask a man for his democratic vote is just to ask him to give back the opinion he's been spoon-fed.
Samantha Harvey. ALL IS SONG, p104.

The Scottish trade unionist, Jimmy Reid, observed that Tony Benn enjoyed "more conversions on the road to Damascus than a Syrian long-distance truck driver".
Telegraph obituary for Benn, 15 March 2014, p33.

"We destroy the beauty of the countryside because the un-appropriated splendors of nature have no economic value. We are capable of shutting off the sun and the stars because they do not pay a dividend.
J M Keynes quoted in Tony Judt. ILL FARES THE LAND, p156.

"It is not sufficient that the state of affairs which we seek to promote should be better than the state of affairs which preceded it; it must be sufficiently better to make up for the evils of the transition."
J M Keynes, quoted in Tony Judt. ILL FARES THE LAND, p153.

(After the fall of Communism) the absence of a historically-buttressed narrative leaves an empty space. All that remains is politics: the politics of interest, the politics of envy, the politics of re-election. Without idealism, politics is reduced to a form of social accounting, the day-to-day administration of men and things.
Tony Judt. ILL FARES THE LAND, p142.

Liberal is a venerable and respectable label and we should all be proud to wear it. But like a well-designed outer coat, it conceals more than it displays.
A liberal is someone who opposes interference in the affairs of others; who is tolerant of dissenting attitudes and unconventional behaviour.. Most genuine liberals remain disposed to leave other people alone.
Tony Judt. ILL FARES THE LAND, p4/5.

Coke Stevenson (LBJ Senate opponent in Texas, 1948) The record was one of economy in government, of prudence and frugality, of spending the people's money as carefully as if it had been his own, of having government do only what the people couldn't do for themselves.
Robert C Caro. MEANS OF ASCENT, p167.

'*You don't have to explain something you haven't said*'
Calvin Coolidge in Congress in the 1920s. Robert C Caro. THE PATH TO POWER, p319

When the Texas Legislature met (to censure Senator Weldon Bailey in 1907), Bailey was in Austin *to drive into the Gulf of Mexico the peanut politicians who would replace me with someone who would rattle around in my seat like a mustard seed in a gourd!*
Robert C Caro. THE PATH TO POWER, p48.

Moral seriousness in public life is like pornography: hard to define but you know it when you see it. It describes a coherence of intention and action, an ethic of political responsibility.
Tony Judt, THE MEMORY CHALET, p31.

With the 'June 25 tape' scheduled for release on Monday, August 5, Nixon told his family: 'It's fight or flight by Monday night.'
Robert Dallek. NIXON AND KISSINGER, p604.

It is difficult for men in high office to avoid the malady of self-delusion. They are always surrounded by worshippers… They live in an artificial atmosphere of adulation and exaltation which sooner or later impairs their judgment.
Robert Dallek. NIXON AND KISSINGER, p488.

'A politician is a statesman who places the nation at his service.' (George Pompidou, 30/12/1973)
Robert Dallek. NIXON AND KISSINGER, p486.

'Woodrow Wilson was the biggest idealist in this office. When he went to Versailles, the pragmatists gobbled him up.' (Nixon)
Robert Dallek, NIXON AND KISSINGER, p460.

Politicians are the same all over. They promise to build a bridge even where there is no river. (Nikita Khruschev in 1963).
Robert Dallek. NIXON AND KISSINGER, p60.

Obama may have campaigned in poetry; like them all he governs in prose.
Ziyad Marar, INTIMACY, p181.

….and the people will remain quiet, not because it despairs of melioration, but because it is conscious of the advantages of its condition.
Alexis de Tocqueville. AMERICAN INSTITUTIONS AND THEIR INFLUENCES.

I find out of long experience that I admire all nations and hate all governments, and nowhere is my natural anarchism more aroused that at national borders where patient and efficient public servants carry out their duties in matters of immigration and customs.
John Steinbeck. TRAVELS WITH CHARLEY, p73

Stalin to Putin:
Shoot all inefficient officials and paint the walls blue!
Why blue?
I knew you'd only ask about the second part.

Why, the English party system is founded upon the principle that telling the whole truth does not matter. It is founded upon the principle that half a truth is better than no politics. Our system

deliberately turns a crowd of men who might be impartial into irrational partisans. It teaches some of them to tell lies and all of them to believe lies… It turns a room full of citizens into a room full of barristers.
G. K. Chesterton. THE BOY. (*Essays*).

…politicians logic☐something must be done; this is something; therefore it must be done.
YES PRIME MINISTER.

The struggle of man against power is the struggle of memory against forgetting.
Milan Kundera. THE BOOK OF LAUGHTER & FORGETTING, p3.

For a country is considered the more civilised the more the wisdom and efficiency of its laws hinder a weak man from becoming too weak or a powerful one too powerful.
Primo Levi. IF THIS IS A MAN, p94.

JFK - a cleverly manufactured politician who happened to catch a nobody's bullet.
John Updike. COUPLES, p343.

Politics is an art: like a pistol shot at a theatre.
Stendahl.

The trouble with radicals is that they only read radical literature, and the trouble with conservatives is that they don't read anything.
Thomas Nixon Carver quote. AGE OF UNCERTAINTY, p31.

What good to us are political doctrines which claim to make man flourish, if we do not know what type of man they will engender?
Antoine de Saint-Exupery. TERRES DES HOMMES.

By depriving white South Africans of sustained exposure to western ideas and thinking, they are being encouraged, possibly, to remain within their laager mentality.
Graham Leach. SOUTH AFRICA.

But what does wisdom mean to a despot? It means skill in the use of power. The wise despot knows when and how to strike. This continual display of power is necessary because, at root, any dictatorship appeals to the lowest instincts of the governed: fear, aggressiveness towards one's neighbours, bootlicking.
Rysard Kapuscinski. SHAH OF SHAHS, p115.

The Shah created a system capable only of defending itself, but incapable of satisfying the people.
Rysard Kapuscinski. SHAH OF SHAHS, p137.

The system (diplomatic, political) itself operated and existed only to the extent in which it was remote, invisible. It was present only in its absence - like God, he thought, in the mind of a good Christian who might commit the most atrocious acts in the pious conviction that it was sanctioned by a Being whose existence was, per definition, unprovable.
Andre Brink, THE AMBASSADOR, p156.

After listening to friends argue for hours about Marxism and how to save the world, Chekhov offered his own contribution - "Everyone should visit a stud farm. It's very interesting."
Quoted by V S Pritchett, CHEKHOV, Hodder 1969.

Before we can make radical changes in the world we've got to learn to see it the way it is.
Milan Kundera. LIFE IS ELSEWHERE, p37.

Artists make disastrous politicians, for artists desire absolute, while the politician must settle, properly, for compromise. When politicians look for absolutes, we have Hitlers and Mussolinis.
Albert Moravia. Irish Times, 17/7/90.

I have attended many editorial conferences where Northern Ireland would come up, like a rat through the floor at a children's party. The response generally was to slap the beast back down the hole, cover it up and hope there would be no further unseemly interruptions.
Cal McCrystal, Independent on Sunday. 21/4/91.

"When you believe in something literally, through your faith you'll turn it into something absurd. One who is a genuine adherent, if you like, of some political outlook, never takes its sophistries seriously, but only its practical aims, which are concealed beneath these sophistries. Political rhetoric and sophistries do not exist, after all, in order that they be believed; rather, they have to serve as a "common and agreed upon alibi".
Milan Kundera. LAUGHABLE LOVES, p112.

Slogans in the mouths of those who have re-cast them for themselves regain painful spontaneity for the tags and faded battle cries of causes the speaker doesn't acknowledge.
Nadine Gordimer. BURGER'S DAUGHTER, p164.

He who has nothing to lose can demand everything.
David Grossman. THE YELLOW WIND, p8.

A lesson of appeasement is that the instantly popular decision is often the most disastrous. Chamberlain was cheered through the streets of London when he returned from Munich in 1938 with Hitler's bogus promise of peace in our time. Joyful crowds would not be seen again in the capital until the war was won, long after Chamberlain was gone and dead.
Andrew Rawnsley. THE OBSERVER, 26/12/1999.

But how brief is the time before the exigencies of political life make it difficult and eventually impossible for the men in power to tell the difference between the truth and the lie!
J M Coetzee. DIARY OF A BAD YEAR, p126.

The only moral justification for capitalism lies in its productivity being harnessed to provide the highest basic income.
Slavoj Zizek. LIVING IN THE END TIMES, p235.

Unbridled capitalism and religious fundamentalism – the two principal dangers today.
Slavoj Zizek.

POVERTY

The leprosy of unreality disfigured every human creature in attendance upon Monseigneur.
Charles Dickens. A TALE OF TWO CITIES, p67.

One must be poor to know the luxury of giving!
George Eliot. MIDDLEMARCH, p102.

Poverty looks grim to grown people; still more so to children: they have not much idea of industrious, working, respectable poverty; they think of the world only as connected with ragged clothes, scanty food, fireless grates, rude manners, and debasing vices: poverty for me was synonymous with degradation.
Charlotte Bronte. JANE EYRE, p20.

(Poverty) is a quasi-embryonic condition, through which a man had better pass if he is to hold his later developments securely, but like measles or scarlet fever he had better have it mildly and get it over early.
Samuel Butler. THE WAY OF ALL FLESH, p380.

You cannot be called poor if you are poor by choice.
Nadine Gordimer. MY SON'S STORY, p89

We are all selfish. Sell up and go to the slums of Calcutta, work with lepers in the jungle......at my most cynical I ask whether even such things are not selfish, because it is easier for you to live with yourself having done that, knowing you have done all you could, rather than suffer the cramps of conscience.
Iain Banks. ESPEDAIR STREET, p242.

They lived on the periphery of the mirage of progress that affected the rest of the country.
Isabel Allende. OF LOVE AND SHADOWS, p40.

Poverty makes a hole in the heart and places hate there.
Victor Hugo.

The greatest obstacle that equality has to overcome is not the aristocratic pride of the rich but the undisciplined egoism of the poor.
Proudhon.

But beggars and performers make up only a small part of the vagabond population. They are the aristocracy, the elite of the fallen. For more numerous are those with nothing to do, with no where to go. Many are drunks - but that term does not do justice to the devastation they embody. Hulks of despair, clothed in rags, their faces bruised and bleeding, they shuffle through the streets as though in chains.
Paul Auster. THE NEW YORK TRILOGY, p109.

POWER

(he didn't believe, as Kafka) that the power in which people are held powerless exists only in their own submission.
Nadine Gordimer. MY SON'S STORY, p17.

Power is the ultimate aphrodisiac.
Henry Kissinger.

As I scribbled this in my notebook, I seemed to hear again Utz's nasal whisper: "They listen, listen, listen to everything but.... they hear nothing."
He had, as usual, been right. Tyranny sets up its own echo-chamber; a void where confused signals buzz about at random; where a murmur or innuendo causes panic: so, in the end, the machinery of repression is more likely to vanish, not with war or revolution, but with a puff or the voice of falling leaves......
Bruce Chatwin. UTZ, p120.

Seek not to enslave all hearts, and all hearts will be yours.
Voltaire.   THE CALLAS AFFAIR, p25.

PREJUDICE

…friends of the family who had never heard of Dupont, and were yet to see the point of him, had the air of mildly offended blankness which is the default expression of any congregation.
Alan Hollinghurst, THE STARNGER'S CHILD, p528 (Kindle)

I haven't a prejudice to bless myself with.
Henry James. THE PORTRAIT OF A LADY, p83.

Cynicism is cheap......it's built into all poor-quality goods.
Graham Greene. THE COMEDIANS, p17.

re Brendan Behan : The salt which makes penury palatable, ironic comment on all forms of possession and ownership, sometimes quite savage, he had in abundance.
A J Cronin. DEAD AS DOORNAILS, p7.

Prejudices, it is well known, are most difficult to eradicate from the heart whose soil has never been loosened or fertilised by education: they grow there, firm as weeds among stones.
Charlotte Bronte. JANE EYRE, p361.

Even Annie Devlin's rich and overgrown garden, with its shooting leeks and roofings of rhubarb leaves, even that natural earth was tinctured with the worst aspects of our faiths, insofar as that lovely flower, Sweet William, became suspect in the imagination from its connection with William of Orange, the King we sent to hell regularly up the long ladder and down the short rope.
Seamus Heaney. THE SENSE OF PLACE in PREOCCUPATIONS, p134.

...every so often another ugly incident takes place, carried out by the merciful hands of people like us, people who never hate, and maybe the fact that we do not allow ourselves to hate actually testifies to the disparagement we feel towards Arabs, since you do not hate a person whom you see as lower that you. It is hard for us, for instance, to hate children, because we sense that they are not our equals.
David Grossman. THE YELLOW WIND, p70-71.

He studied the spindly legs (of the cockroach) seemingly full of joints. The delicate formation of the elongated wings. He was filled with awe at the precise, minute artistry of this creature, which no longer seemed abhorrent but wonderfully perfect: a representative of a hated race, persecuted and confined to drains, excelling in the art of stubborn survival, agile and cunning in the dark: a race that had fallen victim to primeval loathing born of fear, of simple cruelty, of inherited prejudices. Could it be that it was precisely the evasiveness of this race, its humility and plainness, its powerful vitality, that aroused horror in us?
Amos Oz. FIMA, p71.

PROVERBS & SAYINGS

There is a saying that the frog who croaks in the shaft of a well will be frightened by the booming voice of the giant frog who answers him.
Salman Rushdie. SHAME, p91.

An Iranian proverb: Promises have value only for those who believe in them.
Rysard Kapuscinski. SHAH OF SHAHS, p137.

The well's never missed till its dry.
Samuel Butler. THE WAY OF ALL FLESH, p441.

What Cinderella said at midnight:
"Goodness me, the clock has struck,
Alackaday, and fuck my luck."
Kurt Vonnegut. SLAUGHTERHOUSE 5, p69.

Ours not to reason why,
Ours but to flog and fly!
Arthur Daley, MINDER.

An old Russian saying: There are only two things that really exist - one's death and one's conscience.
Vladimir Nabokov. THE ASSISTANT PRODUCER.

a saying: Hate power, hate work, hate your enemies and you'll float like pure oil on sewage.
Amos Oz. ELSEWHERE, PERHAPS, p156.

A man who keeps looking at the moon and stars easily trips over the first heap of dung in his way. And a man who only looks at the dung before his feet will never even know that there are stars in heaven.
Andre Brink. AN ACT OF TERROR, p810.

Sticks to him "as tightly as Formica to an epoxy-coated countertop".
Kurt Vonnegut. JAILBIRD, p59.

QUARRELS

Like all such quarrels it led to nothing except a wound which easily heals. There are places for so many different wounds before we find ourselves breaking an old scab.
Graham Greene. THE COMEDIANS, p108.

I may not be right, but I'm never wrong!

RACISM

However much he loved the blacks, it was in a white world he lived.
Graham Greene. THE COMEDIANS, p143.

England lacks a history of racial guilt.
Martin Amis, quoting Gloria Steinem. THE MORONIC INFERNO, p140

We're making a terrible mistake by regarding 'civilization' as the natural condition of people. We've barely had time to get used to it. If you look at us in perspective, it's only yesterday we started developing from the state of animals. So we're really no more than an aberration, a mutation, something unnatural. Our whole civilization is unnatural.
......try to think of racism in the same way. We regard it as "uncivilized" but actually it's part of our natural condition to resent and hate and persecute whatever looks different from ourselves.
Andre Brink. THE WALL OF THE PLAGUE, p218.

Because he had never yet earned his own living, he thought entirely in abstractions. For instance, he had the conventionally "progressive" ideas about the colour bar, the superficial progressiveness of the idealist that seldom survives a conflict with self-interest.
Doris Lessing. THE GRASS IS SINGING, p226.

To keep things apart, distinct, separate (man and woman; life and death; beginning and end; the inside and the outside of a text; life and story) to define them in terms of their exclusivity rather than in terms of what they have in common, must end in schizophrenia, in the collapse of the mind which tries to keep the distinctions going. In this lies the failure of apartheid, and the failure, as I see it, of structuralism. What is suppressed, Jung said somewhere, comes back to take its bloody revenge. And surely the most terrible revenge must come from the denial of the fluid oneness of things in favour of the principle of isolation.
Andre Brink. STATES OF EMERGENCY, p196.

"You must admit that being white makes it easier for you to believe."
"No," he said quietly......."Judas was white too. So was Hitler. Perhaps there are moments when it may be more difficult for a white to believe, because his faith must overcome all the obstacles of his own whiteness........
Andre Brink. LOOKING ON DARKNESS, p325.

But Africa taught me how necessary it was to touch people. More than a necessity: a need, a natural thing like eating or sleeping.....A man like Richard has a fit if you suddenly touch him. That's also a form of apartheid.
Andre Brink. LOOKING ON DARKNESS, p331.

This one or that has skipped (military service); the laconic phrase contains, for all this generation of white South Africans in the know, dumped by their elders with the deadly task of defending a life they haven't chosen for themselves, the singular heritage of their whiteness.
Nadine Gordimer. "A Correspondence Course" in SOMETHING OUT THERE, p105.

(re segregated areas....toilets!) As some lordly wild animal marks the boundaries of his hunting and mating ground which no other may cross, it was as if the municipality left some warning odour, scent of immutable authority, where the Saturday people were not to transgress. And they read the scent; they recognised it always, it had always been there.
Nadine Gordimer. MY SON'S STORY, p12.

How black they always were, these women; black blackened by labour in the sun, it's as if nature, which supplied our founding parents with the right degree of pigment to inhabit this continent, also supplies them with the camouflage under which to appear to submit to slavery. If you're mixed you don't have the protection.
Nadine Gordimer. MY SON'S STORY, p144.

Racism cannot be fought without plowing under the soil in which it grows. The occupation and the reality of apartheid which was created from its loam are the fertilizer on which racism feeds.
Amos Oz. THE SLOPES OF LEBANON, p84.

Let me tell you, when I walk upon this land, this South Africa, I have a gathering feeling of walking upon black faces. They are dead but their spirit has not left them. They lie there heavy and obdurate, waiting for my feet to pass, waiting for me to go, waiting to be raised up again. Millions of figures of pig-iron floating under the skin of earth. The age of iron waiting to return.
J.M. Coetzee. AGE OF IRON, p115.

READING

It's my habit to read novels like you read poems. I've been rereading the poems of Yeats, Burns, Coleridge and Wallace Stevens since I was young. And I find fresh truths there every year, just as, over time, you find new lines on your face... and the joy is seeing them and knowing they were always just waiting to emerge, and for you to find them. We live in such a period of fearfulness about age – such cultural hysteria about time's expense – that we can forget how lovely it is to advance. There's a kind of vitality that comes only with age, and that matters in several areas of your life, not least in your life as a reader. Simply put: you don't read The Great Gatsby the same way at 50 as you do at 25. By 50, you might know something about the costs of idealism, the penalties of romance, the management of delusion, the persistence of hope or the expanding nature of your capacity for wonder. If so, you'll simply be a better reader of the book.
Andrew O'Hagan, 'The Guardian', 8 April 2012.

Classic criticism has never paid any attention to the reader; for it, the writer is the only person in literature.... the birth of the reader must be at the cost of the death of the author.
Roland Barthes. THE DEATH OF THE AUTHOR.

Such books (good books) arouse false expectations: the noble exterior is assumed to clothe a mind and soul equally great - the Platonic fallacy.
Alison Lurie. FOREIGN AFFAIRS, p61.

There is no end to the making of books and too much reading is a weariness of the flesh.
Henry VIII in A MAN FOR ALL SEASONS by Robert Bolt.

...reading - that individualistic, withdrawn preoccupation.
Nadine Gordimer. MY SON'S STORY, p33.

"One thinks of nothing," he continued, " the hours slip by. Motionless we traverse countries we fancy we see, and you thought, blending with the fiction, playing with the details, follows the outline of the adventures. It mingles with the characters, and it seems as if it were you yourself palpitating beneath their costumes.
Gustave Flaubert. MADAME BOVARY, p97.

"Reading," he says, "is always this: there is a thing that is there, a thing made of writing, a solid, material object, which cannot be changed, and through this thing we measure ourselves against something else that is not present, something else that belongs to the immaterial, invisible world, because it can only be thought, imagined, or because it was once and is no longer, past, lost, unattainable, in the land of the dead....."
Italo Calvino. IF ON A WINTER'S NIGHT A TRAVELLER, p61.

How much of a book is in the words and how much is behind or in between the lines?.......Once you have read it, it may be better not to peer too hard beneath the surface of what it says - or....what it doesn't say.
Graham Swift. SHUTTLECOCK, p214.

I first read "The Castle" when I was fourteen years old. At that same period I admired an ice hockey player who lived near us. I imagined K. as looking like him. I still see him that way today. What I mean is that the reader's imagination automatically completes the writer's.
Milan Kundera. THE ART OF THE NOVEL, p34.

If we watch television and do not read, we are losing the power of reflection.

Books are wonderful things: to sit alone in a room and laugh and cry, because you are reading, and still be safe when you close the book; and having finished it discover you are changed, yet unchanged! To be able to visit the City of Invention at will, depart at will - that is all, really, education is about, should be about.
Fay Weldon. LETTERS TO ALICE, p78.

REALITY

If men define situations as real, they are real in their consequences.
William I Thomas (sociologist), in 1917.

'...because was the only thing that could let me look at reality without being destroyed by it or having it collapse on top of me like a burning house, the only thing that could give it meaning or an illusion of meaning..'
Javier Cercas. THE SPEED OF LIGHT, p277.

How did they all not see? Yet the answer is simple. They saw what they expected to see and did not see what they did not expect.
John Banville. ANCIENT LIGHT, p105.

'There's no remaking reality,' she told him. 'Just take it as it comes. Hold your ground and take it as it comes.'
Philip Roth. EVERYMAN, p5.

We spend our lives 'wanting things and planning things and wishing and regretting - and in so doing, we miss all the accidental gifts. Not only do I believe that the things we set our hearts on ruin our lives, but I also believe that our concept of reality is restricting, that it doesn't matter what is real or what is not real.
Clare Boylan. Irish Times, 28/5/88.

"The frog who croaks in the shaft of a well will be frightened by the booming voice of the giant who answers him." (Salman Rushdie)

The heavier the burden (eternal return is the heaviest), the closer our lives come to the earth, the more real and truthful they become.
Milan Kundera. THE UNBEARABLE LIGHTNESS OF BEING, p5.

In the deserted harbour there is yet water that laps against the quays. In the dark and silent forest there is a leaf that falls. Behind the polished panelling the white ant eats away the wood. Nothing is ever quiet, except for fools.
Alan Paton. CRY, THE BELOVED COUNTRY, p164.

Jung: whatever you are not consciously in touch with happens to you as 'fate'.
Sunday Times, 17/4/88. pG6.

Nothing is important - or unimportant - except as it is perceived.
John Carey.

The truth is that motor cars offer a very happy illustration of the metaphysical distinction between "being" and "becoming". Some are bought all screwed up and numbered and painted.......but still maintaining their essential identity to the scrap heap....
'Real' cars......become masters of men.....vital creations of metal who exist solely for their own propulsion through space....These are in perpetual flux.
Evelyn Waugh. VILE BODIES, p161.

People play with exaggeration as a means of keeping reality at bay.
John Banville.

We imagine that we remember things as they were, while in fact all we carry into the future are fragments which reconstruct a wholly illusory past.
John Banville. BIRCHWOOD, p4.

In a war all is mental, and opinion makes up more than half of reality.
Napoleon.

To live in the real world was to act without knowing the end. The act of living a real life differed, I mused, from the act of making a fictional one, too, because you were stuck with your mistakes.
Salman Rushdie. THE JAGUAR SMILE, p168.

Perhaps I should write like the scribes of "The Anglo-Saxon Chronicle", saying in the same breath that an archbishop passed away, a synod was held, and fiery dragons were seen flying through the air. Why not, after all? Beliefs are relative. Our connection with reality is always tenuous.
Penelope Lively. MOON TIGER, p9

(Impact of the circus in Cape Town) It was so loud and dazzling that it irrevocably changed the perspective of my ordinary life: it was more real than the reality I'd known; it peopled my world with the impossible, so that I could never again successfully escape from it.
Andre Brink. LOOKING ON DARKNESS, p83.

Nothing is real to the corporate mind until it is flashed upon a screen.
Declan Kiberd. Irish Times, 17/8/91.

Just imagine living in a world without mirrors. You'd dream about your face and imagine it as an outer reflection of what is inside you. And then, when you reached forty, someone would put a mirror before you for the first time in your life. Imagine your fright! You'd see the face of a stranger. And you'd know quite clearly what you are unable to grasp: your face is not you.
Milan Kundera. IMMORTALITY, p35.

Moments before sleep are when she feels most alive, leaping across fragments of the day, bringing each moment into the bed with her like a child with schoolbooks and pencils. The day seems to have no order until these times, which are like a ledger for her, her body full of stories and situations.
Michael Ondaatje. THE ENGLISH PATIENT, p35/36.

Reagan at a 1987 speech to business leaders: "One definition of an economist is somebody who sees something happen in practice and wonders if it will work in theory."

Reality is the waste-product of experience.

Proust.

REASON

'Reason is and ever must be the slave of the passions' (Hume). Reason, in other words, can tell you neither what you want nor what you ought to want; but once you have decided what you want, reason can tell you how to get it.
Maurice Craig. THE ELEPHANT AND THE POLISH QUESTION, p91.

RELATIONSHIPS

Robert Putnam, Harvard sociologist, coined the phrase 'Bowling alone' to describe the loss of social capital – networks of reciprocity and trust – in the liberal democracies of the West. More people were going ten-pin bowling, but fewer were joining teams and leagues. Symbol of the West's individualistic, atomistic, self-preoccupied culture. Things people once did together, we were now doing alone. Bonds of belonging were growing thin.
Jonathan Sacks. THE GREAT PARTNERSHIP, p277.

The academic relation of protegér to protegé is a closed electric circuit not subject to the law of entropy: often it sends out sparks until death.
Alison Lurie. FOREIGN AFFAIRS, p162.

To be a man is to be seeded with a fertile treasure of concepts (songs, the universal, etc): that is what determines human relationships - and they are the most important things on earth.
Antoine de Saint-Exupery. FLIGHT TO ARRAS.

(RE PRINCE CHARLES) ...having a platonic relationship with an herbaceous border.......
Sunday Independent, 28/6/87.

Thus they went on living in a reality that was slipping away, momentarily captured by words, but which would escape irremediably when they forgot the values of the written letters.
Gabriel Garcia Marquez. ONE HUNDRED YEARS OF SOLITUDE, p46.

The mystery of what a couple IS, exactly, is almost the only true mystery left to us, and when we have come to the end of it there will be no more need for literature - or for love, for that matter.
Mavis Gallant, a Canadian writer, quoted by Julian Barnes in
A HISTORY OF THE WORLD IN 10 1/2 CHAPTERS, p228.

Youngsters find security in a loving relationship. Getting a girlfriend is what turns them away from crime. It is a crucial institution with an extraordinarily lasting appeal.
Canon David Wyatt. Sunday Times, 15/1/89.

(first half of a Muldoon poem) It is about two people sitting down for a meal and cleverly describes how there was barely enough room at their table for themselves plus their former selves. The same applied to Susan and me - not only were we seated at the table, but also pulling up a chair were myself as her lover, herself as my girlfriend, the James Jones that had bored and irritated her, the Susan Northey that had caused me anxiety and all the other people we had been together - jokers, cooks, drinkers, travelling companions, tired employees and lustful sexual partners. I sensed them

flapping open their napkins and picking up their knives and forks. They were elbowing me in the ribs and crowding the space under the table with their feet.
Joseph O'Neill. THIS IS THE LIFE, p86.

You're like the son I never had.....
And you're like the father I never visit.
The Simpsons.

RELIGION

Christianity is about making peace with a fundamental dependency.
Giles Fraser, THE GUARDIAN, 18 July 2014.

Religion does what none of the great institutions of contemporary society does: not politics, not economics, not science, and not technology. It answers the 3 great questions that any reflective human being will ask: Who am I? (question of identity), Why am I here? (question of purpose) and How then shall I live? (question of ethics and meaning).
Jonathan Sacks. THE GREAT PARTNERSHIP, p282.

Religion is an authentic response to a real presence, but it is also a way of making that presence real by constantly living in response to it. It is truth translated into deed.
Jonathan Sacks. THE GREAT PARTNERSHIP, p197.

'I stopped practicing a long time ago, but some of it holds. If you have it as a child, it gives you a structure of consciousness – the idea that there is something more.'
Seamus Heaney to Andrew O'Hagan and Karl Miller on a visit to Henry Vaughan's grave. (The Guardian, 5/9/2013).

Churches fill on Christmas and Easter because it is on these days that the two most startling moments in the Christian narrative can be heard again. In these two moments, narrative fractures the continuities of history. It becomes so beautiful as to acquire a unique authority, a weight of meaning history cannot approach... Christmas and Easter are so full of church pageant and family custom that it is entirely possible to forget how the stories told on these two days did indeed rupture history and leave the world changed, implausible as that may seem.
Marilynne Robinson, WHEN I WAS A CHILD, p127

...this is a Christian country... attitudes and institutions that are Christian in their origin are profoundly influential in our culture. But this is not good enough. This influence is both unconscious and unforced; and it is therefore invisible to those who think that the majority religious tradition in the country, by virtue of its being the majority tradition, ought to be asserted very forcefully as an intrinsic part of our national identity...They see threat to their religion from secularism and want to enlist society itself in its defence.
Marilynne Robinson, WHEN I WAS A CHILD, p135.

It is a story written down in various forms by writers whose purpose was first of all to render the sense of a man of surpassing holiness, whose passage through the world was understood, only after his death, to have revealed the way of God towards humankind. How remarkable. This is too great a narrative to be reduced to serving any parochial interest or to be overwritten by any lesser human tale. Reverence should forbid in particular its being subordinated to tribalism, resentment, or fear.
Marilynne Robinson, WHEN I WAS A CHILD, p 140.

And it is fully as well attested as America's old-time religion as is any exclusive or backward-looking tradition, though our ill-informed nostalgias elevate what is called fundamentalism to that place, with the result that those who cannot endorse fundamentalist religion scorn the past while those who embrace it despise the present.
Marilynne Robinson, WHEN I WAS A CHILD I READ BOOKS, p. xiv.

Carnival – constitutes a farewell to the flesh before the onset of Lent, 'carne-vale'.
Saul Frampton. WHEN I AM PLAYING WITH MY CAT, HOW DO I KNOW SHE IS NOT PLAYING WITH ME?, p152.

We've subjected religious beliefs to the wrong kind of scrutiny, as if they needed to be true in a scientific sense. So we're desolated by our cleverness, in an empty universe. We need the symbols and stories that embody the idea of another dimension beyond the one we actually inhabit.
Tessa Hadley. THE LONDON TRAIN, p198.

But the Society of Jesus is used to unsettled bills; it works assiduously on the fringe of the aristocracy where returned cheques are almost as common as adulteries, and so the college continued to support me.
Graham Greene. THE COMEDIANS, p66.

The sense of vocation hung around me like the 'grippe', a miasma of unreality, at a temperature below normal in the cool rational morning but a fever-heat at night.
Graham Greene. THE COMEDIANS, p66.

......religious - naive trust in their own righteousness.

a religion of genteel pretence.
John Updike. COUPLES, p108.

But in itself the physical drama only touches us if it shows us its spiritual sense.
Antoine de Saint-Exupery.

I have long concluded that established religions of any kind are in general the supreme example of forms created to meet no longer existing conditions.
John Fowles. A MAGGOT.

But the real legacy of Catholicism is that it teaches you something about the sacramental view of language. Chanting those Latin chants for your formative years is a great help when trying to write English prose. The greatest gift religion can give anybody is the use of language.
Peter Ackroyd. SUNDAY TIMES, 9/4/89.

He became fascinated, as an intellectual exercise, with the idea of power as an abstraction, an extra-religious mystery, since religions explained away all mystery in the person of mythical beings, one religion even awkwardly offering a half-god, half-man, born of a virgin, so as to make that particular myth somehow more credible.
Nadine Gordimer. MY SON'S STORY, p17.

"......And I can't admit of an old boy of a God who takes walks in his garden with a cane in his hand, lodges his friends in the belly of whales, dies uttering a cry, and rises again at the end of three days; things absurd in themselves, and completely opposed, moreover, to all physical laws, which proves to us, by the way, that priests have always wallowed in turbid ignorance, in which they would fain engulf the people with them.
Gustave Flaubert. MADAME BOVARY, p91.

He'd had escapes too, enough of them to want no more. The first had been the roman collar, to hand the pain and joy of his own life into the keeping of an idea, and to will the idea true.
John McGahern. THE CREAMERY MANAGER.

Scripture is a country where men of every sect make raids, as if in order to pillage it; it is a battleground where hostile nations meet frequently in combat, attacking and skirmishing in numerous ways.
Montesquieu. PERSIAN LETTERS No 134.

Religion may be best understood as analogous to a disease such as measles, which nearly everybody gets in youth and recovers from, but which if contracted in later life may have serious effects.
Maurice Craig. THE ELEPHANT AND THE POLISH QUESTION, p33.

RIGHT & WRONG

When I say 'no' I'm always right, and when I say 'yes' I'm always (almost) wrong.
Dwight McDonald. 1980 symposium at Skidmore College on the death of culture in America.

RESPONSIBILITY

We were giddily free of all responsibility and the sweet-and-sour obligations to ensure others were having a good time.
Fionn Barton, 'Taking the Mickey out of Florida' in Telegraph, 1/1/05.

ROUTINE

The ruthless tyranny of the cheap alarm clock; Get up. Go to bed. Sit down.
Amos Oz. TOUCH THE WATER, TOUCH THE WIND, p108.

It was the stubborn conspiracy of objects - to remain exactly as they had been left.
Ian McEwan. THE CHILD IN TIME, p11.

The existence of insignificant people has very important consequences in the world. It can be shown to affect the price of bread and the rate of wages...
George Eliot. ADAM BEDE.

RUMOUR

Rumour exhausted everyone, plucked at nerves, took away the capacity to think.
Ryszard Kapuscinski. ANOTHER DAY OF LIFE.

SAFETY

Is there any instinct more deeply implanted in the heart of man than the pride of protection, a protection which is constantly exerted for a fragile and defenseless creature?
Honore de Balzac. OLD GORIOT, p58.

The only safe place in the world is inside a story.
Athol Fugard.

SARCASM

"There's a hell of a lot of goodwill and understanding in this country, - more than enough to fertilise a whole sewage farm.
Andre Brink. LOOKING ON DARKNESS, p348.

.... no great movement designed to change the world can bear sarcasm or mockery, because they are a rust that corrodes all it touches.
Milan Kundera. THE JOKE, p242.

SCIENCE

Science takes things apart to see how they work. Religion puts things together to see what they mean.
Jonathan Sacks. THE GREAT PARTNERSHIP, p2.

Who thinks of Newton the man? Save, of course, to picture him in that legendary reverie, not unlike Darwin's idyll (Darwin in nature's playground!), ensconced beneath an apple tree - a reverie shattered by the Law of Gravity. The apple, of course, provides a resonantly Edenesque touch. These men of knowledge. These meddlers with the universe. Darwin, they say, was the Newton of biology. If Darwin was the Newton of biology, then Einstein was the Darwin of physics.
Graham Swift. EVER AFTER, p226.

None of the ways we experience the world corresponds even remotely to the scientific truths about it. Not only are our intuitions invariably wrong, it is impossible to imagine what they would be like if they were right.
Michael Dibdin. MEDUSA, 69.

SECRETS

A wonderful fact to reflect upon, that every human creature is constituted to be that profound secret and mystery to every other. A solemn consideration, when I enter a great city by night, that every one of those darkly clustered houses encloses its own secret; that every room in every one of them encloses its own secret; that every beating heart in the hundreds of thousands of breasts there, is, in some of its imaginings, a secret to the heart nearest it!
Charles Dickens. A TALE OF TWO CITIES, p8.

Secrets build their own network.
Don De Lillo. LIBRA, p22.

"When my daughter tells me a secret", Win said, "her hands get very busy. She takes my arm, grabs me by the shirt collar, pulls me close, pulls me into her life. She knows how intimate secrets are. She likes to tell me things before she goes to sleep. Secrets are an exalted state, almost a dream state. They're a way of arresting motion, stopping the world so we can see ourselves in it.
Don De Lillo. LIBRA, p26.

The thing that hovers over every secret is betrayal. Sooner or later someone reaches the point where he wants to tell what he knows.
Don De Lillo. LIBRA, p218.

SELF ANALYSIS

We sculpt ourselves over time with our most persistent moods, as though our faces are dunes and our temperaments the winds that blow them into shape.
Samantha Harvey. ALL IS SONG, p125.

By what am I led, in what do I recognise my past, where do I store all evidence of my past moments? Only in this body walking on through space? Have I more than this? How can I rely on it? Is everything really, finally, reduced to faith?
Andre Brink. AN INSTANT IN THE WIND, p160.

Interview with Michel de Certeau: 'What do you think of Lerinas' idea that "the other" is not just an alter ego but also everything I am not?'
Certeau: 'Because they are what I am not, others bring to me the tidings of my own frontiers, my inadequacies, in the final analysis of my own death.'
Andre Brink. STATES OF EMERGENCY, p165.

Thus it is, in those painful learning years, that circumstance seem to force upon us an inflexibility of character, a remoteness, a self-contained intensity of reflex that is there even in what is usually described as normal circumstances for the adolescent: a sense of him having a coiled spring of action, held by a shallow ratchet, worn down already by time.
Bruce Arnold. A SINGER AT THE WEDDING, p119.

SEXUALITY

I made the oldest of mistakes: every real prostitute must know that the dullest clients have the deepest fantasies – the most wholesome are also the most dangerous.
Chloe Hooper, THE ENGAGEMENT, p135.

No one will buy the cow if they can get the milk for free!

In Fleur's experience.. all men have a sexual hinterland that is more real to them than the place they are living.
Justin Cartwright. OTHER PEOPLES MONEY, p54.

It is time to steer past the Scylla and Charybdis of the elderly sexual farce and sexual tragedy into the wide, clam sunset sea of abstinence, where the tepid waters are never troubled by the burning head and chill, the foamy backwash and weed-choked turbulence of passion.
Alison Lurie. FOREIGN AFFAIRS, p76.

plain women often have a sex life. What they lack, rather, is a love life.
Alison Lurie. FOREIGN AFFAIRS, p10.

As men obsessed with the idea that all knowledge lies within a woman's body, but having entered it to find themselves as ignorant as before, they are driven towards all women again and again: in childish hope that somehow the next time they will find the treasure, and then the equally childish desire for revenge since it cannot be found, that knife in the unfathomable entrails: and they grow full of hatred.
John McGahern. FAITH, HOPE AND CHARITY. (in Getting Through, p51).

...the rebel rod of flesh.
Graham Swift. WATERLAND, p165.

Sex is not love, it is merely the territory love marks out for itself.
Milan Kundera. THE BOOK OF LAUGHTER & FORGETTING, p182.

...you can't remember sex. You can remember the fact of it, and recall the setting, and even the details, but the sex of sex cannot be remembered, the substantive truth of it, it is by nature self-erasing, you can remember its anatomy and be left with a judgment as to the degree of your liking of it, but whatever it is as a splurge of being, as a loss, as a charge of the conviction of love stopping your heart like your execution, there is no memory of it in the brain, only the deduction that it happened and that the time passed, leaving you with a silhouette that you want to fill again.
E.L. Doctorow. BILLY BATHGATE, p226.

Like cunnilingus, tending sheep is dark and lonely work; but someone has to do it.
Martin Amis. THE MORONIC INFERNO, p126.

It is not difficult to deceive the first time, for the deceived possess no antibodies.....
unvaccinated by suspicion, she overlooks lateness, accepts absurd excuses, permits the flimsiest patchings to repair great rents in the quotidian.
John Updike. COUPLES, p132.

Bech- what we are witnessing is the triumph of the clitoral, after three thousand years of phallic hegemony.
John Updike. BECH, A BOOK. p119.

We've only one virginity to loose; and where we lost it there our hearts will be.
Kipling.

...a well-developed schoolgirl - "The Lucan Dairy."
John Montague. THE FLOOD.

Far more than a maiden name
Was cancelled by him on the first night.
Seamus Heaney. VICTORIAN GUITAR.

Any description of the act of love runs the risk of degenerating into either a naming of parts, a purple rain of adjectives, or a pretence of metaphysical agonies and ecstasies.
Andre Brink. STATES OF EMERGENCY. p142.

I am not so interested in sex. For me as a writer it is the key that opens the human heart for inspection, as memory was for Proust, or as Dublin was for Joyce.
Albert Moravia. Irish Times, 17/7/90.

.....but sexual love has the matchless advantage of the flesh as reassurance for anything, everything, for the moment.
The body speaks and all is silenced.
Nadine Gordimer. MY SON'S STORY, p92.

She reveled in all the evil ironies of triumphant adultery.
Gustave Flaubert. MADAME BOVARY, p208.

Sex is a constant life force, and for us copulation is like an amoeba splitting every 16 minutes. One can only hope for its sake that the amoeba has as much fun doing it.
Barbara Amiel. Sunday Times, 21/7/91.

History creates different frameworks for the expression of human sexuality, but one horrid little truth remains constant: there is no free sexual lunch.
Barbara Amiel. Sunday Times, 21/7/91.

We like to laugh - do we not? - at the baroque passions of high adolescence, but we cannot deny that they control and guide us during those few hot palpitating years. It is an unsettling, overwhelming power and one that most people will never feel so vehemently again, indeed, will never want to be so ruthlessly led......What is lust, adult lust, after all, but the desire to recapture the heady sensations of adolescent sexuality?
William Boyd, THE NEW CONFESSIONS, p71.

She put down the basket. A light breeze wafts across the garden and just for a moment it wreathes her hair about her face and flutters her dress against her body with almost sentient, Botticellian tenderness. The bare shoulders are infallible. Their appeal goes to some helpless spot at the centre of the chest.
Graham Swift. EVER AFTER, p86.

The blouse was cream silk (even in those war-pinched days). A white strap, thin and shining like a ribbon and lifting from her skin where it crossed her collar-bone, was visible. The just discernible

fringe of the garment to which it belonged had a filigree tenuosity, curiously evocative of the doily that bore our angel cake and macaroons.
Graham Swift. EVER AFTER, p227.

'I don't know,' he said, 'Cute country girls in their bedsits. They may have lost their virginity but they probably still have the box it came in.'
Dermot Bolger. THE JOURNEY HOME, p31.

And Polly suspected now that erotic pleasure was the bait to a trap, a way to get the squirrel into the cage so that it - or rather, she - could spend the rest of her life running around a wire treadmill, breathless with love and fear.
Alison Lurie. THE TRUTH ABOUT LORIN JONES, p23.

SHAKESPEARE

....with an understanding of Shakespeare there comes a release from the gullibility that makes you prey to the great shopkeeper who runs the world, and would sell you cheap to illusion.
Nadine Gordimer. MY SON'S STORY, p11.

Once a great Shakespearean reader, reverent amateur of the power of words, Sonny must have known that if a term is coined it creates a self-fulfilling possibility and at the same time provides a formulation for dealing with it.
Nadine Gordimer. MY SON'S STORY, p179.

Shakespeare is the happy hunting ground of all minds that have lost their balance.
James Joyce. ULYSSES, p248.

It is true (we know now) that we are descended from the apes. And it is true that an ape, set before as typewriter and given a time-scale of infinity and eternal factor of randomness, might eventually bash out the sonnets of Shakespeare. But, by and large, it is just as well and a good deal neater that Shakespeare appeared when he did to do the job. Which leaves a host of questions still wide open. How Shakespeare came about in the first place   (why he didn't go into sheep farming or die, aged two, of scarlet fever) and why, though Shakespeare is all things to all people, we cannot all be Shakespeares. Why some are poets and some are not. And why not all poets are also explorers, adventurers, courtiers, etc. - all things in one. And why there should be this stuff called poetry, to begin with, which strikes our hearts at such a magic angle. And why there should be certain things in this random universe which cry out to us with their loveliness.
Graham Swift. EVER AFTER, p233.

SHAME

But shame is like everything else; live with it long enough and it becomes part of the furniture.
Salman Rushdie. SHAME, p28.

To face without protection the most shameful moments of the past would destroy us: we would, as George Eliot puts it, "die of the roar that lies on the other side of silence".
Blake Morrison. Independent on Sunday, 16/6/91.

If we had a keen vision and feeling of all ordinary human life, it would be like hearing the grass grow and the squirrel's heartbeat, and we should die of that roar which lies on the other side of silence. As it is, the quickest of us walk about wadded with stupidity.
George Eliot. MIDDLEMARCH, p118.

SICKNESS

Sickness is always a place where there's no company, where nobody can follow.
Flannery O'Connor.

Willard lay face down on his bed, naked. His thighs and buttocks were trenched with purple scars, some just beginning to silver. These injuries had been sustained when his company was retreating across a graveyard under heavy fire, and several tombstone fragments had become embedded in his flesh. 'You want to try it,' he said. 'Lying two months on your belly in a hospital bed with "Requiescat in Pace" stuck up your arse.'
Pat Barker. REGENERATION, p111.

SILENCE

He listened to the silence, chapel silence, with its faint penumbra of excluded sounds – birdsong, periodic rattle of the distant mower, soft thumps that were less the wind on the roof than the pulse in his ear.
Alan Holinghurst. THE STRANGER'S CHILD.

He already knew that there would be no answer. The silence had that coherent quality, like settled soil, which houses only have when they are empty.
Michael Dibdin. A LONG FINISH, p39.

SOCIETY

Society is a partnership not only between those who are living, but between those who are living, those who are dead and those who are to be born.
Edmund Burke, REFLECTIONS ON THE FRENCH REVOLUTION.

We think of ourselves as isolated individuals sometimes, but every self is socially constituted. We make no sense without our audiences, and the social animal needs others in order to live well. For human beings that feeling of being known, that shared and forgiving sense of frailty, is redemptive in a way that nothing else can be.
Ziyad Marar, INTIMACY, p12.

"If you want to know about a society, look at it from the bottom up,"
James Lee Burke.

The cock that crows in the morning belongs to one household but his voice is the property of the neighbourhood.
Chinua Achebe. ANTHILLS OF THE SAVANNAH, p122.

...all the organisations people had devised to bolster their security: state and church, commerce and politics and education, everything; the more laws there were, the more regulations, the more securely one's pattern of existence was predetermined, the easier one could continue without the need to think.
Andre Brink. THE AMBASSADOR, p190.

....but having once discovered the deceit inherent in any custom, any 'system', I suppose one tends to look for hidden meanings everywhere.
Andre Brink. THE AMBASSADOR, p213.

The subterfuges of an illicit love made the frankness of its emotions possible; the subterfuges of resistance made frankness in a lying society possible. Sonny once said, what the oppressors call subversion is the exposure of the rot in the state.
Nadine Gordimer. MY SON'S STORY, p113.

Totalitarian society, especially in its more extreme versions, tends to abolish the boundary between the public and the private; power, as it grows ever more opaque, requires the lives of citizens to be entirely transparent. The ideal of life without secrets corresponds to the ideal of the exemplary family: a citizen does not have the right to hide anything at all from the Party or the State, just as a child has no right to keep a secret from his father or mother. In their propaganda, totalitarian societies project an idyllic smile: they want to be seen as "one big family".
Milan Kundera. THE ART OF THE NOVEL, p110.

All those who extol the mass media din, advertising's imbecilic smile, the neglect of the natural world, indiscretion raised the status of a virtue - they deserve to be called "collaborators with modernity".
Milan Kundera. THE ART OF THE NOVEL, p126.

Yet there is also a seamless aspect to the affairs of man in society, the image of generations handing down their torch - a torch which, in defiance of the laws of the natural world, glows more brightly, stronger, fiercer, with every new possessor. This, then, is the moral continuum,

characterized in its highest form by the sacred relationship between pupil and teacher, bestower and receiver. And just as I have received, so now do I give in my turn: yet only now do I understand that truly it is more an honour to receive than to give. I am old now and I was young. This is the common history of mankind, which each individual must trace in himself as if it were an unique truth and not a universal truism. It is true of our predecessors and shall be true of those countless more who shall come when we are gone, wandering down like white sheep after us to the dark shore of eternity. To you, reader, I reach out my hand. I was a man.
Timothy Mo. AN INSULAR POSSESSION, p671.

SPEECH

Kissinger worked for Nelson Rockefeller in the late 50s. When three speechmakers reviewed an address he had drafted, he was annoyed. 'You tell Nelson that if he had a Picasso, he wouldn't call in three housepainters to touch it up.'
Robert Dallek, NIXON AND KISSINGER, p50.

To say what you think is always a luxury and often a curse.
Kenneth Roberts.

No word is dirty in itself. In general, dirt lies either behind words or between them.
Amos Oz. THE HILL OF EVIL COUNSEL, p19.

There she sat, distilling her reading voice from the still prison of her person.
Vladimir Nabokov. MADEMOISELLE O.

London-born Italians speak with a double-barrelled diphthongs and glottal stops.
Angela Carter. NIGHTS AT THE CIRCUS, p13.

He (the priest) spoke the dignified and beautiful language of a reticent spirituality, but he breathed the fire of instant salvation.
Iris Murdoch. THE BOOK AND THE BROTHERHOOD, p488.

Because lips libertine and venal had murmured such words to him, he believed but little in the candour of her; exaggerated speeches hiding mediocre affections must be discounted; as if the fullness of the soul did not sometimes overflow in the emptiest metaphors, since no one can ever give the exact measure of his deeds, nor of his conceptions, nor of his sorrows, and since human speech is like a cracked kettle on which we hammer out tunes to make bears dance when we long to placate the stars.
Gustave Flaubert. MADAME BOVARY, p214

.......speech is a rolling mill that always thins out the sentiment.
Gustave Flaubert. MADAME BOVARY, p261.

'And what could an auld black Protestant like you know about the lek of that?'
For a moment the talk seemed to cross the ditch of banter into the sheugh of insult.
Eugene McCabe.   DEATH AND NIGHTINGALES, p120.

Speech was invented to cancel thought.
Beryl Bainbridge. MASTER GEORGE, p125.

STORYTELLING

Communication has two distinct functions: passing on information and establishing social relations between participants. To speak in the language of classical communications theory, narratives are as much about relationships as they are about content. The situation in which stories are told is thus often more important than whether what is narrated makes either historical or logical sense. Listeners often forgo questions and requests for explanations because they don't want to disrupt the narrative flow or interrupt the speaker. When captivated by a narrative, they often do not even register whether details can possibly be true or not.
Sonke Neitzel & Harald Welzer. SOLDATEN: On Fighting, Killing and Dying, p104.

Maybe the first stories we are told are the ones we find our way back to.
Chloe Hooper, A CHILD'S BOOK OF TRUE CRIME, p237

The storyteller must divine which episodes of his history hold promise of fullness, and tease from them their hidden meanings, braiding these together as one braids a rope.
J M Coetzee. FOE. p89/90.

Through his ears Friday may yet take in the wealth stored in stories and so learn that the world is not, as the island seemed to teach him, a barren and a silent place (is that the secret meaning of the word story, do you think: a storing-place of memories?)
J M Coetzee. FOE, p59.

"As I relate it to you, my story passes the time well enough," I replied; "but what little I know of book-writing tells me its charms will quite vanish when it is set down badly in print. A liveliness is lost in the writing down which must be supplied by art, and I have no art."
J M Coetzee. FOE, p40.

We all have our little scraps of tale bubbling in us. But what we tell is like the middle of a mighty boa which a foolish forester mistakes for a tree trunk and settles upon to take his snuff.
Chinua Achebe. ANTHILLS OF THE SAVANNAH, p125.

Man - a story-telling animal.
Graham Swift. WATERLAND, p53.

Every story one chooses to tell is a kind of censorship, it prevents the telling of other tales.
Salman Rushdie. SHAME, p71.

......and then over long distances human memory is an erratic instrument especially if it is not reinforced by material mementoes and is instead spiced by the desire that the story be a good one.
Primo Levi. MOMENTS OF REPRIEVE, p144.

To tell a story is to drift on language. To be is to be in motion. The very root of "I am" is inextricably linked to "amo", I love.
Andre Brink. STATES OF EMERGENCY, p48.

"What's so special about habladores?"..

"They're tangible proof that storytelling can be something more than entertainment..... Something primordial, something that the very existence of a people may depend on. Maybe that's what impressed me so. One doesn't always know why one is moved by things.... They strike some secret chord, and that's that.
Mario Vargas Llosa. THE STORYTELLER, p94.

Do stories, apart from happening, being, have something to say? For all my skepticism, some trace of irrational superstition did survive in me, the strange conviction, for example, that everything in life that happens to me also has a sense, that it means something, that life speaks to us about itself through its story, that it gradually reveals a secret, that it takes the form of a rebus whose message must be deciphered, that the stories we live comprise mythology of our lives and in that mythology lies the key to truth and mystery. Is it an illusion? Possibly, even probably, but I can't rid myself of the need continually to decipher my own life.
Milan Kundera. THE JOKE, p164.

SUCCESS & FAILURE

'Anyone who takes a bus after the age of thirty is a failure.'
Attributed to either Margaret Thatcher or Loelia, Duchess of Westminster.
Ferdinand Mount, COLD CREAM, p225.

'....no one dies for having failed, but it's impossible to survive success with dignity.
Javier Cercas. THE SPEED OF LIGHT, p52.

When you're successful you naturally feel more at home.
Henry James. THE PORTRAIT OF A LADY, p51.

Do the thing you most fear: marry fear to the act, go for the coup that balances courage with its dangers; the flow of peace will follow. Success lay in the proper timing, in the moment between danger and safety.
Molly Keane. TIME AFTER TIME, p73.

Success is more dangerous than failure (the ripples break over a wider coastline).
Graham Greene. WAYS OF ESCAPE.

The ventures that succeed best are the ones your enemy thinks you're not capable of.
Primo Levi. IF NOT NOW, WHEN? p136.

On the seventh day God rested and said, "Let's hope it works".
Primo Levi. IF NOT NOW, WHEN? p146.

Besides, nothing was worth the trouble of seeking it; everything was a lie. Every smile is a yawn of boredom, every joy a curse, all pleasure satiety, and the sweetest kisses left upon your lips only the unattainable desire for a greater delight.
Gustave Flaubert. MADAME BOVARY, p314.

What was victory?
The illusory hope that a dream could last; the mad dance of those who are about to die, on the graves of those who have just died. It was a state in which the weeping and wailing of victims was drowned out by shouts of joy.
Ivan Klima. WAITING FOR THE DARK, WAITING FOR THE LIGHT, p135.

SUFFERING

The absent no longer entered our thoughts. One spoke of them – who knows what happened to them? – but their fate was not on our minds. We were incapable of thinking. Our senses were numbed, everything was fading into a fog. We no longer clung to anything. The instincts of self-preservation, of self-defense, of pride, had all deserted us. In one terrifying moment of lucidity, I thought of us as damned souls wandering through the void, souls condemned to wander through space until the end of time, seeking redemption, seeking oblivion, without any hope of finding either.
Elie Wiesel. NIGHT, p36.

(My grandmother) had caught me hobbling around the house as I tried to walk in my new pair of shoes. 'Who knows how much a pretty pair of shoes pinch, except the person wearing them?' she said, because I was always wanting something more, something that somebody else had..
Aminatta Forna. ANCESTRAL STONES, p228.

There is always a tendency to exaggerate any description of suffering, because the person who endured it tends to think it is a virtue or as something to be admired, a noble sacrifice, when sometimes that isn't the cause at all and it was just bad luck.
Javier Marais. YOUR FACE TOMORROW, 3, p274.

Perhaps it is only human nature to inflict suffering on anything that will endure suffering, whether by reason of its genuine humility or indifference, or sheer helplessness. Do we not, one and all, like to feel our strength even at the expense of some one or of something.
Honore de Balzac. OLD GORIOT, p13.

Suffering: its like the sky through which a bird is flying. And only occasionally, very rarely - an instant in the wind - it is allowed to alight on branch or burning stone to rest: but not for long.
Andre Brink. AN INSTANT IN THE WIND, p198.

If you wound the body of a dying man, the wound will begin to heal, even if the whole body dies within a day.
Primo Levi. IF THIS IS A MAN, p147.

For human nature is such that grief and pain - even simultaneously offered - do not add up as a whole in our consciousness, but hide, the lesser behind the greater, according to a definite law of perspective.
Primo Levi. IF THIS IS A MAN, p79.

One uses what weapons one has. Yet suffering offers no redemption; and it gives one no rights. In its own way it corrodes, and corrupts. The only significance of the past is that it is past.
Andre Brink. A CHAIN OF VOICES, p362.

He sat on alone until all unease was lost in a luxury of self-absorption.
John McGahern. AMONGST WOMEN, p56.

Above her bed was a picture of Jesus, head crowned with thorns. Every time he entered the room the first thing he did was glance up at it. To check that face, with its holy grimace of unbelievable, perpetual pain, was looking at him. Pain for which he himself shared responsibility. All men did. But not women. Not mothers. Not his mother lying there, her blood slowing down, her fluttery heart weak as a dying sparrow's. Women who loved the men they brought into the world cancelled out the Crucifixion. The blood shed on the Cross saved the world. And women carried on saving it with womb blood. At school the priest who taught him English said it was pain that made the blind see. Like in "King Lear". The empty pursuit of security and pleasure were the goals of fools. It was a chilling thought.

Shane Connaughton. THE RUN OF THE COUNTRY, p31.

SUICIDE & DESPAIR

How is it possible that, with every step into despair, one also acquires more resistance to the one thing which may end it all?
Andre Brink. AN INSTANT IN THE WIND, p202.

'What will survive us is love.' This is the cautiously-approached conclusion of Philip Larkin's poem "An Arundel Tomb". The line surprises us, for much of the poet's work was a squeezed flannel of disenchantment.
Julian Barnes. A HISTORY OF THE WORLD IN 10 1/2 CHAPTERS, p228.

But how hard it is to kill oneself! One clings so tight to life! It seems to me that something other than the will come into play at the last instant, something foreign, something thoughtless, to sweep you over the brink. You have to become someone other than yourself. But who? Who is it that waits for me to step into his shadow? Where do I find him?
J.M. Coetzee. AGE OF IRON, p109.

SUNSET

Yarinaconcha at dusk, when the red mouth of the sun begins to sink behind the treetops and the greenish lake glows beneath the indigo sky where the first stars are beginning to twinkle, is one of the most beautiful sights I have ever seen.
Mario Vargas Llosa. THE STORYTELLER, p81.

SURVIVAL

We received no food. We lived on snow; it took the place of bread. The days resembled the nights, and the nights left in our souls the dregs of their darkness.
Elie Wiesel. NIGHT, p100.

TALENT

Talent is a gift of fortune, not something that can be chosen.
John Gray. THE SILENCE OF ANIMALS, p111.

TASTE

"Yes, that girl is really nice," said Havel, "but a dog, a canary, or a duckling waddling about in a farmyard can also be nice. In life, my friend, it is not a question of winning the greatest number of women because that is too external a success. Rather, it is a question of cultivating one's own demanding taste, because in it is mirrored the extent of one's own personal worth. Remember, my friend, that a real fisherman throws small fish back into the water."
Milan Kundera. LAUGHABLE LOVES, p186.

TERRORISM

'But that's why you built the towers, isn't it? Weren't the towers built as fantasies of wealth and power that would one day become fantasies of destruction? You build a thing like that so that you can see it come down. The provocation is obvious. What other reason would there be to go so high and then to double it, do it twice? It's a fantasy, so why not do it twice? You are saying, Here it is, bring it down.'
Don DeLillo. FALLING MAN, p116.

Terrorism is not about killing, but about using the fear of death to bring about a political end.
Simon Jenkins. Sunday Times, 4/12/88.

The hardest and most courageous way to defend normality is to stay normal.
Simon Jenkins. Sunday Times, 4/12/88.

We should rather meet terror with the contempt of neglect.
Simon Jenkins. Sunday Times, 4/12/88.

If the defenders don't win, they lose; if the terrorists/guerillas don't lose, they win.
Cal McCrystal. Sunday Times, 10/7/88.

Until we lose this sense of a defeated tribe, we shall continue to admire dangerous heroes.
Nuala Ni Dhomhnaill.

The men at his level were spawning secrets that quivered like reptile eggs. They were planning to poison Castro's cigars. They were designing cigars equipped with micro-explosives.
Don De Lillo. LIBRA, p21.

THEATRE & PLAYS

Opera has plot... but its main function is to deliver the characters as swiftly as possible to the point where they can sing of their deepest emotions.
Julian Barnes. LEVELS OF LIFE, p92.

Personally I would rather play Bingo every night for a year than pay a return visit to *Waiting for Godot*.
Noel Coward.

Lear - crucified on the edifice of his own follies.

Shakespeare has no heroes; his scenes are occupied only by men, who act and speak as the reader thinks that he should himself have spoken or acted on the same occasion.
Samuel Johnson. PREFACE TO SHAKESPEARE'S PLAYS, p128.

Shakespeare's comedy pleases by the thoughts and the language, his tragedy for the greater part by incident and accident. His tragedy seems to be skill, his comedy to be instinct.
Samuel Johnson. PREFACE TO SHAKESPEARE'S PLAYS, p128.

Let him that is yet unacquainted with the powers of Shakespeare, and who desires to feel the highest pleasure that the drama can give, read every play from the first scene to the last, with utter negligence of all his commentators. When his fancy is once on the wing, let it not stoop at correction or explanation.
Samuel Johnson. PREFACE TO SHAKESPEARE'S PLAYS, p163.

a playwright at his own first night is about as useful as a condom in a convent.
Fergus Linehan. Irish Times, 18/7/90.

Both (theatre and newspapers) depend on a capacity for willed self-hypnosis, and only succeed when they manage to infect the public with their own sense of the urgent importance of some event which will probably be forgotten tomorrow.
Irving Wardle. THEATRE CRITICISM, p1.

THOUGHT

The Master said, Learning without thought is naught; thought without learning is dangerous.
Confucius. SAYINGS, p6

There had been a trapped thought about to emerge, something essential and unspeakable, released by the mention of those blank-faced soldiers. Now it was all gone but the image: dead boys with limbs akimbo, staring at the sun.
Donna Tartt, THE GOLDFINCH, p128.

The tendency to revise the history of one's own beliefs in light of what actually happened produces a robust cognitive illusion. Hindsight bias has pernicious effects on the evaluation of decision makers.
Daniel Kahnman, THINKING FAST AND SLOW, p203.

They all seem to be thinking the same thing – finally... But then, feeling the fingernails of their wives, also staring, digging into their arms, their foreheads wrinkle. Their eyes hint remorse, as marriages are scorned (she never lets me do any fun), youth is remembered (why didn't I go to California that summer), first loves are recalled (Roxanne...). All of this happens in a span of about five seconds and then it is over and they are left just staring.
Kathryn Stockett. THE HELP, p321.

That we may accept a limitation on our actions but never, under no circumstances, must we accept restriction on our thinking.
Chinua Achebe. ANTHILLS OF THE SAVANNAH, p223.

He spoke rapidly, with a kind of hunted assurance, as though he were addressing a meeting of sceptical shareholders, as though he feared the silence that would return him to his own thoughts.
Ian McEwan. THE CHILD IN TIME, p32.

An intellectual - that man who does not easily form categorical judgments.
Erasmus.

Isn't the most reliable form of pleasure, Flaubert implies, the pleasure of anticipation? Who needs to burst into fulfillment's desolate attic.
Julian Barnes. FLAUBERT'S PARROT.

She asked him why he did not write out his thoughts. For what? he asked her, with careful scorn. To compete with phrasemongers, incapable of thinking consecutively for sixty seconds? To submit himself to the criticisms of our obtuse middle class which entrusted its morality to policemen and its fine arts to impresarios?
James Joyce. "A Painful Case" in DUBLINERS, p123.

"Rose, human life is too short, not just that it's sad to spend so little time at the play, but it's too short for serious thinking - thinking needs a long training, a long discipline, a long concentration - even geniuses must have felt that they were tiring too soon, giving up when they'd just begun to understand - philosophy, perhaps human history, would be quite different if we all lived to be two hundred.
Iris Murdoch. THE BOOK AND THE BROTHERHOOD, p562.

"Oh, I adore the sea!" said Monsieur Leon.
"Then do you not think," continued Madame Bovary, "that the mind travels more freely on this limitless expanse, the contemplation of which elevates the soul and gives ideas of the infinite, the ideal?"
Gustave Flaubert. MADAME BOVARY, p95.

We had been talking about nothing in particular for three or four hours but now the conversation had hit a lull, and each of us was drifting in the silence of his own thoughts.
Paul Auster. MOON PALACE, p12.

During WW1, Winston Churchill was warned not to meet Siegfried Sassoon, who had written powerful poems about misery and futility of was. Churchill replied: 'I am not a bit afraid of Sassoon. That man can think. I am only afraid of people who cannot think.'
Martin Gilbert. CHUCHILL AND THE JEWS, p29.

TIME

If time heals too well it does so by killing off the intimacy with the loved one, along with the need or expectation of it in the future. So while healing time is a soothing balm for grief, it is a reminder that the purest intimacies will fade and die too.
Ziyad Marar, INTIMACY, p11.

Nothing serious ever appears quite so serious with the passing of time.
Javier Marias. YOUR FACE TOMORROW, vol 2, p278.

Time is not outside us, but inside. Only we live with past, present, and future, and the present is too brief to experience anyway; it is retained afterward and then it is either codified or it slips into amnesia. Consciousness is the product of delay.
Siri Hustvedt. THE SUMMER WITHOUT MEN, p38.

For many years I slept, on average, twice a week. This means that I have been conscious for at least three lifetimes.
Keith Richards. LIFE, p21.

I tried to conjure Ali's frozen face, to really see his tranquil eyes, but time can be a greedy thing – sometimes it steals all the details for itself.
Kallid Hosseini. THE KITE RUNER, p188.

Time is a jet-plane, it moves too fast.
Bob Dylan. BLOOD ON THE TRACKS album.

...for time is not a conflagration; it is a slow grave sequence of grass blade, fish, apple, star, snowflake....
George Mackay Brown. GREENVOE, p237.

Some seem to admire indiscriminately whatever has been long preserved, without considering that time has sometimes co-operated with chance.
Samuel Johnson. PREFACE TO SHAKESPEARE'S PLAYS.

Everything is consumed by the cancer of time.
Amos Oz. A PERFECT PEACE, p363.

Imagine the terrestrial timespan as an outstretched arm: a single swipe of an emery board, across the nail of the third finger, erases human history. We haven't been around for very long. And we've turned the earth's hair white. She seemed to have eternal youth but now she's ageing awful fast, like an addict, like a waxless cable.......We used to live and die without any sense of the planet getting older, of mother earth getting older, living and dying. We used to live outside history. But now we're all coterminous. We're inside history now alright, on its leading edge, with the wind ripping past our ears. Hard to love, when you're bracing yourself for impact. And maybe love can't bear it either, and flees all planets when they reach this condition, when they get to the end of their twentieth centuries.
Martin Amis. LONDON FIELDS, p197.

Mountains are the scribblings of time on the surface of the land, a good place for man to rub life's immediacy and its Jobaic persistence.
Harry Middleton. ON THE SPINE OF TIME: an Angler's Love of the Smokies.

I didn't care about unpacking, but it would have been a logical next step. At that moment I felt I understood about the past. In another century a guest unpacked, and rested, and dressed for dinner, so that everybody had a good long period alone with himself. In the modern age, we have to negotiate vaster expanses of uninterrupted time.
Michael Cunningham. A HOME AT THE END OF THE WORLD, p134.

I've been trying to fit everything in, trying to get to the end before it's too late, but I see now how badly I've deceived myself. Words do not allow such things. The closer you come to the end, the more there is to say. The end is only imaginary, a destination you invent to keep yourself going, but a point comes when you realise you will never get there. You might have to stop, but that is only because you have run out of time. You stop, but that does not mean you have come to an end.
Paul Auster. IN THE COUNTRY OF LAST THINGS, p183.

She awoke in darkness.... And then she realized: for months now she had been woken daily not by the light of morning, nor by a clock, nor by James calling her because it was time to rise and work: she had been roused by the baby who woke independently and, floating inside her, kicked her into consciousness. Now her body was still and quiet as an empty house; the baby was gone. Very quietly she began to cry. The bedroom was slightly ajar, and between the noise of her sobs she could hear the steady and unbroken beat of the big clock in the hall. Time was a trap, coiled like a spring around her, and she could see a life open out beyond her, hours, days, weeks, months, years, spiralling away to her own death, and she would have to live that life.
Deirdre Madden. THE BIRDS OF THE INNOCENT WOOD, p94/5.

Time is merely an expedient invented by man so as to stop everything happening at the same time.
Luigi Malerba.

TOLERATION

We cannot shrink in disgust from our neighbour's touch because his hands, that are clean now, were once dirty. We must cultivate, all of us, a certain ignorance, a certain blindness, or society will not be tolerable.
J M Coetzee. FOE, p106.

"I only mean to say," he replied in less brutal tone, "that toleration is the surest way to draw people to religion."
Gustave Flaubert. MADAME BOVARY, p245.

To "give of one's best" was to surrender to the expectations of those whose values we despised.
Neal Ascherson. Independent on Sunday, 6/5/1996.

TRAVEL & TOURISM

'It is hard to be a traveler.'
'Why is that?'
'A traveler loses all he leaves behind.'
Christopher Hope. MY MOTHER'S LOVERS, p26.

I didn't go straight home, I went up to the hill. No one else was there, with the weather like this. If I still lived there, I'd be indoors too. It's a visitor's privilege to be foolish.
Jeanette Winterson. ORANGES ARE NOT THE ONLY FRUIT, p216.

I don't like leaving the road, my sense of vulnerability deepens, a sort of primal nervousness descends. But this is also one of the most compelling elements in travel, the feeling of dread underneath everything, it makes sensations heightened and acute, the world is charged with a power it doesn't have in ordinary life.
Damon Galgut. IN A STRANGE ROOM, p40.

Travel for the young is an education. Travel for the elderly is an experience.
Francis Bacon. ESSAYS.

Tourism is a self-degrading process, kind of like oxidation of iron.
Alison Lurie. FOREIGN AFFAIRS, p35.

The wise traveller travels only in the imagination.
Somerset Maugham. HONOLULU.

Being in a foreign country means walking a tightrope high above the ground without the net afforded a person by the country where he has a family, colleagues, and friends, and where he can easily say what he has to say in a language he has known from childhood.
Milan Kundera. THE UNBEARABLE LIGHTNESS OF BEING, p75.

Every journey.......is an act of resistance to privation, because we do not travel to arrive but simple to travel, and in our lingerings sparkles the pure present.
Claudio Magris, DANUBE. Irish Times, 15/7/89.

What gives value to travel is fear. It is the fact that, at a certain moment, when we are so far from our country.....we are seized by a vague fear, and an instinctive desire to go back to the protection

of old habits.....At that moment we are feverish but also porous, so that the slightest touch makes us quiver to the depths of our being. We come across a cascade of light, and there is eternity. This is why we should not say that we travel for pleasure....Pleasure takes us away from ourselves in the same way as distraction, in Pascal's use of the word, takes us away from God. Travel, which is like a greater and a graver science, brings us back to ourselves.
Albert Camus. NOTEBOOKS, 1935-42.

The tourist thrives on the uncanny, moving happily through a phenomenal world of effects without causes. This world, in which he has no experience and no memory, is presented to him as a supernatural domain: the language of travel advertising hawks the uncanny as part of the deal. Experience the 'magic' of Bali! The 'wonders' of Hawaii! The 'enchantment' of Bavaria!
Jonathan Raban. Independent on Sunday, 25/7/93.

All bus and train stations are a manifestation of limbo.
Sean Dunne. THE CORK ANTHOLOGY, p6.

The redbreasts and the brooks of Europe, in that dry and songless land; brave old names and wars, strong cities, cymbals, and bright armour, in that nook of the mountain, sacred only to the Indian and the bear! This is still the strongest thing in all man's travelling, that he should carry about with him incongruous memories. There is no foreign land; it is the traveller only that is foreign, and now and again, by a flash of recollection, lights up the contrasts of the earth.
R L Stevenson. THE SILVERADO SQUATTERS, p182.

.....Then there was silence. A long while later it was broken by the sharp, shrill whistle of the Janata Express from Assam clattering down the railway line. He bit down on a cigarette, cursing it: why was there always a train whistle in the dark, calling over vast spaces to all who longed to travel and move on? It promised nothing, it merely reminded prisoners of their loss, mocked them in their cells.
Anita Desai. IN CUSTODY, p132.

TRUTH

Note that venerable proverb: Children and fools always speak the truth. The deduction is plain: adults and wise persons never speak it.
Mark Twain. ON THE DECAY OF THE ART OF LYING, p18.

Zen knew that the truth prevailed, if at all, only after so much time had passed that it had become meaningless, like a senile prisoner who can safely be released, his significance forgotten, his friends dead, a babbling idiot.
Michael Dibdin. RATKING, p229.

It would not come to him, it just lay beyond the breakers, in the deep water, in the dark, slippery moving kelp of the mind.
Peter Temple. TRUTH, p367.

When you tell a lie, you steal someone's right to the truth. When you cheat, you steal the right to fairness.
Kallid Hosseini. THE KITE RUNER, p16.

Better to get hurt by the truth than comforted with a lie.
Kallid Hosseini. THE KITE RUNER, p50.

For how long can one live a lie? A body contains its own truth and will not be denied.
Andre Brink. AN INSTANT IN THE WIND, p92.

When you've eliminated the impossible, whatever remains, however improbable, must be the truth.
Philip Kerr. THE SHOT, p172.

First; observation. Now; suffering. It is easier to trek through the landscape of truth than to comprehend it or account for it.
Andre Brink. AN INSTANT IN THE WIND, p194.

But seen from too remote a vantage, life begins to loose its particularity. All shipwrecks become the same shipwreck.....The truth that makes your story yours alone, that sets you apart from the old mariner by the fireside spinning yarns of sea-monsters and mermaids, resides in a thousand touches which today seem of no importance.
J M Coetzee. FOE. p18.

I was fed up with books, which I still continued to gulp down with indiscreet voracity, and searched for another key to the highest truths.
Primo Levi. THE PERIODIC TABLE, p23.

The truth is merely the lie you most wish to believe.
J G Ballard. THE DAY OF CREATION, p176.

Since it is difficult to distinguish true prophets from false, it is as well to regard all prophets with suspicion.
Primo Levi. IF THIS IS A MAN & THE TRUCE, p396.

Truth is not a collection of facts which can be narrated but a landscape through which one travels in the dark.
Andre Brink. LOOKING ON DARKNESS, p34.

Why should one not speak the truth, laughing?
Horace.

All the best lies have an alloy of truth.
Julian Barnes. METROLAND, p94.

Truth, for any man, is that which makes him a man. But truth.... is that which clarifies, not that which confuses. Truth is the language that expresses universality. Newton did not 'discover' a law that lay hidden from man like an answer to an enigma. He accomplished a creative operation. He founded a human speech which could express at one and the same time the fall of an apple and the rising of the sun. Truth is not that which is demonstrable but that which is ineluctable.
Antoine de Saint-Exupery. WIND, SAND AND STARS, p187.

'You can't talk to anybody here,' Prior said. 'Everybody's either lost somebody, or knows somebody who has. They don't want the truth. It's like letters of condolence. "Dear Mrs Bloggs, Your son had the side of his head blown off by a shell and took five hours to die. We did manage to give him a decent Christian burial. Unfortunately that particular stretch of ground came under heavy bombardment the day after, so George has been back to see us five or six times since.
Pat Barker. REGENERATION, p134.

What use is logic when faced with the power of truth?
Sebastian Faulks. CHARLOTTE GREY, p90.

UNDERSTANDING

The difficult task of knowing another soul is not for young gentlemen whose consciousness is chiefly made up of their own.
George Eliot. MIDDLEMARCH, p74.

We all agree on records that leave you somewhere other than they found you, that provoke thought but explore the tiniest details of very common feelings. The real Holy Grail stuff is when people find a new way to put a familiar feeling.
Guy Garvey (Elbow) in Neill McCormick's interview. TELEGRAPH, 23/8/2011.

Man knows he cannot embrace the universe with all its suns and stars......we all lose in whatever we do, because if it is perfection we are after, we must go to the heart of the matter, and we can never quite reach it.
Milan Kundera. THE BOOK OF LAUGHTER & FORGETTING, p165.

The world enters us through our eyes, but we cannot make sense of it until it descends into our mouths. I began to appreciate how great that distance was, to understand how far a thing must travel in order to get from one place to the other. In actual terms, it was no more than two or three inches, but considering how many accidents and losses could occur along the way, it might just as well have been a journey from the earth to the moon.
Paul Auster. MOON PALACE, p122.

UNIVERSE

By writing books the individual becomes a universe. And since the principal quality of a universe is its uniqueness, the existence of another universe constitutes a threat to its very essence.
Milan Kundera. THE BOOK OF LAUGHTER & FORGETTING, p105.

UTOPIA

We had moved into a realm where sickness and obsession, health and sanity had ceased to be opposites.
J G Ballard. THE DAY OF CREATION, p200.

If everything was right we'd appreciate nothing.
John McGahern. NIGHTLINES, p27.

What is the obsession with redemption? Only a mask for a complete absence of the basic talent for life. This is the talent every cat is endowed with. Whereas we, like the whales that dash themselves against the shore in an impulse to mass suicide, suffer from an advanced degeneration of the talent for life. Hence the popular urge to destroy and annihilate what we have so as to hack a path to regions of redemption that have never existed and are not even possible. To sacrifice our lives cheerfully, to eradicate other people ecstatically, for the benefit of some vague false magic that seems to us to be a "Promised Land".
Amos Oz. BLACK BOX, p231.

Utopias are not for mortals....people are like flies, that the stories they are told must be like flypaper. Utopias are gold-covered paper, he said, and flypaper is covered with everything man secretes from his body and his life. Especially the suffering and our hope is that its measure is the measure of man, and forgiveness.
David Grossman. SEE UNDER: LOVE, p225.

Heaven. I imagine heaven as a hotel lobby with a high ceiling and the Art of Fugue coming softly over the public address system. Where one can sit in a deep leather armchair and be without pain. A hotel lobby full of old people dozing, listening to music, while souls pass and re-pass before them like vapours, the souls of all. A place dense with souls...... A place to which you bring an abstract kind of clothing and the memories inside you, the memories that make you. A place without incident. A railway station after the abolition of trains. Listening to the heavenly unending music, waiting for nothing, paging idly through the store of memories.
J.M. Coetzee. AGE OF IRON, p22.

He and I pressed breast to breast, eyes closed, going down the old road together. Unlikely companions! Like travelling in a bus in Sicily, pressed face to face, body to body against a strange man. Perhaps that is what the afterlife will be like: not a lobby with armchairs and music but a great crowded bus on its way from nowhere to nowhere. Standing room only: on one's feet forever, crushed against strangers. The air thick, stale, full of sighs and murmurs: Sorry, Sorry. Promiscuous contact. Forever under the gaze of others. An end to private life.
J.M. Coetzee. AGE OF IRON, p27.

I suppose everyone has been in heaven once in their life. It is a terrible thing to look down from that height of ecstasy and know that it doesn't matter if you die now because you will never be happier. In amongst the crushing ecstasy is a rotten feeling that you are in possession of the only thing you have ever wanted. For the rest of your life, you are without a plan or ambition. From the moment she first kisses you, it is downhill all the way.
Frank Ronan. THE MEN WHO LOVED EVELYN COTTON, p22.

The first Communists were Adam and Eve. They had no clothes to wear, had to steal apples for food, could not escape the place in which they lived and still thought they were in paradise.
Joke told in wartime Berlin.

VENGEANCE

When it is postponed, vengeance is transformed into something deceptive, into a personal religion, into a myth that recedes day by day from the people involved, who remain the same in the myth though in reality they long ago became different people.
Milan Kundera. THE JOKE, p293.

VIOLENCE

Tobias Wolff had a childhood fascination with a .22 rifle given as a gift. He would often pose with it when his mother was out, aiming it out the window at targets. 'I sometimes had to bite my lip to keep from laughing in the ecstasy of my power. All my images of myself as I wished to be were images of myself armed. Because I did not know who I was, any image of myself, no matter how grotesque, had power over me.'
Review of 'Goat Mountain' by David Vann in Financial Times, 2/11/2013.

Ritual. What it does is make the horrifying normal.
David Vann. GOAT MOUNTAIN, p153.

Katrina was a televised tale of institutional collapse, political paralysis and racial polarisation laid bare by an entirely predictable crisis.
Review of James Lee Burke's 'The Tin Roof Blowdown' in Guardian, 4/12/2007.

But treachery and violence are spears pointed at both ends, they wound those who resort to them worse than their enemies.
Isabella Linton in WUTHERING HEIGHTS, ch 16.

It was another step forward, after Sharpville and Soweto. Each time a step further. There is a terrible logic in the language of violence.
Andre Brink. THE WALL OF THE PLAGUE, p328.

Every week men sit comfortably at the cinema and look on the bombardment of some Shanghai or other, some Guernica, and marvel without a trace of horror at the long fringes of ash and soot that twist their slow way into the sky from those man-made volcanoes. Yet we all know that together with the grain in the granaries, with the heritage of generations of men, with the treasures of families, it is the burning flesh of children and their elders that, dissipated in smoke, is slowly fertilising those black cumuli.
The physical drama itself cannot touch us until someone points out its spiritual sense.
Antoine de Saint-Exupery. WIND, SAND AND STARS, p59.

The reason why writers fail when they attempt to evoke horror is that horror is something invented after the fact, when one is re-creating the experience over again in the memory. Horror does not manifest itself in the world of reality.
Antoine de Saint-Exupery. WIND, SAND AND STARS, p49.

Power is gained and maintained by violence. This is as true of individuals as it is of nations. Both are born in violence, relate to others through violence, and die in violence. This is not cynicism. Nobody who has witnessed a birth can ever forget the tearing of the flesh and the screams. As to our relationships with other people, we play at manners and morals, but we only play, just as states do; the veneer is dangerously thin and what lurks beneath is murderous. As to death, it is the ultimate violation, so it's by nature violent, no matter how it looks on the surface. People who deny

such truths are foolish and dangerous or both, and yet the only thinkers who speak about such things without hypocrisy or sentimentality are the philosophers of war.
Joan Brady. THEORY OF WAR, p59.

VIRTUE

I have not spoken of my faithful vehicle (RocNante) except in formal terms of passing praise. Is it not always so? We value virtue but do not discuss it. The honest bookkeeper, the faithful wife, the earnest scholar get little attention compared to the embezzler, the tramp, the cheat.
John Steinbeck. TRAVELS WITH CHARLEY, p157.

But immaculate virtue does not exist either, or if it does it is detestable.
Primo Levi. THE PERIODIC TABLE, p34.

WEALTH

I am rich in all that I have lost.
Siegfried Sassoon.

WEAPONS

The instrument of survival in the wild is the gun, but the need for it is metaphysical rather than physical. The native tribes have survived without the gun.
J M Coetzee. DUSKLANDS, p80.

You shoot at a series of images conveyed to you through a metal tube. The force of a death should be enormous but how can you know what kind of a man you've killed or who was the braver and stronger if you have to peer through layers of glass that deliver the image but obscure the meaning of the act? War has a conscience or it's ordinary murder.
Don De Lillo. LIBRA, p297/8.

WORDS & PHRASES

Vanity of expectation.
Howard Jacobson. THE FINKLER QUESTION, p289.

brief global philanthropy.
"Gorbeuphoric"
shambolic economy.
dice with their own demise.

So the Parfitt family matured like a tree in its own shade; dense, isolated and firmly rooted in the past.
(Sunday Times Magazine, 11/12/88).

Troubles overcome are good to tell.
(Yiddish proverb).

Like putting a Band-Aid on a cancer.
(Gloria Steinem)

If bullshit was music, she'd be a brass band.
Don De Lillo. LIBRA, p250.

Using one's ignorance as a funnel for one's prejudices.

The intrusion of the gifted outsider.

pluterperfect imperturbability.

with the practiced air of martyred resignation.

To feel like one handcuffed to the rails of the Titanic.

Hi-fi and holidays.
Driving gloves and barbecues.

a bracing sense of the sinister.

Flaubertian syphylitic impotence.

Like a goose farting in a fog.
(Billy Connolly)

a license to shit in the street.
(Billy Connolly)

Don't let the sun go down on your wrath.

chemistry of unrest.

As two-dimensional as weather vanes!

the onion's deceit - where do the skin layers end and the onion begin?

connoisseurs of human oddity.

moral bookkeeping on both sides.

like a snake in the jaws of a mongoose.

that country is one huge historical mistake.

with every bomb, with every atrocity they compromise their own people.

a convenient morality.

Can the Israelis' psychologically handle peace?
(a Mercer play)

In and out like a fiddler's elbow.

post-orgasmic peace.

good natured disappointment.

Are we programmed for survival?

napalm-based curry!

a place so boring that when the tide goes out it never returns.

.....in banks of silt as smooth as pillows of wet sand.
J G Ballard. THE DAY OF CREATION, p58.

a more sensational but just as artfully neutered violence.
J G Ballard. THE DAY OF CREATION, p176.

a layer of response........
J G Ballard. THE DAY OF CREATION, p157.

I imagined my once plump mesentery as a fraying clothes line, on which was strung an ever-more hungry intestine.
J G Ballard. THE DAY OF CREATION, p153.

.......as a soft haze of cerise light lay like a quilt over the sleeping river.
J G Ballard. THE DAY OF CREATION, p145.

He anaesthetised himself with activity.
Ian McEwan. THE CHILD IN TIME, p23.

But their talk had an appearance of embarrased continuity.
Henry James. PORTRAIT OF A LADY, p220.

a pathless desert of virtue.
Henry James. PORTRAIT OF A LADY, p243.

in a wilderness of faded chintz.
Henry James. PORTRAIT, p71.

the house had a "weather-fretted hue"
Henry James. PORTRAIT, p73.

The stringent avoider of pity.
Molly Keane. TIME AFTER TIME, p130.

Most things disappoint till you look deeper.
Graham Greene. THE COMEDIANS, p15.

God uses the good ones, and the bad ones use God.
"Dynamite Man from Glory Jail."

The snatch of renewal was always and everywhere better than the snatch of oblivion.
Dennis Potter. TICKET TO RIDE, p202.

rocks in the stream of time.
John Banville. MEFISTO, p15.

culinary necromancy.
Graham Swift. WATERLAND, p247.

scrabbling without much result at the bars of existence.
Kate Pullinger. Good Book Guide, 37.

an economical use of misery.
John Updike. COUPLES, p289.

or vanished like a good paragraph in a book too bulky to read.
John Updike. BECH, A BOOK, p127.

fragile forest of television aerials.

jammed clockwork of fire-escapes.

the balm of their undeniability.

stunning them with blunt classics
John Updike. BECH, A BOOK, p87.

we reach a point where words seem horrible, maggots on the carcase of reality, feeding, proliferating.
John Updike. BECH, A BOOK, p102.

in a truly lugubrious solipsism.
Martin Amis. THE MORONIC INFERNO, p45.

Worth two fortunes and a sudden death..
John Montague. THE FLOOD.

There is nothing more real than words...I did not say that what they depicted was real.....
Peter Ackroyd. CHATTERTON, p157.

When it came to kissing and telling, Keith was a one-man oral tradition.
Martin Amis. LONDON FIELDS, p167.

pompous psychobabble of the press release.

The trouble with words is that you never know whose mouths they've been in.
Dennis Potter. The Guardian, 2/93.

WORK

When they took a young man into Tellson's London house, they hid him somewhere till he was old. They kept him in a dark place, like a cheese, until he had the full Tellson flavour and blue-mould upon him. Then only was he permitted to be seen, spectacularly poring over large books, and casting his breeches and gaiters into the general weight of the establishment.
Charles Dickens. A TALE OF TWO CITIES, p34.

"Arbeit Macht Frei" - work gives freedom, a sign at the entrance to Auschwitz.
Primo Levi. IF THIS IS A MAN.

Probably no job is done well unless done instinctively.
Anthony Powell.

If work is such a good thing, how come the rich haven't grabbed it all for themselves.
Haitian proverb.

WORLD

Boris was still talking, and I realized if I didn't want to be lost forever in this grainy Nosferatu world, sharp shadows and achromatism, it was important to listen to him and not get so hung up on the artificial texture of things.
Donna Tartt, THE GOLDFINCH, p334.

The details of the world in which we live are always secondary to the fact that we must live in them.
Kevin Powers. THE YELLOW BIRDS, p224.

The world, if it has a future, has an ascetic future.
Bruce Chatwin. THE SONGLINES, p133.

WRITING

Coleridge said that Shakespeare always made apprehension predominate over surprise.
John Mullan. 'THE GUARDIAN' 18/10/2013.

'If you know beforehand, that's bad: you'll just say what you already know, which is what we all know. On the other hand, if you don't yet know what you want to say but you're crazy enough or desperate enough or brave enough to keep writing, you might end up saying something that you didn't even know you knew and that only you can come to know, and *that* might be of interest...
'What I mean is that someone who always knows where they're going never gets anywhere, and you only know what you're trying to say once you've said it.
Javier Cercas. THE SPEED OF LIGHT, p47.

...The only book worth writing is the one you don't know how to write.
Mohsin Hamid, Sunday Times, 17 March 2013, Culture p10.

You have to be disciplined as a writer. I never plan my novels because if I know what is going to happen it bores me rigid. I let the story tell itself.
James Herbert. 'Telegraph Magazine', 3 November 2012, p7.

For me, at least, writing consists very largely of exploring intuition. A character is really the sense of a character, embodied, attired, and given voice as he or she seems to require.
Marilynne Robinson, WHEN I WAS A CHILD, p6.

I was fortunate that most English writing of the time was in the form of undemanding social documentary. I wasn't impressed by those writers (they were spread between South and North America) who infiltrated their own pages as part of the cast, determined to remind the poor reader that all the characters and even they themselves were pure inventions and that there was a difference between fiction and life. Or, to the contrary, to insist that life was a fiction anyway. Only writers, I thought, were ever in danger of confusing the two. I was a born empiricist,. I believed that writers were paid to pretend, and where appropriate should make use of the real world, the one we all shared, to give plausibility to whatever they had made up.
Ian McEwan. SWEET TOOTH, p66.

(Robert Herrick) would study (Virgil's poetry) as he lay with tightened belt on the floor of the old calaboose, seeking favourite passages and finding new ones only less beautiful because they lacked the consecration of remembrance.
R L Stevenson. THE EBB-TIDE, (1894)

Writing by hand forces you to do most of the intellectual work before you make a mark, so you think more carefully. There's only so many times you can cross out and correct before it becomes illegible, whereas with word processing you start with a blank space every time, so there's no sense of responsibility to the initial idea.
Will Eaves, editor of TLS, quoted in Telegraph by Ivan Hewett, 12/3/2011.

Kafka's letter about a doll... when a person is lucky enough to live inside a story, to live inside an imaginary world, the pains of this world will disappear. For as long as the story goes on, reality no longer exists.
Paul Auster. THE BROOKLYN FOLLIES, p156.

The role of the writer is not to say what we can all say, but what we are unable to say.
Anais Nin.

Graham Greene is a Roman Catholic, a partisan of Rome, if you like. Why then does he write so compulsively about bad, doubtful and doubting priests?
Because a genuine artist, no matter what he says he believes, must feel in his blood the ultimate enmity between art and orthodoxy.
Chinua Achebe. ANTHILLS OF THE SAVANNAH, p100.

To give a text an Author is to impose a limit on that text, to furnish it with a final signified, to close the writing.
Roland Barthes. THE DEATH OF THE AUTHOR.

The writer can only imitate a gesture that is always anterior, never original.
Roland Barthes. THE DEATH OF THE AUTHOR.

The text is a tissue of quotations drawn from the innumerable centers of culture.
Roland Barthes. THE DEATH OF THE AUTHOR.

Writing is the destruction of every voice, of every point of origin. Writing is that neutral, composite, oblique space where our subjects slip away, the negative where all identity is lost, starting with the very identity of the body writing.
Roland Barthes. THE DEATH OF THE AUTHOR.

By writing books the individual becomes a universe. And since the principal quality of a universe is its uniqueness, the existence of another universe constitutes a threat to its very essence.
Milan Kundera. THE BOOK OF LAUGHTER & FORGETTING, p105.

In literature we move through a blest world in which we know nothing except by style, but in which also everything is saved by it.
Henry James.

Writing a novel is a little like putting a message into a bottle and flinging it into the sea - unexpected friends and enemies retrieve it.
Graham Greene. WAYS OF ESCAPE.

Writing is a form of therapy; sometimes I wonder how all those who do not write, compose or paint can manage to escape the madness, the melancholia, the panic fear which is inherent in the human situation.
Graham Greene. WAYS OF ESCAPE.

But it's a funny thing about writing. If you are a writer by nature, I don't believe you write for money or fame or even for publication, but simply for the pleasure of turning out the stuff. I don't really care much if these books are published or not. The great thing is that I've got them down on paper, and can read and re-read them and change an adjective for a better one and cut out dead lines.
P G Wodehouse.

I find that writing is like drinking. A man must learn to control it.
William Golding. RITES OF PASSAGE, p29.

The whole business of a novelist's incubatory periods, what can produce or prolong them, is naturally of great professional consequence. Although at times it is certainly necessary to force oneself to write, as one might exert any other form of self-control, while at others a holiday from

writing is obviously needed, the process of occupying the mind with some different mental activity, pleasant but relatively onerous in itself, seems to have a stimulating effect in getting the necessary machinery going.
Anthony Powell. TO KEEP THE BALL ROLLING, vol 3, p195.

(re writing the first novel) It is one of those slightly awkward stepping stones in life, like acne and smelly socks under the bed. Its main function is to purge the young writer of all the grudges and resentments accumulated during adolescence.
Auberon Waugh. Writer's Monthly, 7/89.

A short story is a lazy way to write a poem, and a novel is a lazy way to write a short story.
Muriel Spark. THE INDEPENDENT. 4/11/89.

Stephen King describes his literary style as "the literary equivalent of a Big Mac and large fries from MacDonalds".
THE INDEPENDENT, 11/11/89.

It is the incompleteness of life which makes writing possible.
Roland Barthes. cf STATES OF EMERGENCY by Andre Brink, p134.

Modern writing - a dialogue with despair.
Des Egan.

In my writing, for good or evil, knowingly or not, I've always strived to pass from the darkness into the light, as a filtering pump might do, which sucks up the turbid water and expels it decanted: possible sterile.
Primo Levi. THE MIRROR MAKER, p106.

"The effect of that painting.......will be quite different from anything that we can understand now. Certainly quite different from anything that you intend. It is the same with a poem or with a novel.....The final effect it has upon the world can never be anticipated or measured or arranged.......That is what I mean by its reality.....It can only be experienced. It cannot be spoken of.
Peter Ackroyd. CHATTERTON, p162.

When I watched him work I was reminded of the theory of the French Surrealists with regard to automatic writing, which according to them flowed directly from the subconscious, bypassing the censorship of reason.
Mario Vargas Llosa. AUNT JULIA AND THE SCRIPTWRITER, p130

But how to establish the exact moment in which a story begins? Everything has already begun before, the first line of the first page of every novel refers to something that has already happened outside the book. Or else the real story is the one that begins ten or a hundred pages further on, and everything that precedes it is only a prologue.
Italo Calvino. IF ON A WINTER'S NIGHT A TRAVELLER, p122.

...the power of the journalist is not based on his right to ask but on his right to demand an answer.
Milan Kundera. IMMORTALITY, p122.

Poets, and anyone who ever exercises a creative and individual profession, have in common with chess players total responsibility for their actions......Whoever is on his own, without allies or intermediaries between himself and his work, has no excuses in the face of failure, and excuses are a precious analgesic.
Primo Levi. OTHER PEOPLE'S TRADES, p132.

Writing is not really a trade, or at least in my opinion it should not be one: it is a creative activity and therefore baulks at schedules and deadlines, commitments to customers and bosses. Nevertheless, writing is a way of producing, indeed a process of transformation: the writer transforms his experiences into a form that is accessible and attractive to the customer who will be the reader.
Primo Levi. OTHER PEOPLE'S TRADES, p174.

I don't have a philosophy. I'm correctly cast as a writer because I'm as confused and as ambivalent, selfish and fitful as my characters.
John Updike. The Times, 2/93.

They say, such a life I've had! I really ought to put it all down some day; turn it into a book! And so indeed what a life they've had, but the mere recording of events does not make a book. Experience does not add up to Idea. It is easier for the reader to judge, by a thousand times, than for the writer to invent. The writer must summon his Idea out of nowhere, and his characters out of nothing, and catch words as they fly, and nail them to the page.
Fay Weldon. LETTERS TO ALICE, p22.

Truly, properly invented characters, born out of the imagination, sprung from the head fully formed, as Venus was from Zeus, may appear as wished, or good, or bizarre or foolish, but the writer takes the attitude of God - he forgives and understands, even while condemning. This is, after all, his own creation. He is in a way responsible.
But when the writer describes and does not invent, he suffers the limitations of his own humanity, and he appears spiteful, or bigoted, or not really entitled to comment at all.
Fay Weldon. LETTERS TO ALICE, p88.

'A sentence must flow as smoothly as milk from the Great Tit of the Shuddering Sacred Cow of Cahirciveen. Milk it, Mr. Campbell, sir. Milk.'
Patrick Campbell. MY LIFE AND EASY TIMES, p123.

A house – In the neighbourhood of whispers, it was a shriek!
Augusten Burroughs. RUNNING WITH SCISSORS, p39.

WRONG

But when a man suspects any wrong, it sometimes happens that if he be already involved in the matter, he insensibly strives to cover up his suspicions even from himself.
Herman Melville. MOBY DICK, p90 (Kindle version)

YOUTH

When you are very young, shadows have meaning and their substance fills you. Stretch out your hand and you can feel the flesh. Probe deeper and you touch grieving bone. When you look at the clock, the hands tell you nothing. Only the shadows are real....
Patrick Galvin. SONG FOR A POOR BOY, p105.

Clare waited for us in the car, defeated by the view. I believed, at that moment, that I had never loved anyone but my parents and these two people. Perhaps we don't fully recover from our first loves. Perhaps, in the extravagance of youth, we give away our devotions easily and all but arbitrarily, on the mistaken assumption that we'll always have more to give.
Michael Cunningham. A HOME AT THE END OF THE WORLD, p246.

Youth is terrible: it is a stage trod by children in buskins and a variety of costumes mouthing speeches they've memorized and fanatically believe but only half understand.
Milan Kundera. THE JOKE, p87.

'Find me an uncomplicated child, Pyle. When we are young we are a jungle of complications. We simplify as we get older.'
Graham Greene.   THE QUIET AMERICAN, p174.

It was probably 110-proof red, an evil bathtub brown of bourbon touched up with turpentine and dye, enough to take rust off metal, enough to skin cats alive. But Jonathan was only fourteen or so, and young males are among the stupidest of the stupid young, competitive where the prize is worthless and fiercely proud where pride is meaningless: he drank, shuddered, gasped, choked and recovered, eyes watering, throat aflame.
Joan Brady. THEORY OF WAR, p47.

There is a random, episodic feel to most young lives - the childhood pattern dispensed with, the adult pattern not yet established - which has a peculiar charm all of its own.
Joan Brady. THEORY OF WAR, p82.